WELFARE BUSHED: SOCIAL CARE IN RURAL AUSTRALIA

For Judy, Emma and Simon

Welfare Bushed: Social Care in Rural Australia

BRIAN CHEERS
University of South Australia

LONDON AND NEW YORK

First published 1998 by Ashgate Publishing

Reissued 2018 by Routledge
2 Park Square, Milton Park, Abingdon, Oxon, OX14 4RN
711 Third Avenue, New York, NY 10017, USA

Routledge is an imprint of the Taylor & Francis Group, an informa business

Copyright © B. Cheers 1998

All rights reserved. No part of this book may be reprinted or reproduced or utilised in any form or by any electronic, mechanical, or other means, now known or hereafter invented, including photocopying and recording, or in any information storage or retrieval system, without permission in writing from the publishers.

Notice:
Product or corporate names may be trademarks or registered trademarks, and are used only for identification and explanation without intent to infringe.

Publisher's Note
The publisher has gone to great lengths to ensure the quality of this reprint but points out that some imperfections in the original copies may be apparent.

Disclaimer
The publisher has made every effort to trace copyright holders and welcomes correspondence from those they have been unable to contact.

A Library of Congress record exists under LC control number: 98072806

ISBN 13: 978-1-138-35897-3 (hbk)
ISBN 13: 978-1-138-35899-7 (pbk)
ISBN 13: 978-0-429-43397-9 (ebk)

Contents

List of Figures	vi
List of Tables	vii
Acknowledgements	viii
List of Abbreviations	x

PART 1: FOUNDATIONS	1
1 Welfare Bushed	3
2 Rural Australia	23
3 People in Rural Communities	61

PART 2: SOCIAL CARE	91
4 Rural Social Policy	93
5 Income Support and Housing	109
6 Social Care Development	131
7 Formal Personal Social Care	169
8 Practice	219

PART 3: THREADS	255
9 Threads	257

Bibliography	275
Index	293

List of Figures

2.1　Population Density and Median Annual Rainfall　　　25
4.1　Managed, Sustainable Regional Change　　　107
6.1　Social Planning Process　　　133

List of Tables

1.1	Classification of Rural and Urban Social Places and Related Terms	13
2.1	Rural Settlement Types	28
3.1	Conflicts between Islamic Fundamentalist and Dominant Western Values	64
6.1	Information Relevant to Rural Social Planning	134
6.2	Principles and Strategies of Social Impact Assessment	141
6.3	Ladder of Participation	147
6.4	Constraints on Social Care Development in Rural Communities	155
6.5	Rural Social Care Development Functions and Tasks	161
7.1	Service Designs	196
7.2	Examples of Horizontal Service Coordination and Integration Mechanisms	210
7.3	Examples of Vertical Service Coordination and Integration Mechanisms	212
8.1	Components of the Practitioner's Community Assessment	251

Acknowledgements

A number of people and organisations have contributed to this book. I wish to thank James Cook University of North Queensland for the sabbatical in 1996, during which the first draft was completed. The Department of Agricultural Economics and Rural Sociology at Pennsylvania State University generously provided accommodation, support and a most congenial, peaceful environment in which to work. I also wish to acknowledge the University of South Australia for the funds required to prepare the manuscript for publication, and Amanda Lambden for her help in finalising the book.

Many individuals contributed to the work. I am especially indebted to Lilian Chatterjee of the International Council on Social Welfare, who generously offered to act as editor. Lilian painstakingly reviewed the entire work. Her writing talents, powerful intellect, international perspective, compassion for the human race and insistence that I use the English language correctly have contributed to a vastly improved final product.

Over a long period, I have found many treasures amongst Judy Taylor's experiences of social care practice, policy, service development and management in rural and remote areas of Northern Australia. These, and her thoughts about them, are scattered throughout this work. Judy and her colleagues have been genuine pioneers in a challenging field. Most of all, Judy has relentlessly reminded me that the pristine tidiness of academic speculation cannot match the elegant messiness of the real world.

The list of people who have contributed to my understanding of rural life is limitless. It includes Emilia Martinez-Brawley and Allan Brawley at Arizona State University, Drew Hyman and Al Luloff at PennState, Kim Zapf at the University of Calgary, Geoff Lawrence at Central Queensland University, David McSwan at James Cook University, Peter Munn at the University of South Australia and Bob Lonne at the Queensland University of Technology. Frank Hornby of the Townsville City Council will be surprised to learn that he has contributed more than anyone else to my knowledge of social planning, local government in regional social care. Frank has been one of the true pioneers of regional social planning in Australia.

To all those students at James Cook University who shared my passion for rural Australia - I thank you for joining my journey with such enthusiasm, for contributing to my understanding of rural life and for the many endless debates which challenged my preconceptions and extended my thinking.

Most importantly, this book could never have been written had not the people of rural and remote Northern Australia been so lavish with their hospitality, generous with their insights, and trusting in their souls. From the start, I was fully aware of what an honour it was to be invited into your communities. For very good reasons, you have learned to distrust many of what you call the 'educated idiots' who meddle in your affairs for their own benefit. City folk do, indeed, have much to learn from your strength, courage, love of community and fundamental humanity.

Acknowledgement is given to HarperCollins Publishers and The American Academy of Arts and Sciences for permission to publish the quotation on page 23 from S. Graubard (ed.), *Australia: The Daedalus Symposium*. The extract reprinted on page 80 is from *In Search of Our Mothers' Gardens* by Alice Walker, published in Great Britain by the Women's Press Ltd, 1984, 34 Great Sutton Street, London EC1V ODX.

List of Abbreviations

AAA	Agriculture: Advancing Australia Program
ABARE	Australian Bureau of Agricultural and Resource Economics
ABS	Australian Bureau of Statistics
ACOSS	Australian Council of Social Service
ACSWC	Australian Catholic Social Welfare Commission
AGPS	Australian Government Publishing Service
APEC	Asia Pacific Economic Cooperation Forum
ASTEC	Australian Science and Technology Council
ATSIC	Aboriginal and Torres Strait Islander Commission
CDEP	Community Development Employment Project
Centacare	Centacare Australia and Australian Catholic Social Welfare Commission
DAA	Department of Aboriginal Affairs
DCS	Department of Community Services
DFACS	Department of Family and Community Services
DFSAIA	Department of Family Services and Aboriginal and Islander Affairs
DFYCC	Department of Families, Youth and Community Care
DHCCS	Department of Health, Housing and Community Services
DPIE	Department of Primary Industries and Energy
DPMC	Department of Prime Minister and Cabinet
DSS	Department of Social Security
FFRS	Farm Family Restart Scheme
FHSS	Farm Household Support Scheme
HACC	Home and Community Care Program
IINA	IINA Torres Strait Islander Corporation
Morton	Morton Consulting Services Pty. Ltd.
NADU	Northern Australia Development Unit
NARU	Northern Australia Research Unit
NHST	National Housing Strategy
OND	Office of Northern Development, Department of Housing and Regional Development
ORA	Office of Rural Affairs
ORC	Office of Rural Communities

RAS	Rural Adjustment Scheme
RIRDC	Rural Industries Research and Development Corporation
SIA	Social Impact Assessment
TRDC	The Rural Development Centre, University of New England
UN	United Nations

Part 1
Foundations

1 Welfare Bushed

In Australia, to be 'bushed' means that you are lost, tired, confused and don't know which way to go. This is what happened to the welfare sector when it first moved seriously into rural Australia in the 1980s. Traditional approaches to assessing and providing for human needs did not work as well as they had in urban environments. The sector was in a new world, without a useful conceptual map, confused about how to move around and, for awhile, unable to read the signs indicating how to proceed. Urban welfare was, indeed, poorly adapted to the rural environment.

Since white settlement, Australia's welfare system has been dominated by a number of themes which have worked against successful adaptation to rural contexts. These include a fragmented and centralised policy and service system with respect to decision making, information, control and accountability; a highly professionalised welfare workforce; and a 'provision' approach to social care built on the assumption that it is best provided by a network of formal services which are largely disconnected from natural sources of support. These and other characteristics of Australia's welfare system have made it difficult for rural people to access formal welfare services and resources which, in any case, have frequently been inappropriate to their needs and lifestyles.

The Urbanisation of Australian Social Welfare

The origins and development of Australia's welfare system have been well documented (e.g., Dickey, 1980; Gilbert and Specht, 1981a). The foundations were laid down in England and other European countries between the fourteenth and seventeenth centuries when welfare took shape as an urban response to predominantly urban problems (Trattner, 1981). Prior to the industrial revolution the feudal system ensured that rulers did not need to overly concern themselves with workforce regulation, internal migration problems or social care arrangements. To a greater or lesser degree, the workforce had been controlled, the work had been done and social problems had been contained within locality-based communities. For better or for worse, the well-being of workers and their dependents had relied upon self-help, mutual aid, the largesse and deprivations of liege lords and ladies, medieval churches, hospitals and, in the cities, assistance from social, craft and merchant guilds.

Industrialisation brought major social and economic changes which weakened this system considerably. A monetary economy emerged, characterised by an overriding concern with issues such as capital investment, international trade, credit, interest, rent and wages. There was increasing emphasis on urbanisation of production, centralisation of capital and relocation of labour from rural to urban areas. As industrialisation and the population shift gained momentum, increasing numbers of people found themselves without any means of survival, dislocated from whatever social security had been afforded by the feudal system, living in over-crowded conditions in cities which were ravaged by crime and illness of plague proportions.

> Taken together, these developments - the breakdown of the medieval economy, the social structure and its relatively fixed order of things, and the church with its entire framework of charity - meant for many people the loss of economic security given to a serf by his (sic) master, and the social, economic, and spiritual security given by the church to its members during the Middle Ages. This, in turn, resulted in a tremendous increase in unemployment, poverty, vagabondage, begging, and thievery, especially in the growing commercial centers to which many of the needy naturally gravitated. (Trattner, 1981, p.26)

The rulers of the day believed that for industrialisation to proceed and for capital growth to accelerate, present and future workers and their dependents had to be controlled, socialised into the new order of capital, kept reasonably healthy and later, when increased skills were required, educated. Producers had to be protected from unproductive labour, industrial disputes, illness, social unrest and the aimless wandering of the landless (Trattner, 1981, pp.26-30). Consequently, governments were now forced to provide some, though initially minimal, physical, material and social care, enact industrial legislation, and introduce laws to control the working classes. It was in this context that social welfare emerged. In England, these developments culminated in the English Poor Law of 1601 which introduced the irreversible principle that the state is obliged to care for the material well-being of its members (Gilbert and Specht, 1981a, p.19).

This was the construction of welfare that European Australians brought to this continent when they arrived in 1788. Since then, the development of the welfare system has been a continuing story of increasing government domination of policy and services. Preferred service models have resulted in ever larger and more complex administrative structures, greater centralisation, higher levels of staff training, and tighter government control.

That a highly centralised welfare system would develop is understandable given the penal origins of first European settlement, the high level of urbanisation of Australian society and the political and financial power of central Commonwealth and State/Territory[1] governments relative to local government. As members of a convict colony, European Australians were initially totally dependent on central government for all things, including welfare provision (Dickey, 1980, pp.1-29). During the nineteenth century, the overriding importance of market prosperity meant that the needs of those who could not care for themselves and their dependents were clearly segregated from the ongoing stream of development. In Dickey's (1980, p.95) words:

> The field of social welfare treated the people involved as objects of policy set apart from the prosperous, self-improving middle class dominated colonial societies around them.

This is when social welfare policy first became so thoroughly separated from economic development in this country.

Throughout the twentieth century, central governments further consolidated their responsibility for, and involvement in social welfare. At the turn of the century, the newly established Commonwealth Government accepted responsibility for providing income security, initially through age and invalid pensions (Dickey, 1980, pp.139-40). Later, the 1920s depression convinced us that a system of minimal government provision supported by haphazard non-government charity was insufficient to respond to major social problems such as mass unemployment and destitution (Dickey, 1980, pp.157-63). In the 1940s, Commonwealth welfare programs proliferated as successive Labour governments pursued their vision of a more caring and humane society (Dickey, 1980, pp.167-84). The prosperity of the 1950s and 1960s made this more possible as conservative central governments continued to expand their direct involvement in, and responsibility for providing for the health, welfare and education of the population, though with an emphasis on the middle, rather than the poorer, classes (Dickey, 1980, pp.185-212).

The 1970s brought widespread social and cultural changes, including a renewed emphasis on human values, which resulted in further reinforcement of the structure of social welfare. Commonwealth and State welfare programs proliferated as did non-government services which, following the Bailey Report (Bailey, 1978), were subjected to increased government direction and control. For the most part, however, these were focused on urban localities. Tertiary education programs in social work, social welfare and social policy also proliferated, although virtually all these were offered only in capital cities and predominantly to urban students. Nevertheless, they captured the imagination and idealism of the new generation, many of whom went on to exert a major influence over social policy and social welfare practice, education, administration, research and thought over the next two decades. There was no shortage of employment opportunities in these fields although these, too, were mostly in urban centres.

In the 1980s, recessions and concerns about the international competitiveness of the Australian economy focused attention on economic issues and policies emphasising tight fiscal control. In 1982, the Hawke Labour Government embarked on a program of economic, industrial and labour market restructuring which impacted heavily on all Australians. Unemployment rose to unusually high levels and stayed there, industries were pushed towards greater competitiveness, companies which could not keep up were encouraged to fold, and long overdue social reforms were further delayed. As we shall see in Chapter 2, industry restructuring, droughts and other developments resulted in major changes in rural communities and widespread hardship for rural people (Hungerford, 1994).

Reflecting the economic times, the 1980s and 1990s brought a resurgence of economic rationalism, or an overriding concern with productivity and financial efficiency as the basis of public policy. For the welfare sector, this has resulted in continuing neglect of social goals, concerted attacks on the right of all citizens to adequate levels of social care, and increased centralisation of power and control in urban-based government departments (Riches, 1993). Furthermore, economic rationalism has given overwhelming priority to the financial efficiency of social policy and welfare services, resulting in service 'rationalisation' and an 'accounting' approach to accountability. Unfortunately for rural Australia, 'rationalisation' has come to mean the relocation of infrastructure and services from small communities to larger regional centres and from government to the non-government sector.

This renewed emphasis on non-government organisations and community-based services provided the opportunity to develop innovative services based in, and more suited to rural localities. But the opportunity has only been partially grasped because these essentially sound ideas were exploited to reduce welfare expenditure, withdraw services and infrastructure from small communities, and shift the responsibility for, and some of the costs of services (but not the power or resources) to non-government organisations.

As the evidence presented in Chapter 2 demonstrates, throughout the last two hundred years the social care of rural Australians has been relatively neglected by governments, by large national and State-wide non-government organisations, and by educators, scholars and researchers. For the most part, rural Australia has either been seen as somehow blissfully free of, or capable of solving its social problems. It has also frequently been viewed as an instrument for solving urban difficulties. At different times, the bush has been a place to which people and industry could be sent to ease urban congestion, where poor urban people could be sent for cheap accommodation, where export income could be generated to finance urban imports and discharge urban debts, where the national economy could be regenerated, and as a natural resource pit to be pillaged or sold according to predominantly urban economic interests.

The well-being of Australia's indigenous peoples, the majority of whom live outside the major urban areas, has been severely abused. It is clear that their well-being was far better before 1788 than it is now, that according to most indices it is not improving significantly, that the international community regards indigenous Australians in many remote communities as living in Fourth World conditions, and that the Australian welfare system, based as it is on dominant Western ideologies, has largely failed to help them (Smallwood, 1994; Cheers, 1996).

The fragmentation of our welfare system has a number of roots. First, the Australian Constitution and the federal system of government have resulted in different, and frequently even the same, welfare responsibilities being allocated to Commonwealth and State governments (Sackville, 1973). Second, partly in response to increasing encroachment by successive Commonwealth governments into State powers, State governments have steadily widened their involvement in social welfare over the last 50 years. Third, service programs and welfare categories have proliferated in response to the pressures placed on governments by an ever increasing number of lobby groups. And, fourth, increasing numbers of community-based organisations have been created as the responsibility for service provision has been increasingly devolved to the non-government sector. Consequently, Australia now has an elaborate and complex labyrinth of services, entitlements, policies, programs, service organisations and supervising statutory authorities.

But the federal structure, the founders of our Constitution, politicians and public administrators are not to blame for the system's fragmentation - they, too, are products of the dominant culture. Mainstream Australia has adopted the Western individualistic and atomistic view of human life (Cheers, 1996, pp.24-9). Dominant Western ideology focuses on, and implicitly values, individuals and nuclear families in preference to other social entities such as communities, groups, social networks and natural support systems. Consequently, social policy in this country is overwhelmingly directed at individuals and families rather than communities, regions or localities. The vast majority of social workers and welfare practitioners work with individuals and families rather than whole communities and regions. Furthermore, despite frequent references to concepts such as 'the state', 'society' and 'community', Australian welfare scholars have given scant regard to their reality. Consequently, human needs for accommodation or money, for example, are detached from whole human lives and treated as if they occur in a social vacuum.

It is easy to overlook the fundamental integrity and social embeddedness of people in a highly urbanised country such as Australia. When services are provided to people *en masse*, as most are in large cities, it is difficult to base them on anything but abstract concepts such as 'needs'. Resourcing whole people and whole human lives is anathema to this perspective. For the most part, providing services for, and within the context of, locality-based communities is meaningless in a large city where most residents live in a number of intersecting 'communities' which are not tied to particular localities.

It is not surprising that urban world views would come to dominate welfare in Australia considering that the nation is so highly urbanised, given the overwhelming domination of social policy, social planning, regional development and welfare practice by urban people and urban literature, and given the educational advantages enjoyed by city people. This has been to the detriment of rural Australians.

To summarise, what we have now is a welfare system with the following characteristics:

- It is highly centralised. Virtually all provisions and services are provided directly by government departments, or are funded, heavily regulated and closely supervised by them. Furthermore, most statutory decisions are made in major urban areas.
- The system is urban based in that policies are developed and services are planned and accounted for in cities which are far away from many rural localities. Most services also emanate from cities. For the most part, those in charge are urban people using urban policy paradigms and service models they learned in urban-based training programs.
- It is highly segregated in that a vast array of resources and services are provided in response to narrowly-defined needs. These are 'delivered' by separate government departments and non-government organisations according to equally-segregated funding programs.
- The system is 'provision based' in that formal organisations provide resources and services directly to those who need them. Australia also adopts a 'top-down' approach where welfare is viewed as a function of government rather than an expression of community, and where providers and recipients are clearly distinguished from each other.
- It focuses primarily on individuals and families rather than communities, groups and social networks. Policies, services and provisions are socially contextless in that they are provided to people as if they live in a social vacuum. Furthermore, because it is so focused on individuals and families, Australia's welfare system remains largely unconnected with the communities, social networks and support processes within which they live.
- Social welfare practice is the province of trained, technically-expert professionals to the exclusion of the ordinary people who carry on helping each other anyway.
- The social welfare and economic sectors hardly relate to each other at all.
- Finally, the welfare system fails to respond to the relationship that many rural people have with their natural and spiritual worlds.

How Rural Australia Misses Out

Australia's welfare system has largely failed rural Australians because it is based on these principles. Rural communities usually do not have enough people with a specific need to attract specialised services funded according to total population or target group size. Lacking local services, rural people find it expensive and frequently physically difficult to access those located in urban centres.

A highly complex and fragmented service system is impossible to coordinate, difficult to access and hard to publicise in cities, let alone when users are physically distant from services, when they are widely scattered, and when they lack a local professional to connect them with broader service networks. Furthermore, poor service coordination frequently means that users receive duplicated services or services they don't want, or fall between the cracks of specialised services.

A service which fails to acknowledge the influence of rural communities on human well-being and the knowledge, skills and wisdom of local people will overlook the importance of community ownership or, at the very least, community participation in service provision (Cheers, 1992a). Where the planning, administration and provision of a rural service involves local people, and where staff are well connected with the community the service is more likely to be used by residents. Furthermore, if they don't experience a service as being part of their community, people are less likely to get involved in management and service provision. Failure to recognise community and cultural phenomena can also result in social issues being viewed as individual problems, leading to ineffective intervention and victims being blamed for social ills.

An over-emphasis on formal provisions and professional staff can disconnect services from the support provided spontaneously by relatives, friends, neighbours and local groups (Cheers, 1992b, pp.568-83). In Australia, we have been slow to link formal services with natural supports and provide resources to buttress natural helping processes and reduce costs to carers.

Given that social welfare in Australia has largely been an urban response by urban people to urban problems it is hardly surprising that staff training and selection have not served rural people well. The vast majority of social work, social welfare and community development graduates have been urbanites, many of whom are poorly equipped to live and work in rural areas by virtue of their socialisation, personal values, professional ideologies, or preferred lifestyles (Lonne, 1990). Furthermore, until recently, welfare training in Australia has been dominated entirely by urban models which has only further exacerbated the problems faced by professionals (Sturmey and Edwards, 1991). Rural welfare has only recently been introduced into Australian schools of social work and social welfare, although mostly in a minor way as an elective specialisation or through limited field education experiences. Even then, though, dominant professional ideologies and educational philosophy are prone to view rural communities as inhospitable to the politically correct practitioner, and rural power actors as 'the enemy' (Cheers, 1992a).

Nor have staffing policies been conducive to the development of effective welfare services. Lacking a pool of qualified rural people, government and non-government organisations have used rural positions to induct new graduates into the ways of public administration, test new managers, or side-line mediocre, incompetent or unpopular middle managers. Furthermore, lacking any real incentives to stay in the bush, staff have tended to either suffer rural positions as a temporary, though necessary evil or to use them as stepping stones in essentially urban career paths. And talented rural workers are quickly moved to the city for further organisational socialisation or, if they refuse, find themselves unable to progress their careers further.

Defining 'Rural' and 'Remote'

Rural

Because this book has an applied focus, we will not dwell for too long on the admittedly complex task of defining the concepts *rural* and *remote*. As noted by Nichol (1990, p.5), we need a precise standard definition of the rural-urban continuum which relates to existing definitions, which incorporates categories used by the Australian Bureau of Statistics (ABS), which has the support of the main organisations involved in rural affairs, and which rural people and small organisations find easy to use. For comparative reasons our definition should also relate to those adopted in other countries.

However, this is more easily said than done because of the variety of definitions used in Australia. Population size is the only indicator which satisfies all of the foregoing conditions. The ABS classification (McLennan, 1995, p.25) is as follows:

> Major Urban: All urban centres with a population of 100,000 and over.
> Other Urban: All urban centres with a population of 1,000 to 99,999.
> Bounded Locality: All localities with a population of 200-999.
> Rural Balance: The remainder of the State/Territory.
> Migratory: Offshore Areas and Migratory.

To the ABS, then, rural areas include 'bounded localities' and the 'rural balance'. However, the upper limit of 999 seems unnecessarily restrictive. Within Australian society, communities with much larger populations would normally be regarded as rural.

On the other hand, another Commonwealth report specified less than 100,000 residents as rural (Sher and Sher, 1994, p.11), as did Musgrave (1987) and Powell (1987). Cheers (1990b, p.5) used 49,999 as the upper limit for rural settlements on the basis of his impressions of what are normally regarded as 'country towns' in Australia. This coincides with the limits adopted in the United States by the *Encyclopaedia of Social Work* and by Martinez-Brawley (1990b, p.xv) for what she calls 'small communities'. The United States Bureau of Census also uses 50,000 as the lower limit for urban areas but sets an upper limit for rural communities of 2,500 residents.

Other Australian definitions identify rural areas negatively as all those places left over when certain named large urban places are removed. For good reasons, the concern is to differentiate between the large 'metropolitan' areas of Australia, which have populations in the hundreds of thousands, and smaller cities embedded in rural hinterlands. Epps and Sorensen (1993, p.2), for instance, defined rural Australia as comprising:

> ... everywhere except the six Metropolitan Statistical Divisions of Sydney, Melbourne, Brisbane, Adelaide, Perth, Hobart, the NSW Central Coast, Canberra, the City of the Gold Coast, and such major industrial cities as Wollongong (the Illawarra), Newcastle (the Lower Hunter) and Geelong.

Dunn (1989, p.13) agreed with this definition except that he defined the NSW Central Coast and Wollongong as rural.

Placing these categories along a rural-urban continuum results in the taxonomy presented in Table 1.1. Rural areas include unclustered populations, small towns and large towns.

Table 1.1:   Classification of Rural and Urban Social Places and Related Terms

SETTLEMENT TYPE	DEFINITION
Unclustered population	• One or more people scattered throughout a large geographic area, and clustered settlements with less than 200 residents.
Small town	• A settlement with between 200 and 999 residents.
Large town	• A settlement with between 1,000 and 49,999 residents.
Small provincial city	• A settlement with between 50,000 and 99,999 residents.
Large provincial city	• A settlement with 100,000 residents or more which is not an urban area.
Urban area	• Sydney, Melbourne, Brisbane, Adelaide, Perth, Hobart, the NSW Central Coast, Canberra, the City of the Gold Coast, Wollongong (the Illawarra), Newcastle (the Lower Hunter) and Geelong.

Remote

Rural social places can be more or less remote. When we use the term *remote* we usually mean what the dictionary tells us - "far away or distant" (Harber and Payton, 1978, p.892). The term 'isolated' is frequently used interchangeably with 'remote'. To avoid confusion, *remote* is used here to refer to social places, while *isolation* means remoteness of an individual, family or other type of living group from whatever it is that we are talking about.

A number of studies (e.g., Cheers, 1991) have found that in relation to rural social places *remoteness* is multi-dimensional, incorporating relatively or, in some cases, absolutely limited access to:

- larger population centres;
- a variety of high standard public and private services, facilities and resources;
- good physical infrastructure, including sealed roads, clean water, reliable power and effective garbage and sewerage disposal;
- urban prices for goods and services;
- public and private decision-making processes which affect the community and its residents;

- lifestyle opportunities, including groups of people with similar interests and lifestyle preferences; and
- protective services in relation to situations involving domestic violence and other crime.

It follows, then, that:

> a remote social place is one in which a majority of residents have relatively limited access to services, programs, facilities, goods, resources, opportunities and decision-making processes which affect them.

Here, 'limited access' refers to much more than sheer distance. It also includes travelling conditions, time and costs as well as resources available for the journey or to pay for electronic communication. Griffith (1994), for example, specified a number of 'access elements' in his *Griffith Service Access Frame*, which is a method of measuring remoteness. Elements are how far away the service is from the settlement in question, how much time it takes to get there, the costs involved, and the relative availability of economic resources in the settlement according to the ABS *Index of Economic Resources* (1990). He developed scales to measure each of these. By adding together scores for a given settlement or region on each scale, we can arrive at a service access score for the specified services relative to all other Australian settlements.

From Social Welfare to Social Care

We cannot move forward by simply extending the past. We need a clear vision and some new concepts. If we are to respond more appropriately to rural needs, we must first move beyond the concept of 'social welfare' because it carries some unfortunate conceptual, cultural and ideological baggage.

First, the idea, methods and techniques of 'welfare' are embedded in Western structures and ideologies which suggest an atomistic view of people - that individuals and nuclear families exist as isolated atoms in a social vacuum. For this reason, the term does not sit comfortably with many rural and indigenous people who give higher priority to group, community, cultural and spiritual experiences and to their relationship with the natural world. Second, the concept is historically class based - it derives from a notion of people from one socio-economic class doing something in relation to people from another. Because of this, 'welfare' has frequently been portrayed as a way of getting some people to serve, or at least not to threaten, the interests of those with greater power and resources. Third, the concept has been professionalised. It focuses on some people, usually highly trained, doing things for, or to, some other people. Fourth, as it is used in Australia, the term 'social welfare' is predominantly organisation based. It focuses on provisions made available through formal organisations, rather than social care as part of the very fabric of social life or, in other words, as an expression of 'community'. Fifth, most Western welfare services remain more or less disengaged from the full gamut of social care which people spontaneously provide for each other. There are three tragedies here:

- formal and informal caring fail to support each other;
- the separation makes it easier for governments to devolve responsibility for care to the informal sector, thereby preserving resources for political, economic and militaristic ends; and
- over time, formal welfare services can weaken pre-existing informal caring arrangements within communities (MacPherson, 1994, p.193).

Sixth, in Australia, social welfare systems have been conceptually and administratively separated from market processes, despite the evidence that total human well-being has suffered because of this (Cheers, 1995). Seventh, as discussed earlier, the history and the very idea of welfare is too wedded to urban issues and systems of care to respond effectively to rural needs. Finally, the concept of 'welfare' has largely failed to address global issues, including the obscene distribution of power and resources between as well as within nations, and awful breaches of fundamental human rights.

It is easy to reject established terms. It can be more difficult to replace them with others which are more useful. To improve on 'social welfare', we must first have a clear vision of what we are trying to achieve. Our aim is *social justice*, which is defined here as:

> the establishment and preservation of equal rights of all people and the distribution of power and resources so that this is possible.

Social justice is based on the idea of *social citizenship* which:

> ... refers to the idea that social rights are granted by the state to individuals independent of their participation in the market. It challenges divisions of class, gender and race. It implies an institutional commitment to welfare which is universal, addressing the whole population. As such, it moves beyond the residual idea of welfare which holds that the state should only assume responsibility when the market breaks down; and that its commitment is limited to marginal groups in society. ... As such, social citizenship rejects the idea that a person's worth is only to be measured by economic productivity. (Riches, 1993, pp.8-9)

Human rights usually subsumed under 'social justice' include the rights of a citizen to:

- be treated as a dignified and valued member of human society;
- material security, including adequate shelter;
- an adequate social wage;
- emotional security;
- physical health and well-being;
- social belongingness and social support;
- affordable and accessible health, education, social care and informational services, resources and facilities;
- freedom from unfair disadvantage or disempowerment relative to others;
- information related to their personal well-being;
- develop their life and potentials as they choose;
- access to space, including land, sea and air, which they possess personally or collectively with others through law, custom or heritage;
- maintain and develop their cultural and spiritual heritage and identifications;
- political participation and representation;
- fair, unbiased, visible and accountable public decision making related to their rights and general well-being;
- participation in, access to information concerning, and appeal against public decision-making processes which affect them;
- fair compensation for damage done to their material, psychological, social or cultural well-being, their social standing, or to limitations placed on their rights resulting from the decisions and actions of others; and
- freedom and protection from coercion, abuse and exploitation.

Based as it is on a concept of *individual* rights, the foregoing is good Western ideological stuff. If social justice is to be freed from these shackles, the concept must also be applied to groups of people defined by national borders, culture, ethnicity, religion, filial relationships, socio-economic class, gender and locality. In this context, social justice refers to the establishment and preservation of equal rights for all legitimate groups within a society and the distribution of power and resources amongst them so that this is possible.

If social justice is the aim, *care* is the method:

> 'Care' includes all those arrangements within society, other than the market, which have the primary function of providing for the material, social, emotional, physical, educational and informational well-being and development of citizens, or which help people to access care arrangements.

Material provisions include money, food, clothing and shelter. Social provisions include satisfying social relationships with others; belongingness to social groups; feedback that a person belongs to wider social networks and, through this, has a place within society; and assistance with social problems. Emotional provisions include emotional fulfilment, feedback that a person is held in high regard by others, and assistance with emotional and behavioural difficulties. Physical provisions can be roughly equated with health care broadly defined. Educational provisions include all levels of education. Finally, 'information' includes access to general knowledge, fictional and non-fictional literature, and information about and relevant to rights, policies, services, resources and facilities.

S*ocial care*, which is the focus of this book, is a sub-set of care.

> Social care includes material, social and emotional provisions; assistance in gaining access to information about and relevant to rights, policies, services, resources and facilities; and assistance with accessing care arrangements.

Care arrangements excluded from social care include physical infrastructure provided for the general population such as public transport, health care, education, and information services usually associated with libraries.

Provisions are not limited to goods and services provided by government and non-government organisations; these can also be provided by private individuals. Nor is social care limited to situations in which someone is directly giving something to, or doing something for, someone else. Thus, care arrangements include actions, processes and structures involved in:

- generating policies;
- planning, developing, managing and evaluating programs, services, facilities and resources;
- redistributing power and resources towards marginalised, disadvantaged and disempowered groups;
- community development;
- social change;
- advocacy; and
- social justice research.

Social care is similar to the concept of 'social development' which is well established in international literature (e.g., Midgley, Hall, Hardiman and Narine, 1986; Jayasuriya and Lee, 1994). The latter is not used here because it has three limitations in the Australian context. First, the term 'social development' usually denotes community-based development and provision by and for the people, not development and provision for the people by governments and other large organisations. As it is traditionally used, then, the concept does not adequately describe Australia's 'provision-based' system of care, although this should not be taken to mean that community participation should not be a key component of rural social care in this country. Second, because of its developmental emphasis, the concept has difficulty addressing the needs of communities which are, and will continue to be in long-term decline. Third, as it is used in developing countries, social development normally includes health care and education. In Australia, these are clearly separated both structurally and conceptually from each other and from social care.

What Follows

This is an optimistic book. It is founded on the belief that genuinely rural social care policies and practices can be developed. It is too easy to claim that we are at the beginning, that we know nothing about how to find our way around in this new land. It is also untrue. We know a great deal about rural Australia, and scholars, researchers, practitioners and public administrators have achieved some consensus about the broad parameters of rural social care. Furthermore, government departments and non-government welfare organisations are starting to apply some shared principles. In time, these will be further refined, developed and altered by intelligent public administrators and practitioners in response to the realities in which they find themselves.

We have other tools in our rudimentary swag. We have a sound demographic database incorporating information about population movements. Good community studies have been conducted in Australia over a long period. We have a wealth of information concerning rural life such as social problems and needs, support systems, human services, housing, health and health care, poverty, education, employment and unemployment, indigenous communities, the social, emotional and financial effects of recent recessions and industry restructuring, and much more.

There is an emerging vision of where we are headed. The vision includes innovative, regionally-focused social care policies and services which are negotiated with rural people and which respond to their needs and the realities of their lives. It includes regionally-driven and regionally-coordinated social, economic and infrastructure development. We also know something of the obstacles involved in developing effective rural social care arrangements. Some rural people are politically conservative and will resist social change. Social stratification is strong in many rural areas and powerful local groups sometimes hijack, distort and resist the development of social care policies and services and dilute their impact on disadvantaged groups. Although we may advocate community ownership of service provision, many communities do not have enough people with sufficient time, interest and skills to run community-based organisations efficiently. We also know that the social justice mission of these organisations can be diverted by dominant socio-economic groups. And we know that the economic imperatives which are so powerful in communities with a narrow industry base are usually treated as more important than social needs.

Both the vision and some of the compromises to social justice ideals which are required in specific situations have been documented. We also have documented examples of successful and unsuccessful service programs, welfare practice and social care development initiatives. We have created and tested a range of innovative service models suited to rural areas. And we have some research which identifies the needs and problems of rural people and proposes some solutions for these.

Most importantly, we now know which questions to ask. This book addresses the following:

- How can we develop policies and provide services which are:
  - well coordinated?
  - accessible to rural people given the scattered settlement patterns which are so typical of rural Australia?
  - cost effective, considering that the *per capita* costs of providing most rural services are higher than for equivalent urban services?
  - available to people more or less where and when they are required?
  - relevant to the needs, lifestyles and social, cultural and ecological contexts of rural people given that these vary widely from place to place?
  - acceptable to traditional rural people given their commitment to self-reliance, the distrust with which some of them regard the public social welfare sector, and their general distaste for dependency models of social care?
  - linked with, and supportive of natural helping processes, but which do not destroy their spontaneity, acceptability and effectiveness?
  - responsive to the diversity of rural cultures, groups, regions and communities?
  - based on modern technology? and
  - responsive to the needs of low-income primary producers and other rural business people?
- How can Australia's system of social care respond to the needs, wishes, spirituality and cultural identities of rural indigenous peoples?
- How can we balance the need for public accountability and uniformity of service quality with the importance of community ownership of, or at the very least, participation in planning and providing services?
- How can policy and services respond to the characteristics of rural communities?
- How can we mitigate the social, emotional and financial effects of rural economic, political and social change?
- How can we coordinate regional development in rural Australia?

- How can we attract, select, educate, prepare, support and retain rural social care professionals who understand rural conditions and who want to settle in the bush?

But while it is optimistic, this is not an overly ambitious book. Rural social care is a new field in Australia and relatively undeveloped internationally. Despite apparently wide agreement on essential principles, our knowledge base remains limited. My overriding aim has been to document and organise existing literature and to identify those ideas and principles which seem to have attracted reasonably wide endorsement. Undergraduate and postgraduate students will find in this book a door to existing literature, and ideas and tools to take into their rural work. I have also tried to provide social policy formulators, social planners, human services managers and social care practitioners with some different ways of thinking about and responding to rural issues. Clearly, the demands for instant solutions which they face daily will not wait for the time when researchers and theoreticians feel confident about what they have formulated. And, hopefully, I have provided some food for thought and some new ideas for my research and academic colleagues.

I have tried to build a watershed, a place where we can pause for a while and catch our breath before pushing further along the trail of discovery. I hope that we will look back on this book in another five years and view it as premature and overly general. For that would mean that we have added greater detail to our knowledge base and found more issues to debate. If we do our job well, in a decade or so we will have to write many books to adequately cover the scope of this one.

The book is organised into three sections. Part 1 lays some of the conceptual and empirical foundations for the more applied chapters in Part 2. Chapter 1 has charted the broad terrain, defined key concepts, and identified some of the issues and themes to be explored throughout the book. Chapter 2 describes rural Australia, giving special attention to rural disadvantage and the impacts of recent social and economic change on rural life. In Chapter 3, I discuss rural communities and rural living. The rest of the book draws on these three chapters.

Part 2 organises what we know about social care in rural Australia, develops effective social care responses for rural people, and charts some directions for future development. The aim is to understand the 'differentness' of rural social care, not to regurgitate existing mainstream literature on social policy, social planning, social development, human services provision and welfare practice which is readily available elsewhere. Chapter 4 identifies six frameworks which have informed Australian rural social policy and places rural social care within the broader context of *managed, sustainable regional change*. Four core issues are then identified which weave their way through the rest of the book:

- rural social care as an expression of community as well as a function of government;
- the location of rural social care at the intersection of horizontal and vertical ties;
- the importance of focusing on whole communities as well as individuals and families; and
- the relationship between social and economic development.

In Chapter 5, I examine the fundamental safety net issues of income security and housing and formulate some recommendations for their future development in relation to rural Australians. Chapter 6 discusses *rural social care development*, which includes social planning, community development and community participation, and concludes with a list of functions and tasks which, it is proposed, should be performed in all Australian rural communities. Chapter 7 discusses and formulates recommendations concerning formal social care services, resources and facilities and their relationship with informal social care. Finally, Chapter 8 concludes this section with a discussion of working and living as a practitioner in a rural community.

Part 3 identifies the conceptual threads which run through the entire work. Here I try to chart new territory, erect some sign posts for bushed travellers, provide some tools for their swags, and send them on their way with some encouragement and hope.

Note

1. For the sake of readability, State and Territory governments are referred to collectively as the former.

2 Rural Australia

We live in a dynamic and multifaceted world. Social care is just one component of the social, demographic, economic, political, cultural, spiritual and ecological complexity which is rural Australia. This chapter introduces rural places and people and examines some of the changes which have been affecting them in Australia and elsewhere.

Rural Australia

In Australia:

> There is not the continuity and congruency of land, population, history, tradition and language that knit together a people's soul. (Jose, 1985, p.314)

Australia encompasses 7,682,300km^2 of land and the surrounding sea and air (Castles, 1995, p.3). It is almost as large as the United States (excluding Alaska) and 50 per cent larger than Europe (excluding the former USSR states). 63 per cent of the total land area is devoted to agriculture, making it the most extensive form of land use on the continent (Ockwell, 1990). It is the lowest, flattest and, apart from Antarctica, the driest of all continents (Castles, 1995, p.6). Climate varies widely: temperate conditions in the south-east and south-west; extreme temperature variations associated with desert climates throughout most of the interior; wet and dry tropics in the north; and colder, snowy winters in the south-eastern highlands and Tasmania. The continent has a delicately-balanced ecology (Watson, 1992) and is prone to natural extremes such as droughts, floods, bushfires and tropical cyclones.

Government and Politics

For a long time, Australia was geographically and politically isolated from the rest of the world. Although this isolation afforded some protection against externally-induced change for a long period in our history, it has also resulted in an insular, conservative streak where threats to established values and traditions tend to be resisted.

Australia comprises six States and a number of Territories. The nation has adopted a Westminster parliamentary system which has proven remarkably stable, though frequently resistant to change. There are three levels of government. The *Commonwealth*, or national, government has most of the money and power. It is responsible for the national economy, Commonwealth laws and their enforcement, defence, foreign affairs, immigration and ethnic affairs, postal and telecommunications services, most taxation, major national transportation routes, income security provisions, tertiary education, health insurance legislation, and some areas of health and social care. The *State* and *Territory* governments are responsible for their respective economies, State laws and their enforcement, much of the physical infrastructure (including roads and railways), primary and secondary education, most formal personal social care services, and much of the health care delivery system. Commonwealth and State governments share a number of responsibilities, including physical infrastructure, transportation, main roads, commerce and business, trade, regional development, housing and community services. *Local government* has little power or resources and is responsible primarily for local property-based infrastructure such as roads, sewerage, water and land use. Local governments are also involved in regional planning along with Commonwealth and State governments, and many engage in social planning and community development. Although State and, to a lesser extent, local governments have some taxation powers, the Commonwealth raises most of the nation's revenue which it distributes to the other two levels through a system of grants.

Population and Settlement Patterns

In 1997, Australia's resident population was 18.6 million, growing at an average annual rate of around 1.4 per cent (ABS, 1997; McLennan, 1997, p.76). Australia is one of the world's most highly-urbanised countries and the least densely-populated overall. Most Australians are located in large urban areas, with the remainder spread thinly over vast open spaces (see Figure 2.1). While 1.0 per cent of the continent's total land area contains 84 per cent of all Australians, 50 per cent of the continent contains only 0.3 per cent of the population (McLennan, 1997, p.76). Furthermore, in 1994, 71.5 per cent of the

Figure 2.1 Population Density and Median Annual Rainfall

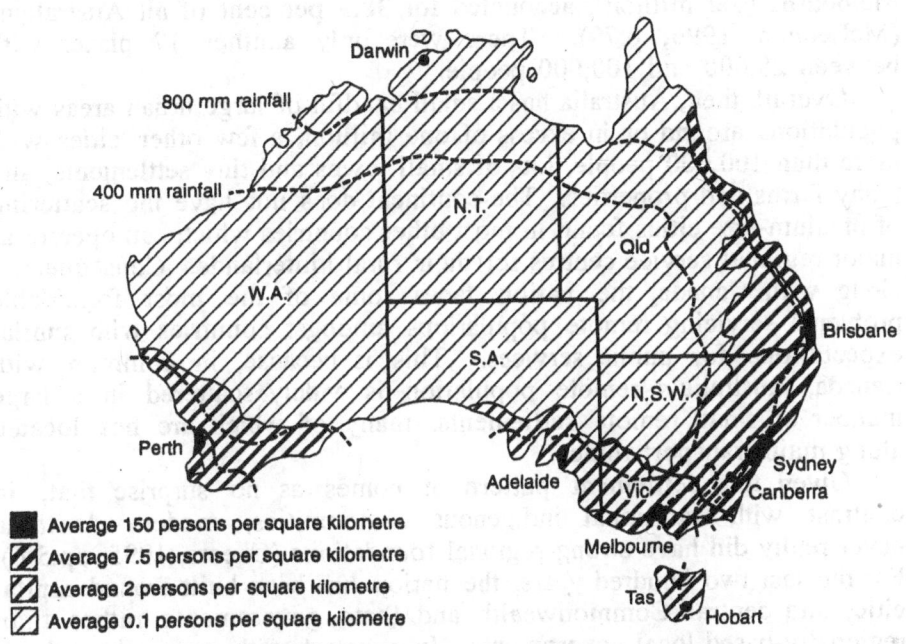

Source: Dept. Immigration and Ethnic affairs, Canberra, AGPS, 1984. Commonwealth of Australia copyright reproduced by permission.

population were living in the eight State, Territory and national capitals and six other major cities of 100,000 persons or more (McLennan, 1996, p.78). At that time, two cities, Sydney (3.7 million) and Melbourne (3.2 million), accounted for 38.9 per cent of all Australians (McLennan, 1996, p.79). There were only another 17 places with between 25,000 and 100,000 people.

Overall, then, Australia has a small handful of large urban areas with populations around or in excess of one million, a few other cities with more than 100,000 people, lots of small towns and tiny settlements, and many farms and properties. The continent does not have the scattering of medium-size cities found in most other countries which can operate as major regional service centres for their rural hinterlands. Consequently, along with Canada, the nation faces some of the most formidable problems servicing remote populations amongst countries with similar expectations for public services. This is because, in common with Canada, Australia's remote population is widely scattered in a large number of small remote settlements, many of which are not located along main transport routes.

Given this settlement pattern it comes as no surprise that, in contrast with traditional indigenous communities, modern Australia never really did have strong regional foundations (Cheers, 1995, pp.5-6). For the last two hundred years, the nation has been built around capital cities and central Commonwealth and State governments rather than regionally-based local governments. In contrast with most other places such as the United States, Europe, Africa and Asia, non-indigenous Australian society does not have a history of local self-reliance and self-government. This is in contrast to the nation's indigenous people who, for at least 60,000 years, were scattered throughout the continent and adjacent islands in self-governing groups, each with their own area of land, sea and air. After their arrival in 1788, non-indigenous Australians congregated initially into a small handful of geographically-separated colonies, each of which came to dominate vast, sparsely-populated, rural hinterlands, politically and economically. From the outset, the lack of natural geographic barriers and the rapid development of long-distance communication and transportation facilitated interaction amongst most communities, thereby reducing the possibility that rural settlements would develop independently from urban centres and from each other. Given this history, it follows that major regional development initiatives have been dominated by urban-based central governments.

How many rural Australians there are depends on how they are defined. In 1991, 14.7 per cent of the total population, or just over 2.6

million people, were living in places with fewer than 1,000 residents and 28.5 per cent, or a little more than 5 million, in settlements with fewer than 100,000 people (McLennan, 1996, p.78).[1] There are proportionately more rural Australians in the Northern Territory (32 per cent), Tasmania (27 per cent) and Queensland (21 per cent) than in the other States or the Australian Capital Territory (Castles, 1995, pp.472-3). The rural population has increased by an average of 1.9 per cent annually over the last two decades, which is slightly faster than the national rate.

Rural Australians are scattered throughout the continent in an enormous number of extraordinarily diverse settlements. As shown in Table 2.1, in 1986 they were living in 1,489 settlements ranging in population size from less than 200 up to 100,000 (Sorensen, 1993b, p.201). Not only is there great diversity amongst rural settlements, but no particular types dominate the landscape.

Castles (1995, pp.472-3) provides an overview of the rural population. Men outnumber women, rural males are slightly older than urban males and rural women are slightly younger than their urban counterparts. There are proportionately more children under 17 years in rural than urban areas, fewer young adults from 17 to 25 years, especially young women, and more adults aged between 30 and 55 years. Rural Australia has relatively more married couples, more nuclear families, and fewer divorced, separated and widowed people, especially amongst women. Rural people are more likely than urban to be self-employed and working in the private sector. They also work longer hours and are more likely to work from home than city people. It is a myth that most rural people are farmers. Depending on how they are defined, only between 3.7 and 17.1 per cent of rural Australians are engaged in farming (Sher and Sher, 1994, p.13).

Economy and Workforce

The rural workforce is small, productive and efficient. In 1991, it delivered two-thirds of all national export earnings, though comprising only 15 per cent of the total Australian workforce (Commonwealth Department of Foreign Affairs and Trade, 1993). At that time, only 24 per cent of rural workers were employed directly in primary industries, including agriculture, forestry, fishing and hunting (Castles, 1995, p.473). Community services, predominantly health and education, accounted for a further 15 per cent of rural workers and the

Table 2.1: Rural Settlement Types

TYPE	SUB-TYPE	NO.	%
Service Centres	Service centres and their satellites.	242	16.3
	Low level services and low income.	213	14.3
Dominant	Local government employment.	22	1.5
Special	Railway towns and transport towns.	9	0.6
Function	Materials processing.	167	11.2
Communities	Primary production and processing.	34	2.3
Farming	Small farming and fishing communities.	108	7.3
Communities	Low level farming and services.	69	4.6
	Farming communities, older age structure.	30	2.0
	Low level services, young unqualified workers.	8	0.5
Miscellaneous	High income professional services.	89	6.0
Service	Upwardly mobile working class.	145	9.7
Communities	Public administration and defence.	16	1.1
Resorts and	High status resorts.	24	1.6
Retirement	Ski resorts.	3	0.2
	Resorts + retirement function.	94	6.3
	Retirement + some resort functions.	13	0.9
	Low income retirement.	61	4.1
Mining	Mining A - multifunction.	40	2.7
	Mining B - heavy mining dominance.	42	2.8
	Low level mining.	15	1.0
Indigenous	Strong professional and service.	11	0.7
	Local government employment.	5	0.3
	Commonwealth and State government.	12	0.8
	Part-time work.	16	1.1
Young Working Class, High Unemployment		1	0.1
TOTALS		1489	100.0

Source: Sorensen (1993b, pp.204-5).

wholesale/retail sector 14 per cent. In 1989-90, more than 90 per cent of the nation's 167,200 agriculture properties were family owned and operated (Mollah, 1993, pp.58-9).

The rural sector has always been a key component of the national economy. In the 1950s, agriculture was earning over 80 per cent of all export dollars, although this had fallen to 20.6 per cent in the early 1990s (Australian Farm Journal, 1993; Epps and Sorensen, 1993, p.1). Meanwhile, the difference has been taken up by mining, another rural-based industry, which increased its share of export earnings from 28.5

per cent to 40.8 per cent between 1974 and the early 1990s (Australian Bureau of Agricultural and Resource Economics (ABARE), 1992).

Rural Australia is important to the nation in other ways (Sher and Sher, 1994, pp.11-3). It is the source of self-sufficiency for the entire nation in relation to food, natural resources and raw materials, the cornerstone of Australia's export economy, and the location of a disproportionately large share of the nation's assets and productive activity. Rural Australia helps to take the pressure off cities and urban people in that it is the preferred destination for people changing their place of residence and the place where most Australians go to temporarily escape the pressures of city life. Rural Australia is also the main source of the nation's international identity and cultural distinctiveness and the magnet for international tourists.

Rural Disadvantage

Given all this, it would come as no surprise should an extra-terrestrial visitor expect rural Australians to be treated like royalty for their contribution to national well-being. Not so - the reverse is actually the case. Time and again, reviews have found that rural Australians are disadvantaged relative to urban residents on almost all indices of social, physical and economic disadvantage and in their access to services, and that those living in the more remote parts of the continent are still further disadvantaged (e.g., Cheers, 1990b; Office of Northern Development (OND), 1994, pp.23-4; Sher and Sher, 1994, p.17).

Indicators

General Indicators Research has consistently demonstrated that rural areas are disadvantaged relative to urban, and the more remote places are further disadvantaged with respect to relative socio-economic disadvantage, social deprivation, life chances, material well-being and statistically-based quality of life indicators (Australian Government Commission of Inquiry into Poverty, 1975; Walmsley, 1980; Rumley, 1983; Glover and Woollacott, 1992). But while they do make the general case, studies such as these are imprecise in that they reveal little about specific indicators or regional variations.

Income In 1991, the median annual income for all persons over 15 years was the same for rural and urban areas, although it was lower for rural families (Castles, 1995, p.473). This was confirmed by OND for Northern Australia[2] where pockets of extremely low income levels were identified in some small remote settlements, especially indigenous communities, and amongst aged people, agriculture workers, indigenous Australians, young people, the unemployed and some small business people (OND, 1994, pp.22-4).

Poverty Rural poverty, both farm and non-farm, is generally higher and more prolonged in rural than urban areas (Department of Community Services (DCS), 1986; Lawrence and Share, 1993, p.5). Even small provincial cities suffer higher rates of poverty than do urban areas (Monk, 1980, p.129). Rural Australians most likely to be poor are indigenous people, farm owners and farm workers (DCS, 1986; Rolley and Humphreys, 1993, pp.248-9).

Living Costs A steady flow of evidence over a long period confirms that prices for goods and services increase as we move from major urban areas to provincial cities, to rural regions, to smaller and more remote settlements (e.g., Loder, 1965; Queensland Office, ABS, 1985, pp.367-82; Hudson, 1989; OND, 1994, p.23). What is remarkable is that higher rural living costs have been documented for more than 30 years, yet nothing much has changed.

Housing In 1991, the median weekly rent in rural areas was around half that paid by urban Australians, and the median monthly rural housing loan repayment was also less (Castles, 1995, p.473). Inevitably, global figures do not account for substantial regional variations. For instance, a recent study by the Northern Territory Department of Lands and Housing (1993) found that rental properties in remote locations in the Northern Territory were far more expensive than in all Australian capital cities (OND, 1994, p.25). Furthermore, rural housing tends to be poorer in quality than urban stock and this can have serious consequences for other areas of human living such as health and education. In reality, savings in housing costs are frequently paid out in other areas of life. It is well established, for example, that housing standards and associated living conditions such as sanitation, hygiene and the quality of water supplies are associated with poorer health, especially in remote Aboriginal and Torres Strait Islander communities (Burnley,

1981; OND, 1994, p.26). Rural housing is also less secure and less available than urban (Hudson, 1992). In Northern Australia, for instance, levels of home ownership are significantly lower than the national average and they reduce further as we move from cities to rural areas to the more remote communities (ABS, 1991a; OND, 1994, p.25).

Unemployment Employment opportunities are more limited in rural than urban areas, even more so in smaller communities, and many rural jobs are seasonal, poorly paid and require low skill levels (Lawrence and Share, 1993, p.5; Rolley and Humphreys, 1993, p.249). Rural unemployment is higher and more prolonged than urban in all States and Territories, with the difference being even greater when under-employment and hidden unemployment are taken into account (DCS, 1986; OND, 1994, p.32). In rural areas, unemployment tends to concentrate in particular regions and groups, especially amongst casual workers, farm labourers, indigenous Australians, junior workers, young women and people with mild disabilities (Rolley and Humphreys, 1993, p.249; OND, 1994, p.32).

Health It is well established that the health status of rural Australians is poorer than that of urban people in relation to premature mortality, morbidity rates, hypertension and psychiatric disorders (e.g., Fitzwarryne and Fitzwarryne, 1982; Wong, 1990; Rolley and Humphreys, 1993; Aoun, Underwood and Rouse, 1994). Furthermore, over the last decade the physical and mental health of many rural people has deteriorated, stress levels have risen, and psychological and social problems associated with dislocation have soared (Bryant, 1991, 1992; Rolley and Humphreys, 1993). Rural suicide rates are also much higher than urban and the gap has been widening at an alarming rate for the last 30 years (Bush, 1990; Wong, 1990; Cooper, 1992; Department of Health, Housing and Community Services, 1992, p.5). For instance, over a twelve month period in 1990, farmer suicides rose by a stunning 67 per cent (Cooper, 1992). More alarming still, though, are the even higher rates of rural youth suicide, especially for men, which are widely acknowledged to be amongst the worst in the world (DHHCS, 1992, p.5; Lohse, 1992; Wilson, 1995, p.7). In 1992, the rate for young rural men between 15 and 24 years was 37.7 per 100,000, which was 50 per cent higher than the urban rate of 24.7 per 100,000 (Commonwealth Department of Human Services and Health, 1995, p.14). Although many factors contribute to rural youth suicide, in recent times it appears to have been largely the result of rising unemployment, declining populations, disintegration of many rural communities, a pervasive sense of hopelessness and despair and, for many, the demise of farming as a way of life.

There has always been a clear rural-urban imbalance in the availability of, and access to, health care services in Australia. In 1992, for instance, the ratio of general practitioners to population was 1:732 for urban areas, 1:1116 for rural areas and 1:1055 for more remote regions (Reid and Solomon, 1992). In Western Australia in 1989, only 9 per cent of the State's specialists were practicing outside the Perth metropolitan area, even though 27 per cent of the population were living in rural areas (OND, 1994, pp.28-9). Nationally, similar trends are apparent for other health personnel including doctors, dentists, community nurses, occupational therapists, physiotherapists and mental health workers (Reid and Solomon, 1992, p.22).

Rural areas have fewer health services, facilities and resources than urban. These include hospitals, specialised equipment, allied health services, rehabilitation facilities, surgical and anaesthetic services, nursing home and private hospital accommodation, women's health centres, family planning clinics, drug and alcohol counselling services, mental health services, health education facilities, rehabilitative and support services for the aged and handicapped, community health nurses, and provision for patients requiring intensive care and resuscitation (Platt and Brentnall, 1985; Humphreys, 1993, p.16).

The health service access difficulties experienced by rural Australians are further aggravated by the large distances many must travel to reach services, by the unavailability in many regions of adequate transportation and communication facilities, by higher levels of rural poverty and by lower incomes. Residents in areas lacking local hospitals, doctors and other facilities can obtain health care only at considerable financial, social and psychological cost to themselves and their supports (Humphreys, 1985; Cheers, 1990b). The more needy, such as the poor, the elderly, the unemployed and people with disabilities, have even greater access problems. All must endure long, time-consuming and uncomfortable journeys, often while in pain or other discomfort.

Education Rural people achieve less educationally than their urban counterparts (Rolley and Humphreys, 1993, p.250; Castles, 1995, p.472) and rural primary and secondary schools, especially non-government, have lower retention and completion rates than urban (National Board of Employment, Education and Training, 1991). The most educationally-disadvantaged young people include those who have physical or mental disabilities, who need remedial teaching or who live in itinerant families (Monk, 1980; OND, 1994, p.30), and indigenous children and youth from the more remote and smaller settlements. In recent times, the rural crisis has further curtailed educational opportunities for many rural children as more families have found themselves unable to afford boarding school fees and as children have increasingly been leaving school prematurely to help on family properties.

Relatively fewer rural than urban adults have post-school qualifications and, even as late as 1991, fewer were enrolled in Technical and Further Education Colleges, Colleges of Advanced Education and universities (Castles, 1995, p.472). Castles suggested that this was due to the small number of tertiary institutions, particularly universities, located in, or readily accessible from rural areas. Thankfully, these disparities appear to be decreasing rapidly (Lewis, 1990).

Social Problems Many authors have commented on the social, emotional and behavioural problems experienced by rural people, their rapid increase over the last two decades, and their association with rising levels of stress brought about by rural recessions, droughts and rural restructuring (e.g., Lawrence and Williams, 1990; Bryant, 1991, 1992; Lawrence and Share, 1993, p.5; Rolley and Humphreys, 1993, p.249). However, in relation to most issues, hard evidence is difficult to find. It is clear to even the casual observer that the vast array of urban welfare services are either unavailable in rural and remote areas or are so inaccessible and under-resourced as to be virtually non-existent. This was supported in 1987 by Coleman (p.5) who reported that remote areas had less than half the range of general community services available in urban areas and by Courtenay (1982, pp.256-70) who found that in 1976 the *per capita* provision of community services was substantially lower in Northern Australia than in the nation as a whole.

Essential Services Many of the essential services which are taken for granted in urban Australia are often unavailable in rural and remote areas. Where they are provided, they tend to be lower standard, more costly and/or less accessible to residents. These include water, sewerage, power, roads, public transport, telephone and postal services, radio and television, retail outlets, commercial and professional services, repair and maintenance services, and recreation and entertainment facilities (Cheers, 1990b, p.8).

Conclusion

The obvious conclusion is that rural communities have been valued less and less for their own intrinsic merit - as places where people live their lives - and increasingly as "... headwaters for an extractive society" (Nachtigal, 1994, p.145). On virtually all indices reviewed here, rural Australians are disadvantaged relative to urban. On many there is a sliding scale of locational disadvantage from urban areas to provincial cities, to large towns, to small towns and remote regions. This is so in relation to general socio-economic indicators, living costs, unemployment, workforce participation, poverty levels, housing availability and security, health status, education opportunities, community and personal support services, and essential services. However, there have been significant improvements over recent years in relation to some health and education indicators.

The concept of locational disadvantage conceals as much as it reveals. Clearly, there are many people in cities who are also disadvantaged, just as there are many rural people who are better off than most urban residents. Furthermore, general figures are averages only and, as such, hide extremes of deprivation in particular regions and amongst specific groups. Income levels are especially low for many indigenous Australians, young people, aged people, farmers, farm workers, small business people and the unemployed. Indigenous people and young rural Australians suffer levels of unemployment which are absurd in one of the wealthiest countries in the world (Walmsley and Sorensen, 1993, pp.64-5). Extremes of poverty are experienced by many indigenous Australians and by farmers and farm workers in economically-depressed regions. Standards of housing and associated services such as water, power and sewerage can be atrocious in some remote regions, and especially in remote indigenous communities. Health status is also extremely poor in many of these communities and, with regard to mental health, amongst young people, especially men. Those hardest hit with respect to educational opportunities and achievement are indigenous people and youth. And we know that women bear the brunt of many social problems.

This discussion has painted a gloomy picture which implies that rural people must be a miserable lot. This is not true. As we shall see in Chapter 3, the joys of rural life are many, so much so that a number of studies from the United States and Canada have shown that, despite being aware of the many material disadvantages of rural living, rural and urban residents alike still claim that the quality of rural life is superior (e.g.,

Campbell, Converse and Rodgers, 1976; Dillman and Tremblay, 1977; Rodgers, 1979; Filson and McCoy, 1993).

Explanations

Two explanations have been offered for rural disadvantage in Australia. *Threshold* arguments suggest that given small settlement sizes and high population dispersion in rural and, especially, the more remote places, it is too costly to provide the array of services required to sustain a quality of life equal to that enjoyed by city people. There is some truth here. As discussed earlier, Australia does indeed face more severe problems servicing the more remote areas than do most other countries.

However, threshold arguments have a number of weaknesses. First, they tend to equate 'the good life' with 'the good *city* life'. It may simply not be true for many rural people that ready access to an extensive array of locally-based, urban-style services, facilities and resources is a major factor in how they assess the quality of their lives. Second, threshold arguments assume that rural services should be similar to urban. This, too, is an urbo-centric position which is challenged throughout this book. Third, threshold arguments fail to explain some of the facts. They cannot, in themselves, tell us why some publicly-subsidised rural settlements, such as company-based mining towns, receive more and higher standard services than other settlements of equivalent size and remoteness. Nor can they explain why some rural people, such as public servants, are assisted more by public policies and services than their neighbours, such as pastoralists and small business people. Nor can high service costs explain why some kinds of services are more highly developed and more abundant in rural areas than others. Why, for instance, are public services and resources relating to communication, transport, roads, mainstream education and curative medicine more abundant in rural and remote locations than those concerned with preventive health care, personal social care services, remedial education programs, the needs of aged people and those with disabilities, and the problems of suicidal youth?

The extension of threshold arguments is the suggestion that, because of cost considerations, Australian society has reduced responsibility for adequately resourcing rural and remote populations (e.g., Lonsdale, 1981; Moran and O'Connor, 1981). This, in turn, assumes that human society has less of a role in producing their social and economic problems in the first place. This is wrong. The formation and utilisation of space, including the very creation of distance, does not occur in a socio-economic vacuum. The need of capital for particular kinds of natural resources, labour and equipment, and the choices capital makes about where these should be located in space so as to ensure maximum efficiency and profitability are key determinants of how space is constructed and utilised (Smith, 1984). The choices made by capital, most of which are supported by governments, have a major influence on where people live, where settlements are located, settlement size, how resources and services are distributed, the sustainability of natural resources, whether and how the natural environment is exploited and neglected, the rise and fall of plant and animal species, and much more.

Political economy arguments, on the other hand, provide more useful explanations for rural and remote region disadvantage than do threshold arguments. These assume that national resources are limited and suggest that they are distributed throughout space and across industries largely according to the perceived needs of capital and the national economy, balancing of competing interests by governments, political expediency, and the primacy which Australian society gives to economic rather than social, cultural, ecological and spiritual values. Proponents claim that political economy arguments also account for some of the facts left unexplained by threshold arguments. For example, communities of similar size and remoteness are treated differently because some have been more effectively represented in decision-making processes and/or because they can better serve national or international economic interests. For the same reasons, some groups receive better treatment than others despite being located in the same region. Proponents of political economy arguments also point out that, in rural areas, some services are more highly developed than others because they better support the interests of capital and governments (Tomlinson and Tannock, 1982; Holmes, 1984, 1985; Humphreys, 1985). It has been claimed, for instance, that improvements in rural services and resources over the last twenty years have occurred primarily in:

- physical infrastructure - such as roads, transport, communication, media and electricity - to facilitate primary production;
- fiscal policies - such as income tax relief, special rural assistance programs, fuel subsidies, some drought relief packages, and some financial assistance schemes - also to facilitate primary production;

- mainstream compared with remedial education facilities to keep people on the land and to maintain a literate, numerate workforce; and
- primary rather than preventive health care to maintain a healthy workforce and because of the influence of a medical profession based on private enterprise.

Indigenous Australians

Australia has many indigenous peoples and cultures which are usually grouped into *Aborigines*, who are scattered throughout the mainland and Tasmania, and *Torres Strait Islanders*, who traditionally own a group of islands just to the north of Cape York Peninsula. In 1994, there were 303,261 Aborigines and Torres Strait Islanders, representing 1.7 per cent of the total Australian population (McLennan, 1996, p.81). Although there are no accurate estimates, it has been suggested that the 'absolute minimum' indigenous population immediately before the arrival of Europeans in 1788 was 315,000 (McLennan, 1997, p.88). Given this figure, by 1921 the indigenous population had fallen by an 'absolute minimum' of 80 per cent to 62,000 (Walmsley and Sorensen, 1993, p.46).

Indigenous people are more likely than other Australians to live outside the national and state capitals (Castles, 1995, p.95) and are more widely dispersed throughout the continent. In 1994, 27 per cent of indigenous Australians were living in capital cities, 50 per cent in towns and rural localities, and slightly less than 20 per cent in rural and remote areas (McLennan, 1996, p.81). While around 90 per cent of the general population are contained within 2.8 per cent of the total land area, 90 per cent of indigenous people live in 28 per cent of the continent (McLennan, 1997, p.90). Furthermore, the propensity of indigenous Australians to live outside capital cities and in small remote communities is highest in Queensland, the Northern Territory, South Australia and Western Australia. For instance, in the more remote regions in Northern Australia, indigenous people comprise around 30 per cent of all residents (McLennan, 1996, p.81).

In recent times, many Indigenous Australians have been returning to their traditional 'homelands' and forming outstations in remote locations. Their main problem has been the lack of physical and social infrastructure such as water, power, road and transport facilities, and health and education services. In 1994, for instance, essential services such as water and power were available in less than half of the newer outstations in Northern Australia (OND, 1994, p.19).

Indigenous Australians have inhabited the continent and adjacent 60,000 years,[3] living in impressive harmony with their natural, spiritual, cultural and social worlds until the arrival of the British a little over 200 years ago (Smallwood, 1994, p.305). The usual accounts tell us that they migrated from Asia, although some indigenous people now claim that they may have originated on the Australian continent (Smallwood, 1994, p.305). Either way, it is inevitable that living for such a long period on a continent which is physically separated from all other societies would result in a unique culture which was well adapted to an equally unique natural environment. Their world was full of spiritual realities and, by all accounts, Aboriginal people managed the land, sea and air, their livelihood and their health extremely well.

This all changed with the arrival of Western capitalism. Shielded (and deluded) with a false doctrine of *terra nullius* - that the land was uninhabited and belonged to no-one - the invaders claimed the continent as theirs and the indigenous culture was rapidly decimated as a result of impoverishment, introduced diseases, kidnapping and murder (Smallwood, 1994, p.305). With regard to kidnapping, even as late as 1994, one in ten indigenous Australians aged 25 years or more claimed to have been taken away as children from their natural families by "... a mission, the government or welfare" (Madden, 1994, p.2).

Indigenous Disadvantage

The level of indigenous disadvantage in this country is abysmal for a nation claiming to be civilised (Department of Aboriginal Affairs (DAA), 1986). Aborigines and Torres Strait Islanders are the worst served groups in Australia socially, educationally, judicially, physically, economically and in all other ways. As Dodson (1993, p.119) pointed out:

> The indigenous peoples of Australia are the poorest, sickest, most ill-educated, most chronically unemployed, most arrested and most imprisoned people in this country.

Smallwood (1994, p.306) tells us of recent reports by the World Bank and the World Council of Churches which described Aboriginal living conditions, health status and health care as being of Fourth World standards, especially in the more remote communities.

Income In 1994, the average annual income for indigenous households was around half that earned by all Australians (Madden, 1994, p.48). This was unchanged from 1981 (DAA, 1986). In New South Wales, and probably in other States as well, indigenous income levels are directly related to settlement size - the larger the community the higher the income (Taylor and Roach, 1994, p.13).

Housing In 1994, the National Aboriginal and Torres Strait Islander Survey (Madden, 1994) found that rural indigenous people reported more severe, and a wider range of housing problems than their urban counterparts. Over-crowding increases as we move from capital cities, to provincial cities and larger towns, to rural areas (averages of 3.5, 4.1 and 4.9 people per dwelling respectively) (p.30). The Survey also found that there were six or more people living in 13.6 per cent of city dwellings, 19.6 per cent of 'other urban' dwellings and 33.1 of rural dwellings (p.30). Over-crowding is particularly severe in the more remote areas. For instance, in 1993 in the Daly River region in the Northern Territory, 44 per cent of households had eight or more residents and as many as 20 per cent had three or more families in the one household (Aboriginal and Torres Strait Islander Commission (ATSIC), 1993). Madden (1994) found that rural households expressed higher levels of dissatisfaction with rental accommodation (31 per cent) than those in capital cities (22 per cent) and other urban areas (24 per cent) (p.25). Dissatisfaction was highest in the most remote communities such as Jabiru (88.4 per cent) and Aputula (72.8 per cent) (p.28). Rural residents fared worse than non-rural on all measures of housing quality reviewed (p.31), although they were paying lower average rentals than indigenous people in other places (p.32).

Unemployment Indigenous Australians suffer far higher unemployment levels than others. The following figures come from the national Aboriginal and Torres Strait Islander Survey (Madden, 1994). In Australia the *Community Development Employment Program (CDEP)* is a government funded scheme, operating mostly in rural areas, which provides limited employment for indigenous people in community projects. The following unemployment figures do not include CDEP employed people.

In 1994, the official indigenous unemployment rate (those registered for employment but without a job) was 38 per cent, which was around four times the national rate. It was 50 per cent for 15 to 19 year olds and 46 per cent for 20-24 year olds. That 32 per cent of those not registered for employment wanted a job demonstrates that the true unemployment figures were far higher than these rates indicate. Disregarding people employed on CDEP projects, indigenous unemployment was about the same level in capital cities, provincial cities, large towns and rural areas. Thus, without the CDEP, rural indigenous unemployment would be far higher than urban. However, because of low wages the CDEP has little effect on relative income levels.

Health In 1991, life expectancy at birth for indigenous Australians was around 20 years less than the national average (Symons, 1992, p.8; OND, 1994, p.26; Mathers, 1995). Furthermore, in 1981 indigenous infant mortality was 2.6 times the national rate (DAA, 1986), although Mathers (1995) has reported some improvement over the last 15 years. Indigenous Australians are far more likely than others to suffer from a variety of diseases including respiratory and infectious diseases, leprosy, tuberculosis, liver cancer, trachoma, chronic renal disease, alcoholism, sexually transmitted diseases, hypertension and diabetes (Symons, 1992, p.8; Walmsley and Sorensen, 1993, p.200).

In 1992, the mortality rate for indigenous Northern Territorians averaged four times the rate for other Australians over a range of age groups (Symons, 1992). It was ten times higher for those aged 30-34 years and six times higher for 25 to 50 year olds. In a recent study, Mathers (1995) found that death rates from preventable diseases for Aborigines living in remote communities in Northern Australia were around 20 times higher than the national average. Remote communities with less than 5000 people, and where more than 50 per cent of residents were Aboriginal, displayed by far the highest mortality rates.

Our main interest here is in comparisons between rural and urban indigenous people. The following analysis draws on studies which make direct comparisons and those which compare the Northern Territory with national figures. The latter reflect the relatively high numbers of indigenous people in the Territory who live in rural and remote areas.

In South Australia, the rural indigenous infant mortality rate is nearly four times the indigenous rate for Adelaide (South Australia Health Commission, 1988). Figures from the Northern Territory also indicate higher rates in remote areas: in 1991, indigenous infants were dying at a rate of 3.7 times the national average (Symons, 1992, p.8) and 1.9 times the rate for non-indigenous infants in the Territory (Gray, 1988).

The 1994 National Aboriginal and Torres Strait Islander Survey also found that indigenous people in rural areas suffer significantly poorer health status than those in capital cities (Madden, 1994). Rural respondents reported higher frequencies of dietary, nutrition, skin, heart and alcohol problems as well as a higher incidence of diabetes, although they also reported fewer substance abuse problems (p.22). In a less direct comparison, the OND (1994, p.28) reported that indigenous children in the Northern Territory suffer higher rates of malnutrition, diarrhoea, skin infections and communicable diseases such as respiratory tract and middle ear infections. There was no evidence to suggest that the situation might be improving.

Further evidence for the extremely poor health status of indigenous Australians living in remote communities comes from a recent study by Torzillo, Hanna, Morey, Gratten, Dixon and Erlich (1995) who found that, regardless of the age group, indigenous people in Central Australia suffer the world's highest levels of serious infections causing pneumonia, meningitis and septicaemia. This situation was attributed to poor living conditions, malnutrition, and high rates of alcohol abuse, diabetes, chronic renal failure and cardiac disease.

Health problems such as these are compounded by and, in some cases, are the direct result of health service access difficulties. To sample just a few figures, Madden (1994, pp.19-20) found that of all indigenous households surveyed throughout Australia, 43 per cent were more than 50km from the nearest hospital, 47.5 per cent did not have access to 'flying medical services', 25.6 per cent were more than 100km from a chemist or dispensary, 74 per cent could not access mental health services, and 43 per cent could not access ante-natal services. As would be expected, indigenous people living in rural areas had less access to all health services than those in provincial cities and towns who, in turn, had less access than people in capital cities (p.12).

Education Indigenous Australians leave school earlier than non-indigenous people, fewer seek tertiary education, and their education achievements and aspirations are lower (DAA, 1986; Cheers, 1990b). But the situation appears to be improving rapidly. In New South Wales, indigenous participation in education improved by a dramatic 67.3 per cent between 1986 and 1991 compared with an increase of only 14.5 per cent for all Australians (Taylor and Roach, 1994, p.7). However, there are no real differences between school participation rates for indigenous people living in rural regions, capital cities and 'other urban' areas (Madden, 1994, p.39). Participation rates for those studying for higher qualifications are also much the same, although they fall a little as we move to smaller and more remote communities (Madden, 1994, p.42).

Legal Justice The evidence concerning imprisonment and arrest of indigenous Australians is simply unacceptable. In 1981, the indigenous rate of imprisonment was 11.6 times the rate for all Australians (DAA, 1986). In 1994, one in five indigenous Australians over 12 years reported having been arrested at least once in the previous five years, 57 per cent of these more than once (Madden, 1994, p.57,62). The figures were slightly higher for rural residents. 31 per cent of males had been arrested at least once and 19.4 per cent more than once. For females, the figures were 9.3 per cent and 4.0 per cent respectively. Narrowing the age range, two in every five males aged 15 to 44 years reported having been arrested at least once, one in four more than once.

Essential Services In 1994, Madden (p.31) reported data concerning essential services and facilities provided to indigenous dwellings. These seemed to be in place for those living in capital cities, provincial cities and the larger towns. However, almost one in four rural households reported that they did not have a garbage collection service, one in thirteen that running water and electricity/gas were not connected to the dwelling, almost one in ten that they did not have a toilet, and more than one in eight that they lacked a shower. As usual, the situation is even worse in the more remote communities. For instance, a 1993 report indicated that more than one in four of all Northern Australian indigenous communities had neither a water supply which satisfied national health standards nor an adequate sewerage disposal system (ATSIC, 1993). Thirty per cent of these communities had no electricity whatsoever.

Conclusion The level of indigenous disadvantage in this country is abysmal for a civilised nation. Indigenous people die 20 years younger than other Australians, their infant mortality rate is 2.6 times the national rate, and they suffer disease and illness far more frequently. What is perhaps even more disturbing is that although the health status of indigenous people in virtually all other developed countries, and many developing countries as well, has improved markedly over the last 20 years, this has not been the case in Australia (Mathers, 1995). The indigenous unemployment rate is around four times the national average and they receive half the income of other Australians. Indigenous

Australians achieve less educationally, although this is changing rapidly. They also live in poorer quality housing and in more crowded conditions. They are imprisoned 11.6 times more frequently than other Australians and 25 per cent of males aged 15 to 44 years have been arrested twice or more.

Indigenous people living in rural areas are generally worse off than those in cities. They suffer higher infant, child and adult mortality and morbidity rates, higher death rates from preventable diseases, and their access to health services is much worse. They receive less income and suffer poorer quality and more over-crowded housing conditions. Their education levels have improved dramatically over the last 15 years, although their participation in tertiary education remains lower than for their urban counterparts. Essential services are poorer in quality in rural areas, extremely so in the more remote communities. Pockets of extreme disadvantage exist in remote indigenous communities in Northern and Central Australia.

Native Title

Many indigenous Australians believe that the *Native Title Act* was a significant step towards changing this situation (Department of Prime Minister and Cabinet, 1994). For many decades now they have been adamant that there will be little progress towards genuine social justice until they secure rights of ownership over their traditional lands. This, they argue, is the foundation upon which their cultural, spiritual, social and personal identity must be rebuilt. For this reason, and for the leadership it provides in recognising the full and unique citizenship of indigenous Australians, the *Native Title Act of 1993* has been viewed as a major step forward. It was the end result of a land claim by Eddie Mabo and other Meriam people of the Murray Islands in the Torres Strait. In 1992, the High Court of Australia rejected the doctrine of *terra nullius* and found that the lands of the Australian continent had indeed belonged to indigenous peoples at the time of white settlement in 1788. The subsequent *Native Title Act* recognises and protects native title. It established legal structures and processes to ascertain where native title exists, what it is, who holds it, to enable future dealings in native title lands and to determine compensation for acts affecting it. The *Act* also created a land acquisition fund to meet the needs of dispossessed Aboriginal and Torres Strait Islander peoples who cannot claim native title. Significant concessions have been made to competing interests, especially the pastoral and mining industries, in that the *Act* provides for the validation of any past grants of land that may otherwise have been invalid because of the existence of native title. However these concessions were weakened slightly in a recent decision by the High Court of Australia (known as the *'Wik Judgement'*) which ruled that native title can survive pastoral leases, although the pastoral lease would prevail where there is a conflict of interests (Fagan, Kennedy and Short, 1996). The Act also provides for the right of negotiation in relation to pastoral and, especially, mining activity on land where native title exists. The Act received widespread support from the Aboriginal and Torres Strait Islander Commission and indigenous communities more generally.

Although qualified, these and the many other positive steps taken towards reconciliation between indigenous and non-indigenous peoples since the 1967 referendum, which gave the Commonwealth the power to make laws in the interests of indigenous people, are now in danger of being reversed by the present Commonwealth Government. Because of political pressures and a complete lack of sociological and cultural imagination the Government has moved a set of amendments to the *Native Title Act* which would, if passed by the Upper House of the Australian Parliament, extend validation of titles and leases to lands not currently covered in the Act and remove legal protection of indigenous people's right to negotiate pastoral, mining and other activities on their legally-recognised land. The Upper House recently rejected the amendments, despite offering compromises on most of the points which were not accepted by the Government. In an act of blatant political cynicism, which has more to do with attempting to restore its ailing electoral fortunes and the timing of the next election than with native title legislation, the Howard Government has threatened to take the nation to what would be a socially and culturally divisive early election based on race should the amendments be rejected a second time. Indigenous people and many other sections of the Australian community are outraged.

Rightly, Patrick Dodson, an Aboriginal leader, has argued that the amendments would set back indigenous rights to before the 1967 referendum by empowering the Federal Parliament to pass laws against, rather than for, the interests of indigenous people (The Advertiser, May 9, 1997, p.13). He commented that "... the High Court Mabo and Wik judgements had left political thinking and ingenuity well behind".

> They are back in the 1830s in terms of the political thinking here. The court says that native title and natives can exist on the land in a co-operative way with pastoralists, subject to those rights the pastoralists have got. We have

got, for the first time in 200 years, a chance to develop friendship, develop genuine trust, develop co-existence. The Prime Minister's proposal sets out to destroy that. (*The Advertiser*, May 9, 1997, p.13)

To make matters worse, the Howard Government stubbornly refuses to offer, on behalf of the Australian nation, an unqualified apology for past injustices suffered by indigenous Australians. In a remarkable act of cultural projection the Government unjustifiably claims that if such an apology was given, indigenous people would lodge an economically-unmanageable log of compensation claims. This is despite the denials of indigenous leaders.

Change

The rural world is constantly being formed and re-formed by a host of global, national and regional forces, most dominantly in the present era by the needs of capital (Smith, 1984; Hungerford, 1994). This century is unique with regard to their power, their geographic reach, and the speed and comprehensiveness of the changes they have induced. Changes discussed here concern market dynamics, the nature of work, communication technology and population movements.

Market Dynamics

The needs of rural people cannot be fully understood without some knowledge of the market forces which shape their lives. The relationship between rural human well-being and market dynamics is more direct than it is for most urban people because rural communities usually depend on a small handful of extractive industries. Unfortunately, the social care sector has largely failed to grasp its relationship with other sectors such as economics, regional development, land use planning, ecology and public administration.

Rural Australia is increasingly buffeted by global and national market forces. These will be reviewed only briefly here because our primary interest is in their impacts on human well-being.[4] Over the last 50 years, the rural sector has steadily increased its participation in the global economy. At the same time, it has become increasingly vulnerable to international market dynamics. Long gone are the days when Australian farmers were self-sufficient producers, economically and geographically removed from mainstream global capital flows

(Hungerford, 1994, p.15). Until the 1970s, they had been largely protected from the full force of international market dynamics through a controlled international economy and a highly regulated national economy involving a variety of protective devices such as fixed exchange rates, price guarantees, subsidies, tariff protection and import restrictions. But, at the same time, these measures had been gnawing away at the initiative, self-reliance, efficiency and competitiveness of agriculture, thereby increasing producers' vulnerability to major international economic upheavals.

Over the last 20 years, the world economy has become more open, more competitive and more global. We have seen the development of huge transnational corporations which possess sufficient financial leverage to influence national and, often, international economic and social policy, as evidenced by the 1997 collapse of the financial markets of the Asian 'tigers'. These also have the capacity to locate and relocate capital, labour, production and even different parts of the production process around the world in response to changes in demand, wages, labour regulations, government policy, growing conditions, climate and ecology (Smith, 1984; Lawrence, 1987). Agribusinesses have also increased their influence on Australian primary industry (Lawrence and Vanclay, 1992). These have the capacity to control the total production process, including the prices which producers pay for production inputs such as seed and fertiliser, and the income they receive from their outputs. Furthermore, international trade barriers are gradually being dismantled through unilateral action by some nations, bilateral trade agreements and trade blocks such as the Asia Pacific Economic Cooperation Forum (APEC). Over the last fifty years, these and other global developments have decreased state control over national economies and public policy, increasingly centralised national and international market power in the hands of fewer organisations and fewer nations, accelerated the movement of capital, labour and production around the world, and decreased the importance of agriculture to national economies (Walmsley and Sorensen, 1993, p.241). They have also resulted in a more competitive environment for Australian primary producers who must now compete more aggressively with each other, their counterparts overseas, and with industries manufacturing synthetic products.

For at least eight reasons, rural Australia was ill-prepared to respond to these changes (Lawrence, 1987; Lawrence and Hungerford, 1994). First, amongst developed nations Australia is particularly vulnerable to international politics and global market forces because it is a weak player on the political stage and has a relatively small economy. Second, we are heavily reliant on export income generated by natural resource based industries. Third, prior to the 1970s, the rural economy had been highly dependent on agriculture. Local diversification had not been encouraged because most existing agricultural industries had been successful and because government policy had assumed that agriculture would continue as the main rural industry. Thankfully, this was to change in the 1980s as tourism and mining increased their contribution to some local economies. Fourth, Australian agriculture has been dominated by under-capitalised, smaller family holdings and marginal properties which could not reap the benefits of large-scale production. Fifth, by the 1980s, farm debt levels and associated interest rates had risen substantially. Sixth, because so much of the Australian continent is ill-suited to European agriculture, land had been depleted in many places. This has contributed to the growing pool of marginal farms (Watson, 1992). Seventh, the continent's susceptibility to natural hazards such as droughts, floods, tropical cyclones and bushfires means that individual producers and whole regions have always been subjected to periodic economic fluctuations. Finally, until 1994, Australia never had a coherent regional development policy designed to strengthen rural communities, reverse the process of decline where it was under way, and help to relocate communities which would probably never recover. In fact, in the 1980s and 1990s, Australian governments and private corporations, such as banks, adopted a negative regional policy involving 'rationalisation' of public infrastructure and services. In effect, this has meant withdrawing support from small communities and from those in decline, and centralising them in large provincial towns and cities.

To make matters worse, in the 1980s the world recession, industry restructuring, escalating interest rates and the dominance of economic-rationalism in Australian public policy resulted in a 'cost price squeeze' for Australian farmers involving higher costs for production inputs and lower prices for their products. Without the range of protective devices to which they had become accustomed, the more marginal farmers were now being squeezed out of the industry by governments intent on developing a more globally-competitive agriculture sector.

There have been many consequences of these and other related changes for rural Australians. Whole communities are losing their capacity to determine their own futures, and some rural populations are being left economically and geographically stranded as local economies succumb to more global and more powerful economic forces. Some communities are being deserted and deprived of public resources. Many are being robbed of their natural resources without just compensation for the social, environmental and material consequences, and some local ecological systems are being destroyed. This ecological decline has only placed additional pressures on more marginal farmers. Furthermore, individuals - both farmers and other residents who depend on local primary industries - are losing control over production processes, their income levels and, along with this, their level of total well-being.

Primary producers who have been unable to meet debt commitments have been forced to leave the industry, suffering major financial, emotional and social losses along the way (Lawrence, 1987; Lockie, 1994). For instance, from the mid-1960s to the early 1990s the total Australian farm workforce decreased by 103,000 (Cribb, 1994, p.13). Farm aggregation has become more imperative economically as farm technology has improved, further contributing to a reduction in the total number of Australian farms which declined from 200,000 in the mid-1960s to 120,000 in the mid-1990s (Cribb, 1994, p.13).

While figures such as these can be reported quickly, we usually don't pause to consider what they mean for the individuals involved. Increasing pressure on farmers has produced or exacerbated the many health and social problems discussed earlier such as stress, suicide and domestic violence. Bryant (1991) investigated the experiences of families displaced from their farms and found that the impacts were different for men and women. Males, she suggested, suffered more than females because they had derived a sense of power and status from land ownership and farming and had, because of this, suffered loss of self-esteem and social standing when forced to leave agriculture. In their new communities they reported higher levels of dissatisfaction with their jobs, their housing, their social networks, their social supports and their social integration. Women, on the other hand, did not appear to experience the same degree of loss or sense of failure, perhaps because they had less difficulty re-establishing their social standing and creating social relationships in their new communities, and because their disposable household incomes were higher and more reliable. Their working hours had also improved. However, as with men, the women were dissatisfied with their new accommodation.

Industry restructuring, local economic diversification, population mobility, and shifts in the location of production have resulted in some communities being overwhelmed by sudden population explosions. While rapid growth of local industries can bring added wealth and improved infrastructure for the benefit of some local people, it also frequently has negative repercussions for others in the form of increased rents, accommodation problems, transportation difficulties and a range of social problems. For instance, a study in the Whitsunday Shire in North Queensland (Bone, Cheers and Hil, 1993, p.43) concluded that rapid recent growth in tourism had increased rents in Cannonvale and Airlie Beach by as much as 50 per cent in one year and had increased over-crowding amongst young people living in rental accommodation. Furthermore, because the local transportation system was focused on tourism, high school students frequently arrived late to school and young people from the Cannonvale/Airlie Beach area found it difficult and expensive to access the well-developed sporting facilities in Proserpine some 30km away (Bone, Cheers and Hil, 1993, pp.102-4).

Rapid population growth can also result in increasing crime rates and other social problems. For instance, Freudenberg and Jones' (1991) review found that crime rates had increased six to seven times in towns experiencing rapid population growth as a result of economic development. They concluded that this was because of the breakdown in social norms and community cohesion which keep social problems in check.

Work

Meanwhile, the nature of work has changed in Australian society. Unemployment has increased dramatically since the 1960s. There has been significant growth in part-time, casual and contract employment and a corresponding drop in full-time permanent employment. This, of course, has meant reduced incomes and job security for many rural people, especially women and youth. In an effort to maintain incomes or simply to stay afloat, farmers and other family members have increased their working hours and diversified their daily activities. This has involved a significant increase in *pluriactivity*, or the practice of farm households earning income from a variety of formal and informal sector activities such as primary production, off-farm employment or on-farm diversification into new industries such as eco-tourism (Le Heron, 1991, p.27). It has been estimated that somewhere between one-third and one-half of all farm households in Australia and New Zealand are pluriactive (Benedikston, Manning, Moran and Anderson, 1990; Le Heron, Roche, Johnston and Bowler, 1991). Pluriactivity has been particularly harsh on women, many of whom have added part-time employment to their usual farm and domestic responsibilities (Alston, 1991b), and to young people asked to delay or sacrifice their education for the good of the farm.

The changing nature of work in Australia over the past two decades has meant that education, training and re-training have become lifelong processes. Because of poor access to education and training programs which are responsive to changing local industry needs it is becoming increasingly difficult for rural people to keep up with technological change and the continual rise and fall of various industries. For example, the Whitsunday study cited earlier found that local tourist operators were employing youth from Brisbane to operate small boats in preference to local youth because the relevant training was not available within the region (Bone, Cheers and Hil, 1993, p.84).

Communication

We are living in a time of rapidly-advancing communication systems, including telephones, pay television and global superhighways. Positively, modern communication technology makes a whole range of public services more accessible to rural people in areas such as distance education, medical diagnosis and treatment, crisis telephone counselling, child development, in-service training and management consultation. Furthermore, in the less developed regions communication technology has the potential to stimulate social change by raising residents' awareness of their marginalised and disempowered position, educating them about the political, social and economic forces shaping their lives, and providing them with the opportunity to join together to improve their collective lot.

However, the new technology can also erode the social glue which binds together rural communities and scattered populations. For instance, one study in remote areas of North Queensland found that many residents believed that the demise of the traditional 'party line' radio had decreased interaction amongst residents in outlying areas (Cheers, 1985). According to one remote area nurse it had actually placed some people at greater risk of emotional, social and physical ill-health because it had increased their social isolation and because she could no longer pick up information about their health by joining the party line every morning. Furthermore, entertainment provided through television and videos may also be replacing the many social activities which have been so important in maintaining cohesion and social control within rural communities. As one resident of a small remote town in North Queensland put it:

People don't get together in each other's houses any more to play cards or just to have a chat - they stay at home now and watch television or videos.

Population shifts

Market changes, the changing nature of work, improvements in communication technology, and other social changes such as ageing of the Australian population have all contributed to some major population shifts throughout rural Australia.

High growth areas include retirement destinations, provincial cities with a broad economic base and located in agricultural growth areas, other provincial cities which are distant from larger competing centres, fringes of metropolitan areas that were once genuine country towns, and individual inland townships serving as destinations for declining hinterland populations (Salt, 1992, p.xiv,64-5). People moving from metropolitan to non-metropolitan areas have primarily been older people seeking cheaper accommodation and comfortable climates for retirement, and families with dependent children escaping the high cost of living in capital cities (Salt, 1992, p.xv).

On the other hand, many regions have recently experienced population depletion. For instance, 210 of the 240 Australian communities which shrank in 1990-91 (87.5 per cent) were rural (Salt, 1992). It is the more sparsely-populated inland regions which have been emptying out (Salt, 1992, p.iii). Greatest decline has occurred in small towns with less than 1,000 people (Henshall Hansen Associates, 1988) and regions in the wheat-sheep zone where farmers have been leaving over a long period (Salt, 1992, p.xv). Other declining places include the central areas of large provincial cities where residents have been moving to the fringes, medium-size towns with shrinking economic and employment bases, smaller settlements subjected to farm aggregation or waning agricultural economies, towns close to provincial cities where local services have become redundant because of improvements in transportation and communication, and regions which lack sufficient locally-based tertiary education and training facilities (Salt, 1992, p.xiv,64-5).

When a rural population declines significantly, community solidarity tends to be weakened along with local social networks and support systems. Governments and non-government organisations withdraw infrastructure, such as public transport, and support services, such as schools and hospitals. Industry reduces investment in the area and associated services, such as banks and accountants, withdraw (Cribb,

1994). This weakening of the local infrastructure only intensifies the cycle of decline, resulting in further community disintegration and personal impoverishment.

People leaving farms and smaller settlements for larger towns and cities include farmers, youth and older people (Salt, 1992, p.iii; Rolley and Humphreys, 1993, p.245). But far from solving people's problems, moving to the city frequently introduces new ones such as unemployment, homelessness, disease, industrial exploitation, crime, social isolation and weakened social support networks (Cheers, 1995). Farmers have been driven from the land by changed market conditions, recession and drought. Older people moving from farms and smaller settlements have mostly been retirees seeking cheaper accommodation, comfortable climatic conditions and health, social care and other support services. And the younger migrants are school leavers, especially young women, in search of work and training (Salt, 1992, p.xv; Rolley and Humphreys, 1993, p.245). For instance, youth surveys in rural North Queensland have found that 41.1 per cent of Whitsunday young people (Bone, Cheers and Hil, 1993, p.96) and 70.6 per cent of Hinchinbrook youth (Cheers and Yip, 1994, p.65) said that they planned to leave their communities within four years to seek further education or employment.

Populations of other areas fluctuate with changing economic circumstances. Included are those dependent on one or two agricultural industries, such as sugar towns in North Queensland, or on mining, such as Croydon in north-west Queensland (Salt, 1992, p.iii).

There are many ugly sights in this scenario: of people, many of them aged, stranded in poverty in towns and on properties without much in the way of public infrastructure or social support; of farmers turning their backs on lifetimes of hard work and inter-generational hopes to sink into the faceless mass of urban poverty; of school leavers and other young rural people forced to leave their homes to vanish into unemployed obscurity in the city; of hopeful low-income families leaving their friends and supports to go to unfamiliar rural environments in search of cheap accommodation and a bearable, though still poor, lifestyle to live amongst strangers, some of whom question whether they should be there at all; of older people retiring to places which lack the support services they need; of country towns, where existing services are stretched beyond sanity by sudden population explosions; and of these same towns losing the cohesion which for so long had kept social problems in check.

The Failure of Welfare

Because of how they are structured, Australia's formal social care arrangements could not respond effectively to the challenges presented by these changes. The evidence for rural disadvantage demonstrates that rural people never had received their fair share of public resources. Until relatively recently, it seems to have been assumed that they could access services in regional centres and capital cities which, given the distances involved, is ridiculous for many of them. A system based on point-specific services, or places where people physically go for help, could not cope with large distances or with highly-dispersed populations. Where they existed, rural services were under-resourced and had difficulty attracting professional staff which, when they could be found, were frequently ill-suited to rural conditions. Furthermore, services which respond to specific components of people's lives have failed many rural people because the new human issues encompass all facets of life. For instance, a financial counselling service for farmers in a declining industry such as tobacco is too narrow if it does not also help them with their social and emotional adjustment problems.

Examples of services and policies ill-suited to rural conditions abound. I am reminded of the rural counselling service which no-one visited because it was prominently located in the centre of town. Another case in point is the Aboriginal women in Northern Australia who ran foul of funding guidelines when they used a government-funded bus to go fishing when family violence erupted in their community, even though it was a time-honoured practice for a group of women to leave the community for a few days with the victim at such times.

Australian social care arrangements do not relate well with natural support processes. For the most part, they do not link people in need with others who can help them. Nor do they focus on facilitating and resourcing natural helping processes. This can be particularly important in declining communities where everyone is suffering because people have fewer resources of their own with which to help each other.

Because formal social care is separate from market forces in Australia, reactive rather than proactive and centralised in urban environments, social administrators neither anticipated nor recognised the developing plight of rural Australians even as the drama unfolded. Had the market-induced changes been anticipated, responses to the social consequences could have been put in place. On a community level, local people could have been involved in developing resources, services and facilities to prepare for the impacts on individuals, families and entire communities. Effective responses could have been initiated for the many farmers and other rural people who were to be displaced from their home communities. Income security provisions would have also been in place to provide for Australia's struggling farmers and other rural small business people.

A service system focused on individuals and families could neither help reverse the process of community disintegration nor contribute to the rebuilding process. Nor could it offer anything to communities which would inevitably decline in the long term or those which were expanding rapidly. Where they existed, community developers were frequently marginalised by the economic sector. Most community regeneration, such as occurred in Tumby Bay in South Australia (Jeffreys and Munn, 1996), has resulted from spontaneous initiatives of communities themselves and through economic, not social, leadership. But where regional development is controlled by economic interests, social issues frequently receive low priority.

Finally, Australia's welfare system is disconnected from the sustenance and sense of personal identity which many rural people derive from their natural and spiritual worlds. It was indigenous people themselves and the legal system, not social care professionals, who recognised and responded to their severed relationships with these worlds. In fact, the welfare system played a major role in wrenching them apart in the first place. Furthermore, while we do have financial readjustment programs and financial counselling services for farming families, we do not respond to the personal anguish and loss of identity which many feel when they lose their land.

Change and Indigenous Peoples

The changes which devastated indigenous Australians started in 1788 with the arrival of European culture. This, of course, was part of the global process of Western imperialism which, in modified form, remains a major force in the modern world. The European scientific view of Australian Aborigines as sub-human provided a rationale for Australian Commonwealth and State governments to treat them as such (Smallwood, 1994). Western land use policies deprived them of self-support and distanced them from their natural world which is the anchor for their material, spiritual, cultural, social and personal sustenance and identity. While it may have helped them to survive the onslaught, Christianity further contributed to the weakening of traditional indigenous culture and spirituality (Gleed, 1996). Dispossessed of their own societies, indigenous Australians were not fully accepted as Australian citizens until as late as 1967. Deprived of self-maintenance, they were not eligible for mainstream income security entitlements until the same year. In any case, these have only delivered dependency. Responding to the needs of capital, Western-style social care arrangements removed children and youth from their communities to be exploited as cheap labour by middle- and upper-class white Australians. In an attempt to breed out the culture, they also contributed to forcibly relocating whole communities and co-locating communities which had never previously lived together. And when it provided anything at all, Western medicine offered curative health care when preventive public health measures such as clean water, effective sewerage and drainage, relevant immunisation programs, adequate nutrition and good living conditions were clearly required (Smallwood, 1994). In the final analysis, Western medicine has been unable to replace what Western society has taken away.

As with any disempowered group, indigenous Australians are more at the mercy of economic and social changes than many other Australians. They are amongst the first to lose their jobs and to suffer the effects of infrastructure and funding withdrawals.

Indigenous Australians are clear that they need the cultural space, the opportunity and the resources to continue to regenerate their cultures. For many, especially those living in rural areas, repossession of their natural environment - their land, sea and air - is a pre-requisite to continued cultural regeneration. In view of this, it comes as no surprise that the recent sharp improvement in infant mortality rates for indigenous people in Northern Australia has coincided with their movement to remote homelands and outstations (Dusevic, 1995).

Recognising the importance of indigenous self-determination, the Commonwealth Government has established the Aboriginal and Torres Strait Islander Commission (ATSIC) with Regional Councils throughout the nation. Through ATSIC, indigenous Australians now have greater input into government policy and resource utilisation than they did ten years ago.

Traditional indigenous ways are embedded in a strong sense of community. Rightly, indigenous people in rural communities have insisted that they manage their own communities and, within limits, many now do so in the Northern Territory and some States. Along with community self-management should go increased control over social care arrangements. However, the extent to which this occurs varies from State to State and from region to region. In Queensland, for example, the Department of Families, Youth and Community Care (DFYCC)[5] has developed a model of 'community services development' (Dale, 1994) which is discussed in some detail in Chapter 7. This approach emphasises the importance of indigenous and other rural communities managing, controlling and providing local services and determining local priorities in negotiation with the Department.

Implications

A number of general implications for rural social policy, social planning and human services can be drawn from this analysis. With regard to social justice, the kind of society which Australia has become has not served rural people well. For this reason, it is important that all human services professionals advocate for disadvantaged and disempowered rural people regardless of their field of practice or whether they are employed primarily as community workers, social planners, managers or direct service practitioners.

Nor are Australia's social care arrangements working well for many rural people. If we are to deal effectively with their personal and social issues we must cease to view social care from within the scaffolding of existing policy, funding and service structures and develop alternative approaches based on the reality of Australia's settlement patterns. We have very few medium-size provincial cities which can operate as regional service centres; rural people are scattered in a great variety of smaller communities, frequently far distant from service centres; and people in remote areas are thinly dispersed in tiny communities.

Nor can we afford to be passive, waiting for problems to develop before devising effective responses to them. We can anticipate at least some changes, project their potential impacts, and plan appropriate services, facilities and resources ahead of time. For example, the State Government and a shire council both knew that a new mine was about to open in one North Queensland town. It should have been easy to plan for the influx of mining families and the extra demands that this would place on local services such as hospitals and schools. At a more general level, the rural recession was predictable, at least to some extent. That a large number of marginal farmers would be forced to leave their farms as a result of primary industry restructuring could have been foreseen because restructuring was government policy. Services should have been put in place ahead of time, including counselling for social and emotional problems and assistance with moving belongings, finding accommodation, locating employment and re-training opportunities, and obtaining information about services and amenities. Furthermore, we know that as the population continues to age, more older urban people will be moving to some identifiable rural communities for retirement. They will require a wide range of services such as social care, health care, transportation and home help.

The well-being of rural people will not be best served by continuing to isolate social care from other sectors of society. We should seek to understand all the changes impacting on rural areas and relate our formal social care responses to them. The close relationship between social and economic issues has been clearly demonstrated in this chapter. Because they are so closely intertwined, social and economic policy should inform each other at national, State and regional levels. Those with the relevant expertise - social planners, social developers, community workers and social care practitioners - should be involved in developing policies which affect the total well-being of rural people. This means locating social care professionals in government departments concerned with areas such as primary industry, regional development, housing, infrastructure development and rural issues more generally. On a local level, they should be relating more closely with local government, chambers of commerce, developers and regional economic development organisations. Most importantly, social care professionals must be trained to take on these roles.

The history of Australian settlement over the last 210 years has resulted in power, decision making and services being centralised in eight State and national capitals and, to a lesser extent, in a small number of large regional centres which are a long way from much of their rural hinterlands. We have not yet developed a regional tradition where local people and local governments are in control of regional social and economic development. Furthermore, social care is still embedded in a 'centre to periphery' framework where policy is determined in, and most services are provided from, major urban centres. This approach is bound to have cost and logistical problems in responding to the needs of far-flung rural populations. An alternative 'periphery to centre' approach where decisions are made on the rural fringes and where the locus of service provision is shifted to the periphery is potentially more useful for rural Australia.

The forces impacting on rural people have localised consequences which vary from region to region, from community to community and from time to time. For this reason, social planning and human services should be tailored to meet the needs of specific regions and be sufficiently flexible to respond to changes over time within the same community. Furthermore, because central planners frequently have difficulty knowing what is going on at the periphery, local people must be involved in decision making.

Most of the changes identified in this chapter have impacted on entire communities as well as individual residents. Consequently, policies, provisions and services should target whole communities and regions as well as specific individuals. Skilled community workers are needed in rapidly-expanding communities to help maintain their identity and cohesion, in declining communities to help regenerate spirit and energy, and in most rural communities to advocate for residents' needs.

These, then, are some of the general implications of this review of rural Australia. Some more specific recommendations can also be identified. First, the long-standing rural-urban price differentials imply that price equalisation policies should be developed for many goods and services and that tax concessions for fuel, road use and freight costs should be continued. Second, in relation to unemployment, we need genuine regional development policies which are supported with adequate resources, public infrastructure and incentives to attract business, especially small business, to the bush. Disbanding the Commonwealth regional development program has been disastrous for many communities and their residents.

Third, in relation to education, many areas need regionally-based education programs which train people for current local industry needs (Cheers and Harris, 1995). Despite recent improvements, tertiary education facilities are still relatively scarce outside the capital cities and, at the time of writing, are in danger of being further reduced. The number of regional tertiary institutions should, at least, be maintained at the present level. There should also be more rural campuses of urban-based institutions, a greater variety of distance education programs, and rural quotas on courses provided on urban campuses. However, in the absence of a national tertiary education policy, current cuts to university budgets could well result in significant down-sizing of regional campuses and substantial reductions in undergraduate distance education places.

Fourth, in relation to health care, appropriate rural services are required which respond to the recent rapid increase in stress-related physical, emotional and social problems. Of all health services, rural people have poorest access to counselling and mental health facilities.

Those who need these, perhaps most notably isolated youth, are literally 'all alone'.

Fifth, support programs such as child care assistance and home help are required for women on pluriactive farms. They should also be eligible for unemployment benefits when they cannot find employment, even though they may be required to continue working on the farm. Furthermore, young people leaving school prematurely to help on family farms need flexible education programs so they can combine work and education. Extending the final two years of school over three or four years, which is now possible in some States such as Victoria, would be one way of providing them with the opportunity to complete their education.

Finally, if this review has shown anything it is that, by and large, those involved in traditional formal social care in this country have not known what to do about indigenous issues. Despite all the resources, all the programs and all the personnel, the situation of many remains wretched. A radically different approach is needed, one which is based on the social, cultural and spiritual realities of indigenous peoples and which takes as its starting point their ownership and control of their traditional space. Only indigenous people themselves can determine the kinds of social care arrangements which will serve them best.

Notes

1. For the most part, specifically rural statistics released by the ABS refer to clustered settlements with less than 1,000 residents and scattered populations.
2. Throughout this chapter, some attention is given to data from Northern Australia because of its proportionately large rural and remote populations.
3. Dating is currently in progress which may indicate that indigenous people have been on the Australian continent for at least 120,000-160,000 years.
4. For more detailed discussion, the reader is referred to Lawrence (1987), Lawrence and Hungerford (1994), Hungerford (1994) and Cheers (1996).
5. The Queensland Department of Families, Youth and Community Care (DFYCC) has undergone frequent name changes over the past 15 years. This was its title at the time of writing. It is also referred to in this book as the Department of Family Services and Aboriginal and Islander Affairs (DFSAIA) and the Department of Family and Community Services (DFACS).

3 People in Rural Communities

This chapter explores what it means to live in a rural community. Throughout this book I examine the reasons why Australia's system of formal social care has failed rural and indigenous Australians. Some of these were addressed in Chapters 1 and 2. However, a more fundamental explanation is that the assumptions upon which it is based are incongruent with how many rural and indigenous people live their lives.

Our formal system of social care is based on dominant Western ideology[1] which separates people from their worlds and compartmentalises human living. While Descartes is usually seen as the originator of this view, he was only reflecting his culture:

> Descartes held that ego and consciousness were separated from the world and from other persons. That is to say, consciousness is cut off and stands by itself alone. Sensations do not tell us anything directly about the outside world; they only give us inferential data. ... Since Descartes ... the soul and nature have had nothing to do with each other. ... We know the world only indirectly. (May, 1958a, p.58)

According to dominant Western ideology people are separated experientially from their social, material, cultural and spiritual worlds, even from their own bodies. With this established, what Norgaard (1994) called 'the cosmos' becomes an objectified thing which is conceptualised and analysed from the detached vantage point of the human being through a series of mental analogues. The person somehow stands outside this cosmos. Accordingly, the universe 'exists' for the individual only as a set of conceptual structures; it is not experienced directly.

By definition, when we conceptualise the cosmos we identify and compartmentalise what we believe to be its components, human experience being amongst these. In this way, dominant Western ideology fragments human living into untold bits and pieces - work is separated from leisure, private from public, person from environment, body from 'psyche', social from psychological, feelings from behaviours, and emotions from relationships. People are viewed as self-contained atoms, disconnected from, and relating to each other only through conscious cognition. Compare this with alternative ideologies, such as those from Pacific Island cultures, which view people as social rather than individual beings.

> The person is not an individual in our Western sense of the term. The person is instead a locus of shared biographies: personal histories of people's relationships with other people and with other things. The relationship defines the person, not vice-versa. (Lieber, 1990, p.72)

Dominant Western ideology fragments human thought into a multitude of disciplines and sub-disciplines each of which is developing along its own separate path. Human issues, needs and problems are segmented and social care is compartmentalised into too many programs, too many government departments, too many non-government organisations and too many occupations. Students are trained to deliver discrete programs from discrete organisations in response to discrete 'problems' using discrete 'competencies'. The concept of 'multi-skilling' merely extends the fragmentation in an even more bizarre way. For now the practitioner is an assemblage of a number of discrete skills rather than an integrated human being. Furthermore, social care has been clearly separated from market processes which has resulted in its marginalisation and enslavement to capital.

This ideology is both the product and the servant of Western industrialism and capitalism (Smith, 1984). The person has become:

> ... an object to be calculated and controlled, exemplified in the almost overwhelming tendencies in the Western world to make human beings into anonymous units to fit like robots into the vast industrial and political collectivisms of our day. (May, 1958b, p.12)

Human beings have been commodified, or viewed as pieces in some economic game. We are now referred to as 'labour', 'units of labour power', 'production factors', 'human resources', 'human capital', 'production inputs', 'markets', 'consumers', and so on (Cheers, 1995).

Western ideology removes people from their natural worlds. Fewer people now work directly with nature. More are kept busy adding value to primary products and moving goods, capital, labour and ideas from one place to another. This distancing of people from their natural worlds is reflected in, and reinforced by, our management of space. Takaya (1995, pp.6-7) put this nicely:

The foremost feature ... [of cities] ... is that ... [they] ... were made as artificial spaces completely independent from the natural surroundings. ... People can react sensitively to wonderfully created artificial space, but they have lost their ability to respond in harmony with nature and to the gods and goddesses of nature.

Social care ideologies that don't mesh with how people experience their lives and their universe are less effective than those which do. It has long been recognised, for example, that one-to-one verbal therapies are incongruent with cultures that accord less importance to verbal discourse than to non-verbal interaction. Similarly, one-to-one counselling tends not to fit with cultures which value social groups, such as kin, rather than individuals and nuclear families. Furthermore, most core concepts of Western welfare such as individuation, self-determination, self-reliance and direct intervention aimed at 'rehabilitating' individuals and nuclear families to mainstream cultures and social structures derive from Western ideology (Midgley, 1981, pp.2-16).

Many in the non-Western world see things differently. For example, Fattahipour (1991, pp.204-5) identified a number of conflicts between Malay Islamic Fundamentalist and Western values, some of which are presented in Table 3.1.

Even in the Western world, there are alternative views. "World", writes May:

> ... is the structure of meaningful relationships in which a person exists and in the design of which he (sic) participates. Thus world includes the past events which condition my existence and all the vast variety of deterministic influences which operate upon me. But it is these as I relate to them, am aware of them, carry them with me, molding, inevitably forming, building them in every minute of relating. (May, 1958a, pp.59-60)

According to the existential tradition, a person and his or her world form a whole. Neither exists without the other and each can be understood only in interaction with the other (see, also, Midgley, 1989, pp.219-25). This is far more than a spatial relationship. While my desk is indeed in this room in a spatial sense, to say that I am in the room means so much more.

Table 3.1: Conflicts between Islamic Fundamentalist and Dominant Western Values

WESTERN	MUSLIM
• Facts constitute reality.	• Beliefs, customs and traditions constitute reality.
• 'Truth' is subject to experimentation and verification.	• 'Truth' is absolute, divine, and irrefutable.
• Enquiry and reasoning (casting doubt on authority) are more important than faith.	• Faith (submission to and acceptance of authority) is more important than reason.
• World view is worldly, secular.	• World view is other-worldly, oriented to the hereafter.
• Economic development is highly valued.	• Human and social development is valued more than economic gain.
• Capital accumulation is encouraged.	• Distributive justice is more important than capital growth.
• Wealth possession is valued.	• Wealth belongs to all, to the 'commonwealth'.
• Competition and individual success is important.	• Co-operation and collective achievement are important.
• Land belongs to individuals.	• Land belongs to God and the community.
• One's worth is measured by money and power.	• Piety is the true worth of the individual.
• Self, I, Me, the individual is important.	• We (Ummah) is the goal.
• Independence and individual freedom are highly valued.	• Dependence on Allah, king, government, or elders is necessary; security is more important than freedom.
• The future is different from and more important than the past.	• People are past-oriented, and the future is a replica of the revered past.

Source: Fattahipour (1991, pp.204-5)

May (1958a, pp.61-5) identified three *modes of world*, within which we exist. The first is *Umwelt* ('world around'):

> ... the world of natural law and natural cycles, of sleep and awakeness, of being born and dying, desire and relief, the world of finiteness and biological determinism, the "thrown world" to which each of us must in some way adjust. (p.61)

The second is *Mitwelt* ('with world'), "... the world of interrelationships with human beings" (p.62). The third mode is *Eigenweld* ('own world'):

> ... the basis on which we see the real world. ... It is a grasping of what something in the world - this bouquet of flowers, this other person - means to me. (p.63)

A fourth, the *spiritual world*, can be added. This is constituted by the forms which a person believes exist, but which cannot be accessed through the physical senses. The importance of the spiritual world to the lives of many rural people was nicely portrayed in Dylan Thomas' (1971, p.viii) little story of:

> A shepherd who, when asked why he made, from within fairy rings, ritual observances to the moon to protect his flocks, replied: 'I'd be a damn' fool if I didn't!'

Takaya illustrated the fundamental integrity of these four *modes* with an example from Indonesia:

> The people there still live alongside the spirits of their ancestors. When a person dies, his (sic) family immediately begins to prepare for the funeral. They have to prepare a buffalo and clothes for the dead person to take with him (sic) to the other world. The preparation takes several months and the dead person waits on the nearby hill. When the preparation is completed, all the villagers send him (sic) off to the other world. As the travel from the hill to the other world is long and full of danger, the villagers accompany him (sic). They dance all night in the village square. They advise him (sic) and guide him (sic) along the correct way by saying "to the right", and "to the left." When they have sent the dead person safely to the other world in such a manner, they have another ceremony several weeks later. Then the dead comes back home as an ancestral spirit. As the ancestral spirit is a member of the family, he (sic) eats together with, and gives advice to, the family. (Takaya, 1995, pp.7-8)

The point of the present discussion is that elements of dominant Western ideology do not mesh with how many rural and indigenous people experience their lives. In Australia, as elsewhere, it is well established that Western and indigenous ideologies are fundamentally different. Indigenous cultures tend to emphasise community over individualism, a different relationship with time and integration of personal, social, physical and spiritual worlds. This integration, and, for many indigenous Australians, their experience of their own identity, are anchored in the natural environment. This is why changing patterns of land use on this continent have had such severe social, cultural, spiritual, emotional and material consequences for indigenous Australians (Smallwood, 1994).

What is less well recognised is that the ideologies of many Western rural people may also differ significantly from dominant Western ideologies. For instance, in Australia many of those who work directly with nature, such as farmers, small scale miners ('tin scratchers') and genuine 'bushies' experience greater connectedness with their natural world than Western ideology suggests. This may be part of the reason, though yet unexplored, why Australian farmers displaced from their properties suffer the stress, depression, despair, disorientation and social problems identified by Bryant (1991, 1992) and Gray (1991).

Many rural people also emphasise their identification with, and commitment to, their community and their social and support networks, not only to personal and family interests (Martinez-Brawley, 1990b). Etzioni (1989) challenged the view that the over-arching goal of people is to satisfy personal wants. He suggested that most of us evaluate our desires according to a number of criteria including internalised moral and social values which reflect shared community ideas of what is right and wrong and what is and is not good for our community, no matter how this is defined. Sometimes personal desire wins out, sometimes community interests, and sometimes the same action serves both ends. Many rural people experience this dual commitment keenly because they know that personal and community well-being are interdependent, because strong sanctions can be applied to those who transgress community expectations and because, as Etzioni pointed out, human beings are simply like that. Consequently, many of them view social care as a responsibility of 'community' and not only the responsibility of formal societal structures such as government and non-government organisations (Martinez-Brawley, 1990b).

In sum, then, dominant Western ideology and the system of social care derived from it, such as we have in Australia, do not adequately recognise or respond to the fundamental integrity of human life and the embeddedness of many rural and indigenous Australians in their natural, spiritual and social worlds.

Rural Communities

For many rural people, their community is a key component of their social world. The concept of *community* takes us to the heart of rural life and distinguishes it from much of urban existence. Although a number of different kinds of communities can be identified, we are interested here primarily in locality-based communities.

A *locality-based community* exists as an entity, or has *entitivity*, to the degree that people who live there invest themselves in it. Its existence is a matter of degree rather than an all or nothing affair, depending on the proportion of people living in the locality who invest in it and the extent to which they do so. Here, *investment* means committing energy and time and deriving some sense of identity from the community. Investment can be ideological, physical, social, psychological, cultural and/or infrastructural. *Ideological investment* occurs when a person recognises and supports the idea of the community as something more than a simple aggregation of people. For example, a resident who actively champions their community in the wider world has ideological investment. *Physical investment* is demonstrated by how much time a person spends in the locality. For instance, the country school teacher who escapes to the city every weekend has low physical investment. S*ocially invested* people are actively involved in local social, recreational and sporting activities and in local social structures and institutions. For the most part, they choose other local people as members of their intimate social networks and for social support. *Psychological investment* involves deriving some sense of identity from the locality. Although now long ago, having been a 'North Ryde boy' remains part of how I continue to experience myself. A *culturally invested* person is one who identifies with and supports local structures, institutions, values, norms and interaction patterns. We do this, for example, by attending local celebrations and volunteering to work in community organisations and committees. Finally, a person with high *infrastructure investment* uses local services, facilities and resources rather than those located elsewhere.

Personal investment in a community can have a number of sources. It might be based on local capital investments, land inheritance or the fact that a person's work is tied to the locality. Most of a person's social supports and close friends may live locally. Or the person might have grown up in the community, survived a common threat with other local people, such as a natural disaster or economic recession, or simply love the place.

When, over time, a significant proportion of people who live in the same place invest in their community they generate a shared history which is transferred orally and through symbols and documentation. For example, as part of my preparation for one study, residents insisted that I read an account of their community's history reported in the local newspaper. When *community* exists, people take an interest in each other, their interaction and their shared locality. They interact in more or less consistent ways and develop a host of socio-cultural processes such as social structures, social groupings, sub-cultures, power structures, leadership patterns, social networks, social institutions, normative systems, rituals, myths, legends and much more. When newcomers arrive and when babies are born into a more or less established community, they enter into its ways and, over time, invest or don't invest themselves in it to varying degrees.

A number of qualifications should be added to this idea of community. First, an individual's level of investment, and the extent to which it is conscious and intentional, are matters of degree and can vary from one dimension to another. Second, investment is not a 'once and for all' thing. It can ebb and flow over the course of a person's life. Third, community entitivity fluctuates as people move in and out of the locality. Fourth, people - such as children in boarding schools and young people employed elsewhere - don't have to live in the community to be part of it. Fifth, community entitivity and community cohesion are not identical. It is entirely possible, for example, that a community high in entitivity can be torn by conflict, factionalism, power struggles and general negativity. Sixth, although most rural Australians live in clustered communities, many are also scattered thinly throughout vast areas. In Northern Australia it is common, for instance, for people on cattle properties to live up to 100km from town and still belong to a 'local community'. For this reason, in Australia our concept of community should extend beyond towns to people living in their hinterlands.

The rest of this chapter presents some information about rural communities. Although it is supported by research, much of this information is based on the personal and professional experiences of countless rural people who have shared their thoughts with me. This is not a critical, comprehensive and detailed review of literature. Material has been selected to meet the needs of practitioners, students and educators rather than the interests of researchers, theoreticians and community sociologists.[2]

Economic Base

Until recently, the economies of most Australian rural communities relied heavily on one or two primary industries. This is now changing as more communities 'uncouple' from these and diversify into additional agricultural products and other industries such as tourism, leisure, retirement and mining (Stayner and Reeve, 1990; Campbell and Phillips, 1993). Diversification provides some protection against rapid market changes and the vagaries of climate, and usually results in more stable economies and more reliable development. However, it can also lead to sudden social changes when, for instance, vacationers flock into town, or more permanent demographic restructuring when, for example, retired people settle in the area. It may also lead to changes in community social structures and normative systems which can threaten community integration. As we saw in Chapter 2, if social planners are unprepared for such changes, communities can find that essential infrastructure and social, health and education services are lacking or stretched beyond their limits.

Place, Culture and Nature

In rural areas, the material form of a place interacts with local cultures. Many have written about how culture influences material form (e.g., Arensburg, 1955; Takaya, 1995, pp.6-7). Clearly, capitalism has transformed the planet, and Australia's natural environment has been severely damaged by unsuitable methods of agriculture imported from European cultures. At the local level, the old unchanging shop-fronts in the main street of Proserpine reflect a stable, close-knit business community and an elite power structure while the new glossy motels and resort shops of nearby Airlie Beach are the product of recent rapid economic and social change and a more fluid power structure. Similarly, the tall chimney just outside Georgetown stands as testament to the historical and continuing importance of mining to the character of the district, as does the stately old stock exchange at Charters Towers.

An insightful police sergeant once made the following comment about the influence of culture on the material form of country towns in which he had worked.

The first thing I do when I'm posted to a new town is visit the cemetery and the dump. I can tell a lot about a place by the way people look after these. If they look after their dead and their rubbish, they have pride in their community.

The reverse is also true: the material form of a place also influences local cultures. This is succinctly captured by the simple comment that *'tough country breeds tough people'*. For example, partly because of the natural environment in many regions, Northern Australian beef cattle producers tend to live on huge, remote, largely self-sufficient properties. Consequently, most settlements are small and widely scattered. This settlement pattern and the cycle of 'Wet' and 'Dry' seasons mean that property people, truck drivers and others spend long periods away from home during the Dry mustering, trucking cattle and working on outlying properties. Many children are also away at boarding school. Furthermore, in many towns people are unavailable during the Dry because they are busy servicing the tourism industry. These characteristics of life in many areas of rural Northern Australia have a number of implications for local cultures and for how people relate to each other. For instance, residents of many remote towns focus on their community mostly during the Wet because this is when people are in town, and because there are no tourists around to dilute the sense of togetherness. One resident put it this way.

How is life different in the Wet? That's when we all get together. The property people are around town. The business people aren't so busy. And there are no tourists to get in the way. The Aboriginal men are at home then - they're not off working on properties or in the (larger) towns. That's when we have time for each other. We get together as a community in the Wet.

Other characteristics of the natural environment also affect rural life. In Australia, rural climates can be harsh and unpredictable. Conditions vary widely - from the incessant heat and humidity of the north, to the snow and cold of the south, to the dust and dryness of the interior, to floods and bushfires in most places. Natural disasters can devastate rural economies and the well-being of residents overnight, although they can also galvanise a community by increasing cohesion and strengthening local social and support networks.

Tuning in to Macca's *Australia All Over* on a Sunday morning will quickly convince even the staunchest urban sceptic that many rural Australians are deeply attached to their natural worlds, an attachment which, for many, carries over to their local community. Whether soft or tough, pretty or desolate, inviting or threatening, rural places on this continent have a power which relates to the soul.

Less poetically, rural Australia can also be an uncomfortable and expensive place to live. For example, many North Queenslanders saw the 1996 Mundingburra by-election as an opportunity to persuade the Queensland Government to air-condition North Queensland State schools. The proposal was rejected on the grounds that it would be too expensive. Air-conditioning, four wheel drive vehicles, cyclone resistant homes, property insurance in high risk areas, boarding schools and the like can be expensive.

Gemeinschaft, Gesellschaft and Community

The terms *gemeinschaft* ('community') and *gesellschaft* ('society' or 'association') have been central in literature concerning rural communities for more than a century (Harper, 1989, p.162). Tonnies (1955, pp.ix-xxvii) saw these as two kinds of social patterns which are present to some degree in all social structures. He proposed that *gemeinschaft* is stronger in rural communities and *gesellschaft* in urban places. *Gemeinschaft*, he suggested, is generated from intimate social relationships based on kinship, friendship, co-location, a shared history, cooperation and coordinated action for the common good. In *gemeinschaft*:

> Status is ascriptive, roles are specific and constant, culture is homogeneous and the people bound to place through mutual understanding, sentimentality, hopes, aspirations, beliefs and emotions. (Tonnies, 1955, p.53)

In contrast, he saw *gesellschaft* in the newly industrialised cities of his time.

> [In *gesellschaft*] ... we find no actions that can be derived from an 'a priori' and necessarily existing unity; no actions therefore which manifest the will and spirit of the unity ... ; no actions which, in so far as they are performed by the individual, take place on behalf of those united with him (sic). (Tonnies, 1955, p.74)

Bell and Newby (1972, p.23) viewed *gemeinschaft* and *gesellschaft* as modes of daily interaction (see, also, Rivera and Erlich, 1981; Martinez-Brawley, 1990b, pp.6-7). They saw *gemeinschaftlich* (*'gemeinschaft*-like') interaction as "... intimate, enduring and based on a clear understanding of where each person stands in a society" (Bell and Newby, 1972, p.23). People tend to relate to each other as they are rather than according to formal roles and contractual obligations. This results in an intricate web of interrelationships where what happens in one role relationship can determine what happens in another. For example, a parent and teacher discussing a child's progress might also be mayor and councillor of the shire council. By acceding to the parent's wishes in relation to the child, the teacher can gain his or her support for an important proposal at a shire council meeting later that day.

Gemeinschaftlich interaction is based on roles and expectations built up over many generations of living in the same place. People and families have relatively fixed positions in the socio-economic hierarchy, and social structural divisions based on class, occupation, culture, gender and length of residence are usually strong and fairly stable (Wild, 1974). As with other distinctions, those based on occupation can be between two or more groups (such as private entrepreneurs and public servants) or between one occupational group (such as property workers) and all other residents. In one town, for example, men group together in different places around the bar according to whether they are public servants, property workers, railway workers or miners. Many towns also distinguish between cultural groups. An extreme example is the bar in one North Queensland hotel which is divided into two halves, one side for Aborigines and one for others. There is even a wall down the middle and separate entrances. And the literature is full of examples of 'insiders' being clearly distinguished from 'outsiders' perhaps, as suggested by Martinez-Brawley (1990b, pp.38-41), to protect the identity, culture and even the size of the community.

Communities characterised by *gemeinschaftlich* interaction are relatively homogeneous:

> For it must be so if roles are not to conflict or human relations to lose their intimacy. The moral custodians of a community, the family and the church, are strong, their code clear and their injunctions well internalized. There will be community sentiments involving close and enduring loyalties to the place and people. ... [*Gemeinschaftlich* interaction results, therefore,] ... in a personalising of issues, events and explanations, because familiar names and characters inevitably become associated with everything that happens. (Bell and Newby, 1972, pp.23-4)

Gesellschaftlich interaction, on the other hand, occurs through specific roles based on formal exchange and contractual obligations. Relationships are fleeting and impersonal. People don't share a common history - they remain virtually anonymous to each other. In this interactional pattern, normative expectations attach to roles and contractual obligations rather than to people, and these are not usually internalised. Consequently, what happens in one interaction normally has little effect on what happens in another. Societies characterised by *gesellschaftlich* interaction are heterogeneous, with high mobility across social divisions. People feel little loyalty to their locality or to each other. Public issues and events are seen as detached from the ongoing stream of personal life and there is little unity of action for the common good.

Following Schmalenbach (1961), Wilkinson (1991) suggested that a third category, simply called *community*, is needed to complete the typology. According to Schmalenbach, community is a natural state of 'being-in-relationship' with other people. Wilkinson (1991, p.16) continues:

> It is natural because the formative conditions of this state ordinarily are unconscious. Community simply exists in the fact that people have multiple and natural relationships with one another and these, taken as a whole, make up a common life. ... Recognition of community can arouse feeling, but community itself simply refers to the fact that one naturally is connected to other people.

Community, in other words, emerges from the natural flow of interaction. It simply 'is', regardless of whether participants are aware of it or whether it is celebrated through various rituals. In this sense, then, *gemeinschaft* and *gesellschaft* patterns of interaction are properties, rather than types, of community.

Horizontal and Vertical Ties

Warren (1963, pp.237-8) distinguished between *horizontal* and *vertical* ties. *Horizontal ties* are relationships characterised by interdependence between people, groups and organisations within the locality. *Vertical ties*, on the other hand, are links between a local community unit and wider society; between, for example, a community-based human services organisation and a government funding body. Warren suggested that horizontal or vertical patterns of organisation tend to be relatively more or less dominant in a given community.

In the horizontal pattern, or what Warren referred to as 'the locality type of participation':

> ... individuals and families who share the same locality associate in neighbourly fashion with others in the immediate vicinity. A unifying basis of interest underlying such association is that of the common locality. ... Such important functions as production and distribution, socialization of the young, social control, and mutual support are performed largely within the locality by such relatively undifferentiated groups as family and neighbourhood. (Warren, 1963, pp.59-60)

The vertical pattern, on the other hand, involves:

> ... a differentiation of interests among people in the locality and differential association based on their respective interests. The individual often turns away from other individuals in his (sic) locality and associates himself (sic) with individuals from other localities on the basis of selective interests. (Warren, 1963, pp.59-60)

Warren believed that the increasing dominance of vertical ties has undermined the intimacy, supportiveness, cohesion and integration of horizontal ties. So, too, did MacPherson (1994, p.193).

> Whatever the overall economic situation, the long-term solutions to the fundamental problems of development ultimately lie in local communities. Everywhere, there have been tremendous changes taking place in local communities, especially the rural communities, where most of the world's population still live. These changes have been so great as to precipitate the breakdown of the social geographic units which are basic to people's lives. Throughout the world, people have become more dependent on aid from government. Government aid has almost always been in the form of service delivery, not genuine development assistance. People are less and less able to bring about and maintain sustainable development at the local level.

On the other hand, though, rural communities with weak vertical ties can be poorly connected with wider networks. Because of this they may be inward-looking and prone to miss political, economic and funding opportunities.

As we shall see in later chapters, distinguishing between horizontal and vertical ties is a key to understanding rural social care. As Martinez-

Brawley (1990b, p.13) commented: "... perhaps, the local practitioner stands at the point where the vertical system meets the horizontal". She quoted Buck (1982):

> This is the point where policy is transformed into action. It is here that the worker must perform the magic of 'taking a recipe and baking a cake'. (Martinez-Brawley, 1990b, p.13)

Social Provisions

Rural communities with reasonably strong horizontal ties and a modicum of *gemeinschaftlich* interaction have the potential to provide identity, distinctiveness, significance, solidarity, constancy and, in some ways, liberation for their members. They can also limit individual freedom and punish unacceptable behaviour.

Rural communities can give a person a sense of *identity*, including the experience of belonging somewhere in the social and physical universe, and a feeling of *distinctiveness* (Martinez-Brawley, 1990b, pp.13-5,48; Martinez-Brawley with Buck, 1990, p.96). Most of us derive some sense of who we are from where we grew up or where we live. For instance, I once motivated a father who was about to drop out of family therapy by commenting that "I didn't think that Bushtown [pseudonym] boys gave up so easily". The challenge had emotional significance because of his identification with his community and he returned with renewed determination to face his problems. Furthermore, our immediate geographic and social environments - our localities and the small social units to which we belong such as family and friends - provide us with the only concrete connections we have with the wider world. Broader entities such as 'the State of Queensland' or 'Australia' are too abstract and our relationships with them too vague to provide order and meaning in daily life.

The other side of identity is *distinctiveness*. I may have been *a* 'North Ryde boy' but I was also *this* 'North Ryde boy' - the school football captain, the folk singer, the mediocre student, the surfer and so on. Being part of a community provides a variety of relationships through which we see different reflections of ourselves. These we integrate as best we can into a sense of identity. A series of isolated, narrow, purely functional role relationships cannot provide this to nearly the same extent. As the different reflections come together we experience distinctiveness, perhaps even uniqueness, and this inevitably entails a feeling of separateness as well (Martinez-Brawley, 1990b, p.38).

One consequence of being known as a person is *visibility*. It is more difficult in rural communities to hide behind roles. In a city shop I can be simply a customer, but in a rural community I also stand at the counter as the social worker, the football coach, the secretary of the Parents' and Citizens' Association, a friend and so on. To protect themselves from the intrusions of others, many people and families in smaller and more remote communities erect some social boundaries. They do this, for example, by never discussing family or personal financial matters with other residents, by restricting interaction between families, *qua families*, to clearly demarcated occasions, by maintaining strong active links with non-local people, and by retreating regularly from the community (Cheers, 1985). For instance, in one study I found that many families would escape to a favourite spot just outside of town, such as a waterhole, for a few hours most weekends. This was especially important for families, such as those of publicans, whose work involved constant interaction with other residents.

People in rural communities constantly receive feedback that they are *significant* (Morganthauw et al., 1981, p.29; Martinez-Brawley, 1990b, pp.13-5). For instance, walking through the retail centre of Croydon (about 50m) can take an hour or two by the time I greet and chat with the store-keeper, the butcher, the sergeant, the publican, and a few others. They are interested in me and I in them. They want to know how my research is coming along, how my family is faring back in Townsville and so on. In Townsville, I go shopping on Saturday morning and perhaps bump into one or two people I know and we chat briefly. In Adelaide, chances are that I can ride buses all week, do the shopping and go to a football game without ever accidentally meeting anyone I know. Furthermore, because the opportunity to participate in community activities is higher for the average rural person there is also a greater chance that they will be recognised for their efforts through citizen awards, medals, trophies or simple expressions of gratitude.

Rural communities also provide a sense of *solidarity*, or a feeling of 'we-ness' (Martinez-Brawley, 1990b, pp.13-5; Martinez-Brawley with Buck, 1990, p.96). Frankenburg (1966, p.238) suggested that this is based on commonalities amongst residents, common interests such as the local economy and the weather, and on people frequently doing things with each other. For example, most residents participate in civic ceremonies and other community rituals, major sporting fixtures such as the annual rodeo, and social occasions such as Friday night at the pub (Frankenburg, 1966). Many are also involved in running them. Consequently, these social rituals have greater influence on community solidarity than similar events in cities which are more socially remote from most citizens. They play an important role in perpetuating the awareness amongst local people that they do, indeed, form a community.

Many authors have commented on the atmosphere of *constancy* which pervades rural settlements. This can provide people with a feeling of security and a sense of permanence. In relation to space, there are the unchanging familiar landmarks such as the sugar mill at Giru, the shop-fronts in Proserpine, the Shire Council yard in Burketown and the creek crossing just south of Laura. Compare these places with the more transient and facade-like qualities of cities, where the skyline constantly changes, buildings are demolished, new ones are built, roads are re-routed, bus routes change and so on.

Constancy can also be found in social interaction. Each day the same people greet each other in the same ways at the same times in the same places. Freilich (1963) used the term *interaction centre* to refer to the places in a community where regular significant interaction occurs. In one town, for example, the same men gather in much the same groups in much the same places each evening around the bar to chat and do business. After school, the same children play together on the stretch of road between Mrs Thompson's house and the hotel. And in another town the school is where local people gather together during, before and after committee meetings to discuss local issues and make decisions.

Communities with a shared history, a strong sense of community identity, and more or less established interaction patterns tend to develop strong and clear normative systems, or expectations for each other's behaviour (Martinez-Brawley, 1990b, p.41). These also help constrain potentially socially disruptive reactions in communities where people relate more on a personal level. For it is when people step out of formal roles and carefully circumscribed contractual expectations, as they so often do in rural communities, that they tend to react more passionately to local issues and to each other.

Rural normative systems are buttressed by strong public rewards for conformity and just as strong sanctions for transgressions. *Community gate-keepers* make a major contribution here. These are the *information hubs* - the people who acquire and pass on information about their community. Many are placed strategically around the community in various organisations and groups. They are frequently found in interaction centres, which often include their own homes. One example comes from Peter Dunn (1982) who tells the tale of the postmistress in a small town who stuck her head out the window of her house/post-office in curiosity when, in the days of local switchboards, he adopted a false foreign accent while on a long-distance call from the nearby telephone booth. She was clearly in the habit of listening in on calls. *Gossiping* - the well-known 'bush telegraph' - is part of this information system. Gossip keeps information circulating and provides a way of commenting publicly on questionable, unacceptable and also exemplary behaviour without the source becoming known. It helps to keep the normative system in place by applying sanctions and rewarding good behaviour.

By definition, rural communities with strong normative systems place strong pressures on people to conform to expectations. To quote an extreme example, as recently as 1981 in one small town in the United States, Reese and Malamud (1981, p.28) reported that:

> The Peterborough Transcript now lists births to unwed mothers (sic) along with marriages and deaths - while the town's annual report includes those who fail to pay their taxes.

Although most forms of deviancy by *locals* (long-term permanent residents) - such as alcohol dependence or mental illness - are accepted, it is different for *outsiders* (more temporary residents) who are more likely to be labelled negatively, marginalised, ostracised and even pressured to leave town. Genuine community members usually remain just that despite deviations from community norms and, because of this, they have to be found a social place. Sometimes, communities will attribute positive characteristics to them while accepting their deviance. For example, in one community the consensus about a man who was alcohol dependent was that "he might be the town drunk but he has a heart of gold" (resident). In another town, locals agreed that one particular woman could "... talk the leg off a chair, and she is a little touched in the head you know, but she does so much good for the community" (resident).

Sometimes the deviancy will be re-framed as a positive attribute, although only for that particular person. For instance, Pearson (1985, p.10) tells of the advancing eccentricity of Miss Pettigrew in his small town in North Carolina.

> That was the day Miss Pettigrew stopped being just peculiar. She'd been peculiar ever since I'd heard of her and ever since I'd known what being peculiar meant, but now, when folks spoke of her they would say she was Not Right, which was an advancement of a sort. The town of Neely had seen a blue million peculiarities in its history, but those among its citizenry who were genuinely not right were rare and cherished.

This is not to say that country towns cannot be ostracising, at times making life so uncomfortable for outsiders who deviate substantially from community norms that they are forced to leave town (Martinez-Brawley, 1990b, pp.38-41). I recall, for instance, the professional man and his wife who left town because he no longer had the respect of locals which he needed to do his job after it became public that one of them had been involved in an affair with another local person. Sometimes residents manage to have unwanted people actually removed. For instance, a group of residents once told me proudly of the police sergeant who was "... suddenly transferred somewhere else - he never knew how this came about, you know, but we did!" (resident).

Rural communities will put newcomers to the test. I have become accustomed during initial visits in research towns to endless cups of coffee, shouts at the bar, and dinners in private homes. Of course, this is just one example of the hospitality for which rural Australians are famous. But it is also a way of testing my values and attitudes and what I think about local people before being granted entry into the community. In reality, most people would not agree to research interviews or tell me anything of value until I had passed their tests. This was summarised succinctly by an influential female pastoralist who, after an hour of grilling me over coffee and biscuits, exclaimed: "Well put! - Now who do you want to talk to around here?"

In many small rural communities, residents can be quick to label people on the basis of very little information. Once this happens, the label tends to stick because it is constantly reinforced by local gossip networks. For instance, in one community, a male nurse was labelled as gay when, shortly after his arrival in town, a male friend came to stay with him for a few days.

The other side of a strong and enduring normative system is low tolerance for change and for alternative views of reality. For example, in one place residents firmly believed that all youth problems emanated from what they thought were the many young, unemployed, homeless "blow-ins from down south" (prominent resident) sleeping in cars and on beaches. Despite ten days of diligent searching by our research team we could find only one young homeless transient in the area who was leaving the next day after only a three day stay. The local power elite simply refused to accept our evidence that it was local youth who were engaging in under-age drinking and anti-social behaviour.

Clearly, rural communities can limit residents' freedom to behave as they choose. But more personal forms of interaction can also be *liberating* compared to the restrictions placed on people by the narrow roles of more superficial contractual interaction (Martinez-Brawley, 1990b, p.44; Martinez-Brawley with Buck, 1990, p.96). Moreover, for rural people, the security and solidarity provided by their home community, knowing that they belong somewhere in the social world, knowing that they are significant to others, and being secure in their values and attitudes can also provide a solid existential base from which to build a positive self-concept, self-confidence, self-reliance and a pro-active approach to life. If the home base is securely in place, a person can forge their way into the wider world. For example, Walker (1983, pp.85-6) wrote the following about Zora Neale Hurston, a black anthropologist, novelist, and folklorist:

> She ... had a confidence in herself as an individual that few people, black or white, understood. This was because Zora grew up in a community of black people who had enormous respect for themselves and for their ability to govern themselves. Her own father had written Eatonville town laws. This community affirmed her right to exist, and loved her as an extension of itself.

Power, Influence and Leadership

Although power, influence and leadership are closely interrelated, they are not identical:

> Powerful actors are people who have the potential to exert influence, influentials are people who do exert influence, and leaders are people who exert influence by mobilizing others to join in their causes. (Martinez-Brawley, 1990b, p.53)

Nor are these necessarily the same people. For example, a mayor might have the potential to influence (power), while the shire clerk is the one who actually influences (influence), and another councillor has the local connections necessary to mobilise others (leadership). The generic term *power actor* will be used to refer to all three collectively.

We can distinguish between local power actors such as shire councillors, and those located outside the community such as bankers in regional centres. Local power actors know about their communities, they focus on local issues and they are well connected with other residents. Their influence is within the community where they can quickly mobilise local resources. However, they frequently lack the connections with the outside world which can be important in attracting resources and influencing policy. Conversely, while non-local power actors can influence what happens in the outside world they are not well connected within the community and, because of this, may find it difficult to generate local support for, and compliance with, their policies and plans.

Local power actors can be further divided into *local influentials* who focus on local issues and *cosmopolitans* who are more interested in issues which extend to the world beyond their community (Merton, 1957; Martinez-Brawley, 1990b, pp.78-9). Local influentials use well developed personal connections to draw support from local people and organisations and tend not to be interested in extending their influence beyond the local arena.

> They crowd into those organisations which are largely designed for making contacts, for establishing personal ties. ... Their participation appears to be less a matter of furthering the nominal objectives of these organizations than of using them as contact centres. (Merton, 1957, pp.398-9)

Cosmopolitans, on the other hand, see themselves as players in the wider society and, because of this, join organisations which extend beyond their community. In contrast to local influentials, they draw their power from the functions, structures and processes of these organisations and their areas of special expertise rather than from personal relationships. While locals base their influence on personal relationships built up over a long time, cosmopolitans are more recent arrivals who have brought prestige, skills and, sometimes, capital from other places.

Cosmopolitans are frequently temporary residents, such as school principals, bankers and senior police officers, who move into prestigious and powerful local formal positions bringing knowledge, skills and prestige from the outside world. They expect themselves, and are expected by employers and other residents, to be power actors within the community, even though they don't usually have the local connections required to support this role. Their ability to influence depends on the support of local people. One police sergeant, whose closest colleague was more than 150km away, put this succinctly:

> When a bloke pulls a knife on me at the pub, I want to be sure that the other men in the bar will stand with me and not him. This is why I put a lot of work into gaining the respect of the town during the first few months in a new posting.

Local influentials and temporary cosmopolitans frequently work together. While the former identify the directions in which they want their community to develop, the latter do much of the actual work. One highly influential local woman put it this way:

> We make a deal with them, even though it is never spoken. We call the shots, they help with the work. It suits them because they want a good report from the community for the sake of their own careers. Most also genuinely want to help out, and they do realise that it is our community. We want our community to run how we want it to run - after all, we'll still be here when they're long gone. But we locals are short on numbers and time. So we need these people to help with the work. Usually it works just fine.

In rural communities, power, influence and leadership are close to most residents. Many are either powerful themselves or they personally know people who are. This makes the power structure all the more real, a daily presence in their lives. Power is more abstract and remote in cities where most people only read about it in the newspaper and see it on television. Most urbanites do not participate in it directly. Because local issues are more immediately real for rural people, they tend to be more passionate about them than most city people and are more likely to attempt to influence outcomes. In this climate, issues which seem trivial to an outsider can come to dominate local interaction.

But while ordinary rural people might debate local issues endlessly, this does not necessarily mean that, individually, they have more influence over decisions than urban residents. To understand why, we need to look at the different kinds of power structures. Powers (1967a, p.156) defined a power structure as an "... identifiable interaction pattern composed of power actors who may relate to each other in a number of different ways". Martinez-Brawley (1990b, pp.60-5) identified two kinds of power structures: *elitism*, where power, influence and leadership are highly concentrated amongst a small number of people; and *pluralism*, where they are more dispersed across a wider range of people and organisations and where the power structure changes from issue to issue. Powers (1967a, 1967b) suggested that power structures can be identified according to where they fall along a continuum from more centralised to more dispersed.

- In *one-person* power structures, power lies with one individual or family and has been accumulated slowly over many generations.

- In *tightly knit groups*, power rests with a small number of people and organisations which form a cohesive bloc.
- In *segmented* power structures, a relatively small number of people, groups or organisations are powerful in different spheres of influence, but do not form a cohesive power bloc.
- In *diffused* power structures or *power pools*, a large number of people, groups and organisations have different spheres of influence but don't act together. In these, coalitions form and re-form according to the issue at hand.

Smaller communities which are not economically diversified, which do not have competing political parties, and which lack a number of voluntary associations tend to have more centralised power structures (Magill and Clark, 1975, pp.38-40; Menneghan, 1976). In more centralised structures power actors tend to be the same across issues which, partly because of this, are highly interconnected. For example, decisions concerning staffing of hospitals and schools can be very much interrelated if membership of the hospital and school committees overlaps.

Entrenched elite power structures, clear social structural divisions and strong normative systems can make it difficult to challenge established ways of doing things. This is why attempts at major social change frequently don't work in rural communities. Consequently, an incremental approach to social change can be especially effective in rural areas where mobilising resources and securing support for more acceptable smaller changes can be quicker and easier because of the overlap amongst power actors. Furthermore, when the power elite is on side it is usually easy to gain the support of the whole community.

In most rural communities, men tend to be more structurally powerful than women. There are usually fewer women in powerful formal positions such as mayors, shire councillors, school principals, senior police officers, or executives in the more influential government departments. However, after reviewing the evidence from the United States Martinez-Brawley (1990b, p.56) concluded that rural women are increasingly filling these positions. Although she found that men remained more powerful than women overall, "... generally women influentials were found in traditionally nurturing or expressive issue areas (health, welfare, human rights, and the environment)" (p.56).

Politics

Politics in rural communities tends to be simple, close to residents and highly participatory. It is simple in that usually only a handful of issues are debated, these are immediately real to virtually everyone, and debates often involve clearly differentiated groups. Furthermore, the small size of rural communities means that most people relate to office holders and political aspirants in a variety of roles and have personal feelings about them, their families and their associates. For this reason, who to support is frequently determined on the basis of personal feelings rather than the issues at hand. For example, elections in one North Queensland town have always been fought between two local families and most residents vote according to their relationships with these. This personalisation of issues can result in passionate political debate amongst ordinary residents which can influence interaction in other spheres and dominate local social life more generally.

A memorable example comes from a small town in Northern Australia which some years ago experienced a classic struggle between property owners and workers for control of the shire council. For many decades the wealthy beef producers had held the power. However, over the years the council had grown, gradually employing more blue-collar workers. There were two candidates for the position of shire chair - a property owner and a blue-collar small business man - and candidates for other council positions were clearly aligned with one or the other. One issue concerned replacing the gates across a main access road to the region with cattle grids. According to local reports, Council had offered to pay half the costs involved although property owners had so far refused to pay the other half. The election was close to the people because everyone knew all candidates and because the main issues directly impacted on all residents. It was highly participatory in that everyone seemed to be involved in ongoing debates and informal 'party' meetings. Feelings amongst residents were so intense that they could not focus on anything else in the run-up to the election, so much so that I suspended my research for two weeks. To complete the story, the workers won the chair and a council majority. However, despite this, a decade later cattle grids still have not been laid and travellers still have to open and close the gates along the road. And some town residents continue to leave them open in protest.

Factionalism and Conflict

Given strong normative structures, clear social structural divisions, elitist rather than dispersed power structures, highly participatory political processes, the predominance of personal rather than contractual relationships and the intensity of interaction in rural communities, it is not surprising that conflict can develop between rival factions. Once established, factionalism and conflict can become entrenched and, although not active all the time, can continue as interpersonal undercurrents of town life. Community conflict can have any number of bases. For example, the conflict in the town facing a local government election concerned control over resources and influence over decision making. Another town was divided over whether to condone, ignore or condemn the affair of a local married business man and a local woman. The intense rivalry in another seemed to emanate from railway workers' loss of power to local private entrepreneurs and property owners. And another community was divided according to residents' allegiances with two dominant kin groups.

However, it would be wrong to conclude that divided communities do not have unifying themes as well. Rural communities seem to have both to varying degrees. For example, the town in political turmoil united around the hospital. Another intensely divided town came together around the primary school and their children's education. In this community, the school grounds and buildings were immaculately maintained and the Friday 'fish and chip night' at the pub which was run by, and for, the school was always well attended.

Remoteness and Isolation

Possibly the most obvious characteristic of many rural communities in Australia is their remoteness from most services and facilities. Individual residents are frequently isolated from their social and support networks and many lack the protection afforded by police and service organisations in situations such as domestic violence and child abuse. This is why transport and communication are so important. Good public transport is a key to effective rural human services. Without access to private transport many rural Australians, such as women on properties, can be cut off from friends, relatives, supports and services. The importance of public transport and access to private vehicles is vividly illustrated by the woman on a property in north-western Queensland who had been abused over a long period. She managed to escape to a town some 20 km away and caught a train bound for Townsville. However, because there was only one train daily her husband was waiting at the next station to take her home.

Rural telecommunications have been improving rapidly over recent years. Still, though, timed long-distance *STD* calls means that, although the technology is there, rural people do not use it as much as they would if costs were more comparable with urban rates. And, in some areas, telephone zonings do not coincide with regional boundaries as these are defined by settlement patterns, transportation routes and residents' natural geographic identifications.

Social and Support Networks

It is frequently claimed that rural social networks are stronger than urban. On the one hand, some people living in the same locality may be close emotionally because they have known each other for a long time. Perhaps, too, the constant interaction involved in living in the same locality strengthens ties. And perhaps rural people are more likely than urban to have close kin living nearby. Overall, though, the empirical evidence indicates that there are no overall differences (e.g., Korte, 1980, 1983; Fischer, 1982, pp.56-61).

It is also frequently claimed that rural people have stronger support networks than urban residents and that they are more likely to seek and receive help from others within the same locality (e.g., Melton, 1983, p.9; Urey and Henggeler, 1983; Craig and Killen, 1984). However, with only occasional exceptions (such as Scott and Roberto, 1987) empirical evidence consistently suggests that there are no overall rural-urban differences (e.g., Lee and Cassidy, 1981, 1985; Lee and Whitbeck, 1987). The proposition that rural supports are stronger can be challenged on three grounds. First, as discussed in Chapter 7, research on social support has consistently demonstrated that who helps whom depends on the need in question, characteristics of the support and the recipient, their relationship, and other contextual factors rather than whether the recipient lives in a rural or an urban place (Wellman, 1979; Fischer, 1982, p.175; Martinez-Brawley and Blundall, 1989, p.515; Cheers, 1992b). For some needs, people seek the help of their neighbours, while for others only their closest friends and relatives will do, no matter how far away they are. Second, the earlier view that the support networks of urban people have been weakened by high mobility and the urban environment has been shown to be incorrect. In general, urban people do have fairly strong support networks - it is just that they are now spread over greater distances (Wellman, 1979; Fischer, 1982). Third, reports that rural communities have key local helpers - people to whom a number of other local people go to for assistance - are inconsistent. Although Martinez-Brawley and Blundall (1989) found key helpers in rural communities in Pennsylvania, Kelley and Kelley (1985, pp.361-2) failed to find them in rural Iowa as did Cheers (1992b, pp.484-8) in North Queensland.

Media

The media, especially the country newspaper, plays an important role in rural life. It provides a communication point for private individuals, organisations and power actors and is a significant source of information about social and recreational activities, meetings and so forth. As Wild (1983, p.1) noted:

> The usual interpretation of the role of the country or community newspaper is that it reflects what is happening in the surrounding region, that it communicates valuable information to disparate groups and individuals and that it helps to integrate a community by providing a focus for the emotional feelings that people have for a locality.

The media supports important rituals and events which help bind a community together. Local newspapers, for example, report births, deaths, weddings, engagements, anniversaries and civic ceremonies. In this way, the media supports not only the things which bind a community together, but also the very idea that a community exists.

But in reinforcing, sometimes perhaps creating, an awareness of community amongst local people, the media can also reinforce existing power structures. It does this partly by promoting a positive view of the community. For example, in their study of Springdale in Upper New York State, Vidich and Bensman (1960, p.32) commented that:

> The newspaper always emphasises the positive side of life; it never reports local arrests, shotgun weddings, mortgage foreclosures, lawsuits, bitter exchanges in public meetings, suicides or any other unpleasant happening. By this constant focus on warm and human qualities in all public situations, the public character of the community takes on those qualities.

Rural newspapers also tend to avoid significant or controversial political and social debate. For instance, Wild's (1983, p.2) content analysis of the newspaper in Bradstow from 1883 to 1969 found that 91.6 per cent of all news and editorial columns were non-controversial. Janovich (1967, pp.76-7) arrived at a similar figure of 93.2 per cent for all items in a sample of small newspapers in the United States.

In this way, the rural media can serve the interests of the powerful and the wealthy by promoting the concept of community and by reducing class consciousness.

> Ideas of community are consistently asserted by dominant economic and political groups ... [and] ... echoed by subordinate groups and thus used to foster a sense of fellow feeling, local attachment and relative contentment. Identification and solidarity therefore is encouraged along the local/non-local, rural/urban cleavage, and in this way, class consciousness based upon economic interest is avoided. (Saunders, Newby and Bell, 1978, p.78)

Local social and normative structures are central to all rural communities and tend to serve the interests of the powerful and the wealthy. By generating support for the concept of the local community, the media is also generating support for 'the way we do things here'. By supporting the prevailing culture, the media is supporting existing power structures. Wild (1983, p.1) put it this way:

> The dominant ideology surrounding the country newspaper concerns its roles as an integrating mechanism and as the upholder of local democracy. In practice this means support for consensus and the status quo rather than for conflict and social change. If such newspapers reflect the underlying social structure then to some extent they must support the values, ideas and interests of the powerful. ... When matters of conflict and change are discussed it is usually with reference to perceived threats from outside the community. Here bureaucratic government departments or the big city or national and multinational companies are the source of concern. Conflicts and disputes internal to the community are down-played in comparison to such external issues. Such small town values as parochialism, provincialism and xenophobia are emphasised at the expense of worldly-wide values.

But existing power structures can also be more direct in their influence of country newspapers. Wild found a clear example of this in relation to the *McIvor Times*:

> The Councillors exercise considerable influence over what is published in the McIvor Times. In the meeting of 9 July 1981, one Councillor, who had criticised the infant welfare sister, turned to the editor of the McIvor Times and

said 'don't write that down'. In the same meeting another Councillor told the editor not to write down comments he had made concerning a caravan park owner's refusal to pay rates. The latter issue had also been discussed in the June meeting when the Council had gone into committee and asked the editor to leave the Council Chamber. The Shire Secretary spoke to the editor and asked him not to publish anything about the issue. The editor generally acquiesces to such requests but becomes annoyed when Councillors telephone him to complain about stories asking such things as 'who authorised the release of that?'. (Wild, 1983, p.3)

Conclusion

An overriding thesis of this book is that effective rural social care must be informed by an accurate, useful understanding of rural people, the places in which they live, and the interaction between the two. People are buffeted by a vast sea of determining forces but, within limits, can influence their respective destinies through their choices and actions. We are all embedded in our respective social, natural and spiritual worlds which, at some level, most of us experience in an integrated way. A person shapes their world as does world the person. In Australia, Western ideology has generated a system of social care which breaks human living and social care into a multitude of bits and pieces and which focuses on individuals and nuclear families at the expense of communities and other social groupings. It has been suggested in this chapter that this does not fit with how many rural and indigenous Australians experience their lives and their worlds. I have also reviewed some characteristics of rural communities, primarily for the benefit of practitioners, students and service managers. We are now ready to develop some different ways of thinking about social care in Australia which might prove more useful for rural people.

Notes

1. The term 'ideology' is used here in the broader sense of a 'system of ideas' including, but not limited to, beliefs and values.
2. In this section I am indebted to the work of Martinez-Brawley (1990b). Readers are referred to her book for further discussion of what we know about rural communities. Also see Wilkinson (1991).

Part 2
Social Care

4 Rural Social Policy

In Part 1 we examined rural Australia, the structure of Australia's formal social care arrangements, and their shortcomings in relation to rural issues. In Part 2 we focus in greater detail on existing rural social care arrangements and generate recommendations for more effective responses to the personal and social needs of rural Australians. The present chapter identifies six frameworks underlying rural social policies, introduces four key issues which thread their way through the remaining chapters and presents a framework for examining rural social care within the broader context of managed, sustainable regional change.

Frameworks

The history of Australian rural social policy, both before and after European settlement, is yet to be documented. Consequently, only a beginning analysis can be conducted here. Most Australian rural social policies since 1788 can be grouped according to their emphasis on one or more of the following frameworks:

- urbo-centricity;
- economic reductionism;
- mainstreaming;
- rural targeting;
- reactive residualism; and
- development.

Urbo-centricity occurs when ostensibly rural policies are introduced primarily to solve urban, not rural, problems. For instance, from time to time, some State governments have tried to reduce urban public housing shortages by providing cheap accommodation in country towns for low-income city people. At a more general level, escalating social problems in cities and concerns about the economic inefficiencies of urban over-population, urban sprawl and increasing urban housing and transportation costs have prompted sporadic efforts to relocate city people and businesses to rural areas (Alexander, 1994; Hurley, 1994, pp.3-6). In the 1970s, urban pressures for decentralisation came from what the Cities Commission (1973, p.9) described as the:

> ... relatively sudden ... [awareness of] ... problems of congestion, overcrowding, lack of essential services, excessive noise, air and water pollution, urban social isolation, poverty and increasing crime rates.

Similarly, the 1994 Commonwealth regional development policy (Keating, 1994) was mainly an attempt to regenerate the national economy, primarily for the benefit of urban interests. The fact that around 30 per cent of regional development outlays in the *Working Nation* strategy were allocated to develop the airport at Badgery's Creek - for the benefit of Sydney, Quantas Airways and international air traffic generally - demonstrates that the strategy was, in large measure, an urban policy (Hurley, 1994, p.8).

Economic reductionism involves re-framing social and personal problems as economic issues. Once this is done, simplistic logic suggests that we should deal with them through economic mechanisms, ineffective as they may be. For instance, the *Working Nation* statement (Keating, 1994), which was primarily an attempt to enhance economic growth and planning, equated social development with increasing regional employment opportunities. Policies such as these are especially dangerous because they provide a rationale for ignoring other social issues such as the needs of people who are not in the labour force and of those, such as abused children and women in violent relationships, whose problems will not be solved by creating employment opportunities for others. Besides, it is well established that regional economic development strategies alone do not alleviate rural poverty (Larson, 1989; Lichter, Johnston and McLaughlin, 1994; Lichter and McLaughlin, 1995).

Mainstreaming rural social justice issues dominated the policy landscape until recently. Here, rural needs are viewed as identical to those of urban populations and dealt with through the same policies, programs and services. For example, approaches to youth suicide have generally assumed that young people have access to sophisticated mental health facilities and accessible referral points such as general medical practitioners. This is frequently not the case for rural youth. Clearly, the evidence presented in Chapter 2 demonstrates that this approach is not working in rural Australia.

In contrast, *rural targeting* responds to the distinctiveness of rural contexts and rural needs. Examples include multi-purpose centres, innovative funding programs such as combined services funding, and services such as mobile counselling (Dale, 1994, pp.332-4; OND, 1994, pp.95-8). These are reviewed in Chapter 7.

Assistance following natural disasters such as droughts, floods and cyclones, and responses to more long-term situations such as the effects of rural restructuring, industry downswings and population depletion can be classified as *reactive residualism*. They are 'reactive' in that they react to events after they have occurred rather than plan for them ahead of time, and 'residual' because they care for people who cannot benefit from normal market processes. Drought assistance programs and packages designed to help the human casualties of rural restructuring such as the *Household Assistance Scheme* (see Chapter 5) are applications of this framework.

Finally, *development* policies involve planning and establishing social care arrangements in response to current and projected social issues through data-driven planning and participative community development. For example, the *Australian Assistance Plan* of the 1970s established regional councils for social development to initiate and coordinate ongoing locally-based social care (Munn, 1993). On a more localised scale, some communities, such as Mackay in Queensland, have been involved in ongoing social care development through the *Mackay Regional Council for Social Development* (Jones, 1993) while others, such as Tumby Bay in South Australia (Jeffreys and Munn, 1996), have spontaneously launched into integrated social and economic development in response to threats to community survival.

Issues

Social policies, programs and services also vary according to the extent to which they:

- assume that social care is a function of government or an expression of community;
- locate care in horizontal or vertical ties;
- focus on whole communities as well as individuals and families; and

- relate to economic development.

Social Care as a Function of Government and an Expression of Community

Gemeinschaft and *gesellschaft* patterns of interaction were introduced in Chapter 3. It will be recalled that *gemeinschaftlich* interaction is more personalised, happens between whole people, and is based on feelings of mutual identification with, and commitment to, the community. *Gesellschaftlich* interaction, on the other hand, is less personal and more circumscribed by formal roles and contractual expectations. Whilst *gesellschaftlich* interaction occurs through positions and roles located in impersonal formal societal structures, *gemeinschaftlich* interaction happens between whole individuals within the context of community sentiment and intersecting personal histories.

These two concepts help us to identify different approaches to social care policies, programs, services and practice. At one hypothetical extreme, social care can be provided by people filling strictly circumscribed organisational and professional roles through formal societal structures and programs. Here, government controls social care arrangements by providing services and resources directly, and by imposing stringent accountability requirements on non-government organisations. The strengths of this approach are that government has the jurisdictional power to provide a fairly standard basic safety net for everyone, standardise quality of care across regions, and ensure target effectiveness and an equitable distribution of resources. The weaknesses are that centralised decision makers can misread needs; plan, provide and fund services which are inappropriate to local issues, conditions and lifestyles; discourage mutual aid; and lose those potential users who are reluctant to use government services.

At the other extreme, social care can be viewed as an expression of community, a normal function of community life. It is something which people do for each other in the normal course of human living and through small, local community-based organisations (Hadley and Hatch, 1981; Martinez-Brawley, 1990b, pp.213-9; Cheers, 1992b, pp.568-72). The spirit of this position was nicely portrayed by Martinez-Brawley with Buck (1990, p.96) when they wrote that:

> Government bureaucracy, civic organization, and goodwill and welfare agencies regardless of their sensitivity and compassion cannot substitute for the

nurturing and identity-enhancing aspect of the rich social mosaic of day-to-day association interlacing landscapes of familiarity.

In this approach, there is greater emphasis on informal care, greater responsiveness to local conditions, needs and priorities, local control of service planning and delivery, and autonomous decision making by non-government community-based organisations.

Where community is emphasised, the community takes responsibility for identifying and prioritising local needs and developing social care arrangements through local structures and organisations. The main advantages claimed for this approach are more accurate understanding of local needs, encouragement of mutual aid, strengthening of horizontal ties within communities, and care which is more appropriate to local needs, priorities and conditions (Cheers, 1992a). However without government support, local resources, initiative, time and energy may be lacking and local power structures, normative systems and social processes can interfere with the effectiveness of social care arrangements (Wade-Marshall, 1982; Coorey, 1988). Further, some people may not get what they need, resources could be distributed inequitably and social care might be neglected.

In Australia, policies and programs vary according to their relative emphasis on each approach. Only governments can ensure that everyone has a basic social safety net and that resources are distributed throughout society according to consistent and accountable principles. On the other hand, given Australia's settlement patterns, limited social care resources and the importance of local communities to many residents, it is naive to believe that government has all the answers.

Horizontal and Vertical Ties and Rural Social Care

Rural people and social care practitioners move constantly through a sea of complex horizontal and vertical interdependencies. It is romantic nonsense to claim that rural communities are isolated from the rest of the world in enclosed cocoons. The idea that urban ways of living have flooded rural communities to the point where they have lost their social identities is equally naive. Rural communities exist as does the wider world and deal with each other they must.

In many rural places, horizontal ties have been progressively weakened by developments in communication and transportation technology, the spread of urban-based national media, market globalisation, population mobility, the sprawl of urban metropolises, increasing dependence on direct government assistance, and a programatic approach to social policy. As Martinez-Brawley (1990b, p.12) commented:

> The vertical system is strong and often is needed to mitigate the lack of resources and know-how in many local settings. Herein lies the dilemma. Although often necessary, the growth of the vertical system results in further strains - financial, intellectual, and moral - in the horizontal ties. Both intellectual and moral dimensions must remain strong for cohesive communities to survive.

Sher and Sher (1994, p.21) also concluded that the vertical programatic emphasis of Australian social policy has weakened rural communities.

> Government social programs inadvertently have worked against community cohesiveness by segregating small, rural populations along the lines of eligibility criteria - and thus, atomising these little communities into disparate, rival "client groups". ... Cumulatively, they exacerbate existing rural community tensions. ... From a rural development perspective, social policy has a dark side that only rarely is brought to light. It is relentlessly individualistic. It does undermine community cohesiveness. And, it will continue to foster more dependency on government than community self-reliance. Seen in this light, Australian social policy looks surprisingly anti-social. (Sher and Sher, 1994, p.21)

In a similar vein, Quixley (1993) suggested that "the conventional, urban, program-based approach" to youth marginalisation does not work in small communities.

> It is inadequate ... to attempt to break the cycle by simply providing houses, or establishing training programs, or extending secondary schooling provisions. [Such measures] ... will not deal with the problems faced by young people in rural and remote communities. Solutions must be tackled in the context of a response to the whole problem faced not only by young people, but by the entire community. Community ownership of the process of change is critical to a successful outcome. (Quixley, 1993, p.20)

It does not help, for instance, when a shire council rejects an independent consultant's report on local youth problems because councillors want to blame them on mythical transients from southern cities, especially after a large representative sample of local young people have just expressed the view that they feel alienated from their community. Funding and facilities provided from outside the community will not change the marginalisation of youth issues and the defensiveness of the power elite which lie at the communal heart of this issue.

In recognition of the fact that vertical ties cannot build community, some Commonwealth and State governments have recently introduced policies to strengthen horizontal ties. Community development has been undergoing a minor resurgence in rural areas. More local governments are developing social plans (Callaghan, 1993, pp.84-92; Madden, 1993, pp.18-9). The *Working Nation* statement (Keating, 1994) provided a locally-driven regional development framework aimed partly at rebuilding rural economies, although this has now been dismantled. Commonwealth and State governments are introducing new funding structures for community-based, multi-function social care services and locally-driven community services development initiatives (Dale, 1994, pp.332-4; OND, 1994, pp.95-8). Some have also recently increased their emphasis on regional level administration (Disney, 1992, p.12). But establishing regional offices, relocating staff and giving them executive titles does not automatically provide them with the freedom to respond to local circumstances on their own initiative or with real influence in central policy development. Nor do such measures ensure that regional managers will involve local people and organisations in policy development and program administration. Less progress has been made on these, the more telling issues (Disney, 1992, p.12).

Both horizontal and vertical ties are clearly necessary in social development. Strong horizontal ties enhance community cohesion. They also contribute to social development by providing energy, enthusiasm, material and human resources, and local wisdom concerning cultures, problems and needs. Vertical ties, on the other hand, can provide access to resources, decision-making processes and additional expertise. Bringing new external resources into a community can stimulate enthusiasm, energy, commitment and involvement of local people in both community and economic development (Luloff and Wilkinson, 1979; Martin and Wilkinson, 1984; Wilkinson, 1989, 1991). New resources also help to revitalise local organisations. But, as we shall see in Chapters 6 and 7, both horizontal and vertical ties are also potential sources of constraints and complications.

Rural social care practitioners, whether they are involved in direct practice, social planning, community development or management do, indeed, stand at the intersection of horizontal and vertical processes. While being immersed in these processes, they must also stand outside the web, maximising their respective contributions to human well-being, minimising their negative impacts and, where necessary, trying to change them.

Community Focus

Australian social care policies focus primarily on individuals and families, rarely on whole communities. Clearly, social problems do affect individuals and families and many must be resolved at that level. But for four reasons a community focus is also required. First, the social, emotional and material well-being of entire communities is affected by many social, economic and environmental issues. Second, community processes such as self-help groups, natural support processes and mutual aid can provide effective care to individuals and families (Martinez-Brawley and Blundall, 1989; Cheers, 1992b). Third, many of the problems affecting rural people are the result of community factors and must be resolved at the community level. Examples include physical infrastructure deficiencies in remote indigenous communities and the problems created for many women by local social and power structures (Coorey, 1988; Alston, 1995). Fourth, given that rural disadvantage is often locality specific, it is important that rural community developers help residents band together to represent common local interests.

The Relationship between Economic Development and Social Care Development

In Australia, the social and economic sectors have been clearly separated for the last two hundred years (Cheers, 1995)[1]. (Such was not the case prior to this in traditional indigenous communities.) Government departments and non-government organisations focus on one or the other, seldom on both. Personnel have been trained to work in only one sector. Scholarly and research literature are clearly separate. And each sector is infused with a different ideology - economics with capitalism and social care with Fabian socialism.

There are two overriding reasons why social care and economic development should be more closely interrelated (Jones, 1993; Cheers, 1995, pp.9-16). First, as shown in Chapter 2, social and material well-being are tightly interwoven. Second, each sector has much to contribute to the other.

[Economic well-being] ... should provide a springboard for overcoming social service difficulties and a well developed community encourages economic growth. (Office of Rural Affairs in Victoria - ORA, 1991, p.61)

Clearly, economic growth can provide benefits for local people such as employment (where labour is not imported), personal and business income (where cash and financial investment flow back into the community), recreational facilities, improved roads, and better services. Successful development projects can have other social spin-offs. They often involve investing in infrastructure such as local roads and community health facilities. When development projects attract local support they can provide a 'rallying point', or a focus, for community cohesion and involvement. Economic development also often brings new people into a community such as managers, engineers, accountants and tradespeople with skills that can be turned to community projects. Perhaps more subtly, social care development can benefit from being touched by the more 'tough-minded' approach of the economic sector.

Good economic development projects will anticipate a variety of social impacts, both positive and negative. Negative impacts include, for example, increased demand for public facilities, increased social dislocation, higher living costs, and general weakening of the host community's social fabric and personal support systems. Inappropriate infrastructure developments also frequently accompany economic development. For instance, as late as 1992, young people living on the Whitsunday Islands off the coast of Central Queensland were ignored by a public transport system geared to the needs of tourism. Consequently, they were frequently late to school because of a poor connection between the ferry and the bus. We also found many Whitsunday young people crowded together in small apartments as a result of a recent 25 per cent average annual rent increase (Bone, Cheers and Hil, 1993).

Perhaps not so obvious are the contributions of the social care sector to economic growth. Investing public resources in rural areas fuels economic development and invariably brings public investment in the form of buildings, facilities and personnel. Building is always good for business, facilities such as offices and equipment such as computers can be used by other residents, and staff bring skills and local spending power. Conversely, withdrawal of public infrastructure limits development (Cribb, 1994, p.13). In Northern Australia, for instance, differences in public resource investment have been found to explain some of the differences between economically-growing communities and those which are stagnant or declining (Hudson, 1989, 1991, 1992; Hudson and Jensen, 1991).

Development projects can be quicker, cheaper and more successful when they respond to human needs. The Magnetic Quays development on Magnetic Island just off the coast of Townsville provides one example. Some years ago, plans were made to establish a major resort complex on the island, and building was commenced. However, lack of community input contributed to a major public outcry and cessation of work. The developers eventually pulled out having started but, by no means, completed the job. They suffered a substantial loss and left a little piece of the North Queensland paradise dominated by an ugly pile of rubble.

The point here is not that a project should be stopped if a handful of local residents whinge about it. It is that skilled community negotiation - a social care development strategy - can result in considerable time and cost savings. Where development involves residents in planning and responds to their concerns it is more likely to proceed with their support. The Barramundi Fishing Lodge on Escott Station in the Gulf of Carpentaria has done so well partly because it has used local knowledge about the best fishing spots and acceptable locations for the resort, and because it has harnessed the knowledge and skills of local people. Placing the Lodge closer to Burketown may well have exacerbated community conflict, damaged the local Aboriginal community, fuelled community resistance, and resulted in poor catches for tourists and, consequently, lower profits for developers.

Good social development also generates community cohesion, involvement and commitment which can flow over to economic initiatives. Therefore, the developer is in a better position to access local knowledge about culture, resources and ecology as well as residents' energies and skills. Furthermore, the social care sector reminds people of their social obligations as well as their rights, and provides them with the opportunity to exercise them. As one Queensland Transport Department executive commented during a seminar in which I was trying to persuade regional managers to take account of the social implications of their road investment decisions (Cheers, 1993b):

> I know that everyone in this room is a human being when we are not at work. We have to take that into our jobs on Monday morning.

Managed, Sustainable Regional Change

If economic development and social care are, and should be, so closely interrelated then we need a framework which encompasses both; one which also incorporates the other two components of care - health care and education. The concept of *sustainable, integrated regional development* has frequently been used as an organising framework (Cheers, 1995). Here, *regional development* refers to the development of economic resources, physical infrastructure and care aimed at preserving, and possibly increasing, natural, human and social resources and maximising personal and community well-being. Economic development is a more or less planned and directed process resulting in economic growth, increased wealth and enhanced material well-being for residents and others (Cheers, 1995, p.3). It incorporates improvements to physical infrastructure - concrete facilities and services such as roads, buildings, transportation, power and water supply and emergency services.

Integrating all components of development maximises total human well-being.

> Development means the development of people. Roads, buildings, the increase of crop output and other things of this nature are not development; they are only tools of development. ... An increase in the number of school buildings ... [is development] ... only if the buildings can be, and are being, used to develop the minds and the understanding of the people. ... An expansion of crops is development only if these things can be sold, and the money used for other things which improve the health, comfort and understanding of the people. ... Every proposal must be judged by the criterion of whether it serves the purposes of development - and the purpose of development is the people. (Nyerere, 1968, pp.59-60)

If material and social well-being are integrated in human living then surely both would benefit from being approached as such. Total human well-being is maximised when economic development takes account of its potential social impacts and, conversely, when social development takes account of its economic impacts. We who are involved in social care cannot ignore the economic sector. Morally, our commitment to social justice demands that we should try to harness and, where necessary, change processes which affect the distribution of power and resources.

Improved human well-being is a short-term proposition unless its sources are maintained. The principle of *sustainability* demands that we preserve and, where possible, further develop natural resources, people's cultures and spirituality, and those social structures, processes and institutions which enhance human well-being (Smailes, 1995). Sustainability is morally binding because the concept of social justice is not generationally specific. It refers to the distribution of rights, power and resources between, as well as within, generations. It means that the total well-being of future generations will be at least as high as it has been for present and past generations, and that present generations are responsible for ensuring that this eventuates.

Sustainable, integrated regional development can now be defined as:

> planned processes aimed at enhancing the total well-being of present and future residents of a region through sustainable integrated development of financial, material, physical, social, cultural, educational, health care and spiritual resources.

But although it is attractive, this concept has three limitations. First, through its focus on development, it refers only to localities which are growing economically or which have the potential to do so. History is dotted with communities which, for one reason or another, have died economically and there is no reason to believe that this will change (Disney, 1992, p.4). The social care sector is also morally obliged to respond to the needs of these communities and their remaining residents.

Second, the implication is that sustainable, integrated regional development can be controlled through careful, rational planning. This is clearly not so. Change is too complex, too multifaceted to be 'planned' in this sense, for much happens of its own accord. Perhaps the best we can hope for is to 'manage' change as best we can.

The third limitation of the concept is that, given the structure of Australian society, integrated regional development will not be achieved in the foreseeable future except, perhaps, for a few isolated localities. At all levels, economic development and social care are clearly separated in policies, programs and organisational structures. This separation was strengthened by Keating's (1994) *Working Nation* statement and is currently being further reinforced by the Howard government. Integration is simply not possible when some government departments focus exclusively on economic and physical infrastructure issues and others just as exclusively on social care. Narrowly-specialised government departments, ever eager to protect their own 'turf', are often at odds with each other and can exacerbate conflict between competing local economic and social interests. Nor does integration seem possible when economic interests are forcefully represented by tightly-knit, powerful local organisations while social care issues remain the province of less powerful people and agencies which have their hands full simply ensuring that those who need immediate help receive it.

There are three other problems involved in trying to integrate social care and economic development (Cheers, 1995, pp.15-6). First, if integration actually happened in the present climate, economic agendas would dominate and experience shows that these often conflict with social justice ideals. Second, history demonstrates that each 'side' is prone to denigrate or disregard the other's priorities and to make assumptions about their motives. While economic developers are often seen as uncaring and exclusively profit-driven, social workers and community developers are just as often viewed as woolly-headed, soft-hearted do-gooders who deny the reality of economic imperatives. Third, we should not underestimate the sheer complexity of trying to coordinate, let alone integrate, all components of social and economic development. Regional developers are trying to bring together land use planning, town planning, preferred settlement patterns, industry development, road and transport planning, architectural and landscaping considerations, social planning, community services development, environmental and social impact assessment and much more. At the same time, they are coordinating the contributions of a variety of Commonwealth and State government departments, several local governments, a number of industries and private firms, non-government community service organisations, local groups and organisations, indigenous peoples, ethnic groups, and developers, all with their differing priorities. And all this in a context where many sectors, organisations and groups have had little experience of working with each other, where Commonwealth, State and local governments and government departments compete with each other for resources and influence, and where no-one has had much experience with integrated development.

So although it clarifies some issues, the concept of *sustainable, integrated regional development* will not work as an over-arching framework in Australia. Perhaps it is more realistic to think in terms of coordinating the sectors rather than integrating them. To account for the social care aspects of communities in economic decline we need to think more broadly in terms of change rather than development. The idea of social, emotional, cultural, spiritual and environmental sustainability remains important as does the need to plan for change or, at the very least, its repercussions for human well-being. Perhaps the concept of *managed, sustainable regional change* is more useful. This can be defined as:

> managed processes aimed at enhancing the total well-being of present and future residents of a region through sustainable, coordinated improvement or maintenance of material, physical, social, cultural, educational, health care and spiritual resources.

Figure 4.1 presents the components of managed, sustainable regional change. The community's boundaries are indistinct - it stretches out into the wider world. Economic development, social care, health care and education are represented as four braids, each comprising a number of entwined cords. How tightly the cords are interwoven varies from cord to cord and from time to time. The braids are linked, but not rigidly. In declining communities, economic development may cease completely although social care, health care and education may continue to be provided. Vertical and horizontal ties intersect in the local community. These, and their interaction, have a major impact on directions taken by the configuration as a whole, by each braid and by each cord. Social care includes social care development (social planning and community development), formal and informal social care arrangements and direct practice. In keeping with my thesis that rural social care should adopt a community (or regional) frame of reference, rural social care development is discussed first to provide the conceptual context for discussion of formal personal services in Chapter 7 and practice in Chapter 8. But before moving on to these issues we should first examine Australia's basic social care safety net in relation to rural people. For if this is not firmly in place then all the rest can come to nought.

Note

1. Although this discussion focuses on interaction between social care and economic development, we should not ignore relationships between these and the education and health sectors. The same general point could be made about education and health: they tend to be disconnected from the economic sector, perhaps slightly less so for tertiary education. In rural Australia, the social care, health and education sectors tend to be fairly closely interrelated.

Figure 4.1 Managed, Sustainable Regional Change

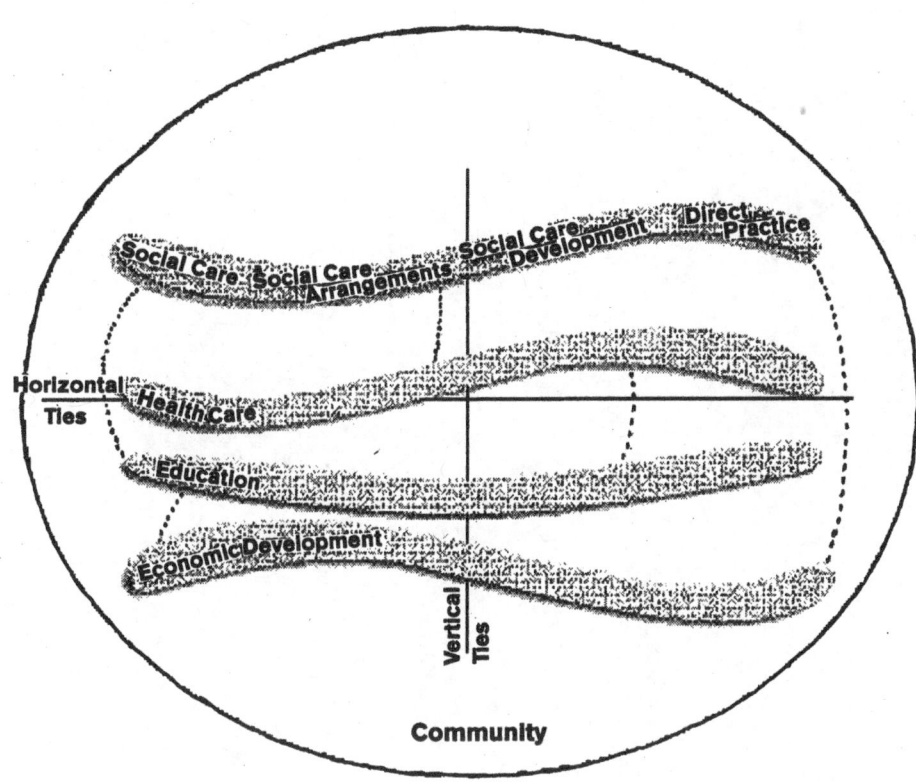

5 Income Support and Housing

This chapter discusses problems and issues involved in providing rural people with basic safety net provisions concerning income support and housing, and suggests potentially useful policy and program guidelines.

Income Support

Programs

Australia's income security system provides an impressive array of pensions, allowances and other benefits for people who are unable to earn a basic income either permanently or because of temporary circumstances such as illness or unemployment. Because it was designed primarily for people who are normally, previously had been, or potentially will be, wage earners rather than the self-employed we, in the social care sector, usually think of income support in terms of payments made to people from the formal income security system. But for rural private entrepreneurs, especially farmers, this is only part of the story. Special income security provisions introduced for farmers since 1993 are components of broader packages aimed at contributing to industry restructuring and enterprise development as well as providing social care. Furthermore, private entrepreneurs also receive financial concessions and direct income support through purely business support programs. For these people, there is substantial overlap between the social care and economic sectors with respect to income security.

From a rural perspective, Australia's income security system reflects urbo-centric, reactive, residualist and, in relation to primary industries, developmental policy frameworks. Historically, it is urbo-centric in that it has been designed primarily for wage earners, the majority of whom (both absolutely and proportionately) live in urban areas. It is reactive in relation to rural people because specifically rural policies introduced since 1993 have responded to problems which became apparent during recent economic crises, primary industry restructuring and droughts. Overall, the system is residualist because these policies were designed specifically for people who are market casualties. However, in contrast with mainstream income security provisions, they have been linked with broader rural economic development policy. Finally, recent income security provisions for farmers and, to a lesser extent, other rural private entrepreneurs have been developmental in that they have aimed, amongst other things, to support primary industry restructuring induced by global, national and regional market changes and government economic intervention.

Because Australia's income security net was designed primarily for wage earners, it has a number of gaps and inconsistencies in relation to farmers and other rural self-employed people. For this reason, the present discussion concerns these groups and the programs introduced recently to try to remove these anomalies. The main focus is on Commonwealth programs because, for the most part, the Commonwealth is responsible for providing Australia's income security safety net. Recent Queensland Government programs are also mentioned as examples of those available from State governments. What follows is a critique of Australia's income security system in relation to rural people focusing on farmers and other self-employed people. A comprehensive and detailed description of available provisions will not be provided. Commonwealth programs are described in *the Information Handbook: A Guide to Payments and Services* (Department of Social Security (DSS), 1995), *The Rural Book* (Department of Primary Industries and Energy (DPIE), 1995) and *The Independent Social Security Handbook* (Raper, 1994).

Prior to 1993, Australia's mainstream income security provisions had two major limitations in relation to farmers and other low-income rural private entrepreneurs. First, because of the net value of their assets, many were ineligible for assistance or received reduced payments, even though they were on low, sometimes even negative, incomes. This has since been rectified through special 'hardship provisions' applied to all pensions and allowances offered by the DSS (Raper, 1994, 384-6; DSS, 1995, 79-82). These help people whose assets would otherwise exclude them from receiving pensions and benefits or would reduce their level of payment, even though they receive little, if any, income from those assets. They allow DSS to disregard the value of assets which are 'unrealisable' in determining eligibility and payment rates. By 'unrealisable', DSS means that they cannot be sold or used as security for commercial loans. Assets which DSS believes it would be unreasonable to expect the claimant to sell are also excluded.

The second limitation of mainstream income security provisions prior to 1993 was that unemployment benefits, such as the *Newstart* and *Job Search Allowances*, could not be paid to people who were unavailable to engage in, or even seek, full-time employment because they had to maintain their properties or businesses. In bureaucratic terminology, they failed the 'Activity Test'. Consequently, many impoverished farmers and other rural business people had been excluded from what was, in most respects, a reasonably sound and comprehensive income security system. In 1991, in response to the rapidly growing numbers of poor farmers, the Commonwealth Government attempted to resolve this problem by tinkering with benefit rules. The attempt failed dismally. Twelve months later, in April 1992, only 63 farmers had availed themselves of the new arrangements and only slightly more than $200,000 of the allotted $10 million annual budget had been spent (Alston, 1992, p.2). Consequently, in March 1993 these special provisions were replaced by the *Farm Household Support Scheme (FHSS)* which was a more direct, though still substantially flawed, attempt to deal with the issue. In turn, this was replaced in December, 1997, by the *Farm Family Restart Scheme (FFRS)*.

The *Farm Household Support Scheme* was introduced specifically for farmers who were ineligible for a *Job Search* or *Newstart Allowance* (DPIE, 1995, pp.73-4; DSS, 1995, p.72). The *FHSS* was a loan at commercial interest rates to help farmers meet day-to-day personal and family living expenses for periods during which they had insufficient income, when they could not access further commercial loans, and when they were not available for full-time employment because of farming commitments. Assets were taken into account in determining the level of the loan, although 'farm assets', as well as life insurance and superannuation policies, were disregarded. The maximum rate of payment was equal to the maximum amount of the *Job Search Allowance* although, because it was a loan, the farmer could choose to be paid at a lower rate.

The *FHSS* was part of a more comprehensive package, the *Rural Adjustment Scheme (RAS)*, which was discontinued in 1997 (Anderson, 1997, p.6). The *RAS* was an example of a program which attempted to provide income support through a combination of social care, industry restructuring and business development policies. The overall purpose of the *RAS* was to "promote an efficient and competitive rural sector by providing support and services to help farmers to adjust to changing economic, technical, and institutional circumstances" (ORC, 1994, p.23). It incorporated a number of provisions in addition to those of the *FHSS*. These included: interest subsidies on new and existing commercial finance; grants for training and professional advice to improve farm performance; additional subsidies for producers experiencing exceptional hardship in the wool industry or because of drought; and a re-establishment loan to help primary producers exit the industry and re-establish themselves elsewhere. Re-establishment support was available as a loan in the first instance, although it was convertible to a grant in certain circumstances. In 1996, the maximum amount of support was $45,000 with an additional $30,000 available for people in drought-affected areas. To dovetail with the *FHSS*, this assistance was provided only after the farm had been sold or when it was no longer the farmer's principal source of income.

Because it was embedded in a program with industry restructuring, enterprise development and social care purposes, the *FHSS* included a number of provisions to encourage farmers to either sell their farms or become self-supporting. First, payment was for a maximum of two in every eight years. Second, if farmers sold their properties - which usually included their homes - within two years, the first nine months of the loan was converted to a grant. Third, if their properties were sold within nine months they received the balance of the loan (up to the nine months) as a re-establishment grant. But if they could not sell their properties within two years they had to repay all monies received and interest accumulated. These provisions may have made sense from the perspective of primary industry restructuring which, as discussed in Chapter 2, was a major national concern through the 1980s into the early 1990s. However, they were indefensible from a social justice point of view. On the one hand, they discriminated against farmers compared with unemployed wage earners while, on the other hand, they discriminated in favour of farmers compared with other rural business people.

The *FHSS* discriminated against farmers in three ways. First, it imposed limits on how many times, and for how long, during a specified period they could receive benefits. Conditions such as these do not exist for unemployed wage earners. Second, under certain circumstances, farmers had to pay their benefits back to the government with interest. This has never been the case in Australia for other unemployed people except where they have obtained the payments illegally. By providing repayable loans rather than grants in the first and, for many, in the last instance, the *FHSS* made social justice aims secondary to industry restructuring and enterprise development. It was unfair that farmers could not obtain a grant equal to *Job Search Allowance* rates, rather than a loan, when they suffered a temporary loss of income because of industry downturns or between 'jobs' regardless of how quickly they managed to sell their farms. Moreover, the inducement to sell quickly became punishment for farmers who failed to sell their farms or become more profitable. After two years, they were left with unsaleable and unprofitable farms and additional debts resulting from what was supposed to be a 'welfare' provision. This, indeed, was what happened. A recent media release by John Anderson, Minister for Primary Industries and Energy, reported that in September, 1997, there was "... approximately $5 million in outstanding FHS debts owed by mostly low income farmers who do not have the capacity to repay it" (Anderson, 1997, p.9). The third inequity in the *FHSS* was that receipt of benefits was tied to whether, and when, the farmer sold the property. No such conditions have ever been applied to unemployed wage earners. Thankfully, in 1997, the Commonwealth decided to convert all outstanding *FHSS* loans to grants, and farmers who had previously repaid their debts were reimbursed the full amount.

In December 1997, the *FHSS* was replaced by the *Farm Family Restart Scheme (FFRS)*, which brought to an end some of the injustice done to farmers. As with the *FHSS*, the *FFRS* aims at "... delivering improved welfare support to the farm sector, as well as providing adjustment assistance to farmers who wish to leave the industry" (Anderson, 1997, p.6). More specifically, it provides:

> ... a welfare safety net for low income farmers experiencing financial hardship who cannot borrow further against their assets and/or who are not ready to make a decision to place their farm on the market and access welfare support under the Social Security hardship provisions. (Anderson, 1997, p.6)

The *FFRS* has two components:

- *Restart Income Support* for up to 12 months at a rate which is equivalent to the *Newstart Allowance* and not subject to the 'Activity Test' plus up to $3,000 financial counselling assistance; and
- the *Restart Re-establishment Grant* of up to $45,000 for families who sell their farms, although this is only available to farmers who join the scheme during its first two years.

The *FFRS* redresses two of the major sources of discrimination against farmers compared with unemployed wage earners contained in the *FHSS*: it is a non-repayable grant rather than a loan; and it does not require farmers to put their properties on the market to obtain benefits. From a social justice point of view, then, the *FFRS* is a major improvement on the *FHSS*.

As with the *FHSS*, the *FFRS* is part of a package, *Agriculture - Advancing Australia (AAA)*, which has a multiplicity of social and economic purposes. The *AAA* package aims at providing incentives for ongoing farm adjustment and increased farm profitability, ensuring an adequate welfare safety net for farmers, and encouraging social and economic development in rural areas (Anderson, 1997, p.1). It contains a number of other programs in addition to the *FHSS* including:

- a *Farm Management Deposit Scheme* which allows farmers to equalise their income by depositing funds in prosperous years so that they are available, with interest, during lean years;
- the *Farm Business Improvement Program* which supports farm management training;
- provisions whereby older farmers can transfer ownership of the family farm to their children and have immediate access to the *Age Pension*;
- an *Exceptional Circumstances Relief Payment* which is available to farmers suffering hardship as a result of rare and severe events, including droughts and, depending on their circumstances, an associated *Partner* or *Parenting Allowance* and *Family Payments*;
- a *Rural Communities Program* to kick start community development projects and provide professional assistance to develop strategic regional plans in rural areas;
- a *Consultative Rural Finance Forum* to improve communication on farm finance issues between farmers, government and banks; and
- several programs supporting research into the social impacts of changes in rural communities, climate research and the development of decision support tools for farmers to aid risk management (Anderson, 1997).

Positively, the *Exceptional Circumstances Relief Payment* extends the previous *Drought Relief Payment* to other kinds of natural hazards. However, valuable as it is, the scheme remains discriminatory in that it is not available to rural private entrepreneurs other than farmers. These can be equally affected by natural hazards.

Because it is part of a package with social and economic aims, the *FFRS* places some pressure on low-income farmers to sell their properties, although this is not nearly as great as in the *FHSS*. First, the allowance is limited to one year. This continues to disadvantage farmers compared with low-income wage earners, many of whom are unemployed for longer than this. Second, to receive benefits, recipients are required to obtain professional advice on future business viability. Third, the *Restart Re-establishment Grant* provides an inducement to farmers to sell their farms, which usually includes their homes. A further incentive to sell quickly is introduced through the provision that the value of income support received is deducted from the grant. Thus, the more quickly the farm is sold, the more finance the farmer has available to meet re-establishment costs. Of course, the effect could be to reduce the selling price of the property to the detriment of the already impoverished farmer who is impatient for an early sale.

Both the *FHSS* and the *FFRS* have only been provided to farmers. Consequently, they have discriminated against other rural business people who are equally affected by rural restructuring, recessions, technological developments and droughts. Some of these receive a limited amount of assistance through purely business support schemes such as Queensland's *Small Business Debt Assistance Scheme*. This program provides concessional loans to meet up to 12 months of debt servicing commitments to help small businesses in specified regions survive temporary downswings caused by factors which are beyond their control (ORC, 1994, p.26). But it should not be regarded as a social care program because it takes the form of a repayable loan, not a grant.

In addition to the provisions of the *AAA*, emergency assistance is available to people who have no immediate means of support through a one-off payment from *Emergency Relief Funds* (DPIE, 1995, p.166). *Disaster Relief Payments* are also available for victims of natural disasters declared 'major' by the Commonwealth Government such as the Ash Wednesday bushfires of 1983, the Newcastle earthquake of 1989 and the NSW bushfires of 1994 (DSS, 1995, pp.70-1). People subjected to natural disasters which have not been declared major might still be eligible for a DSS *Special Benefit* because they are in severe financial hardship (DPIE, 1995, p.167). Finally, a *Remote Area Allowance* is added to pensions and allowances for people living in designated locations, and the taxation system provides *Remote Area Rebates* for some taxpayers.

The *RAS* and the *AAA* are examples of programs which combine income and business support. Others include the *Natural Disaster Relief*

Scheme which assists primary producers and other small businesses affected by natural disasters through low-interest loans for business carry-on and restocking purposes (ORC, 1994, pp.24-6). This has been one of the few financial assistance packages aimed at rural business people generally, not only farmers. There have also been a number of rural counselling programs focusing primarily on financial issues, but also providing information about social care provisions, referral to other sources of help for emotional, social and family difficulties and/or a little direct counselling for these problems. Most of these are provided exclusively or primarily for farmers, although a strong network of business advice and development services also exists around Australia for other kinds of small businesses. Some counselling programs, such as Lifeline's *Rural Support Unit* in the Darling Downs (Lifeline, 1992), provide substantial help for emotional and social problems.

There are also many programs with the sole purpose of providing business support through training, advice and assistance with farm development. Many also provide financial assistance, mostly in the form of interest subsidies. Although discussion of these is beyond the scope of this chapter, three points should be made about them. First, given the overlap between private and business financial affairs, even programs which focus exclusively on business support have direct implications for a family's more general level of well-being. Second, as with other programs reviewed here, most are not available to rural business people other than farmers. Third, in recent years it has been recognised that threats to primary industry incomes, such as industry downswings and natural disasters, do occur in most regions at fairly regular intervals and, in this sense, can be anticipated with effective social and economic policies. This change of thinking has led to the introduction of income-equalising programs such as the *Farm Management Deposit Scheme* discussed earlier.

Issues

Although it is fairly comprehensive, Australia's network of income support programs is multifarious and fragmented. It serves most people who have been and/or potentially will be earning wages through employment reasonably well, including those living in rural Australia. Our general emergency relief provisions and programs for people experiencing natural disasters are also necessary, although they contain some bias towards farmers. This bias has probably developed as a result of the importance of farmers to national and regional economies (Sher and Sher, 1994, pp.11-3), the power of the farm lobby, and perhaps, too, from lingering urban myths that most rural Australians are farmers.

But Australia's income support system still contains many gaps and inconsistencies. As the casualties of rural restructuring, rural recessions and drought became more visible we tacked more measures onto an already fragmented system in an attempt to meet the needs of farmers and, to a lesser extent, other rural business people in affected areas. In the process, social injustices occurred: many programs have been available to farmers but not to other small business people; income support is still time-limited for farmers but not for unemployed wage earners; in the past, asset tests unfairly disadvantaged many rural people in relation to their wage-earning neighbours; and similar income assistance programs have provided more help to some rural people than to others. Even amongst farmers, some primary industries, such as wool, have been favoured over others for reasons other than the sheer level of income deficit.

These inconsistencies have resulted from electoral considerations, public sympathies, and the historic and continuing importance of particular industries to national and State economies. Historically, there have been more votes in the farm lobby than in attending to the needs of other rural small business people. Furthermore, droughts, rural recessions and primary industry restructuring have resulted in mounting national sympathy for rural people. Unfortunately, though, this sympathy has focused more or less exclusively on farmers partly because of the strength of the farm lobby and partly because of Australian mythology which equates 'rural' with 'farming'.

The inconsistencies have also resulted from trying to pursue economic and social care aims through the same programs. For example, although from a social justice perspective the *FFRS* is a definite improvement over the *FHSS*, it still imposes limits on farmers, such as a maximum payment period and encouragement to sell their farms - and their homes - which do not apply to unemployed wage earners.

Policy Directions

Australia's income security policies need further review and modification in relation to farmers and other self-employed rural people. Given the foregoing review, we need to:

- conduct systematic research on the issues involved in providing a comprehensive and secure income support safety net for all rural Australians;
- re-balance our income security system so that all privately employed rural people are provided with a financial safety net similar to that which is available to wage earners;
- distinguish more clearly between industry and enterprise support and development programs and those aimed at providing income security for people on low incomes as a social care measure;
- base income security provisions for self-employed rural people more squarely on their level of income deficit rather than on considerations concerning business viability, support and developmental needs;
- re-design assets and income tests to ensure consistency across programs, and so that discrepancies are justified according to specific program goals and individual circumstances; and
- remove from our income security system biases favouring some rural people over others when their level of income deficit is the same.

In fairness to public administrators, it is acknowledged that designing specific policies and programs is not so simple. In 1993, our policy formulators and social planners did an admirable job in rapidly cobbling together a number of income security measures in response to the plight of many of the human consequences of recent rural recessions, primary industry restructuring and droughts. This pioneering work was further developed in 1997 through the *AAA* and the *FRSS*. There is no question that, because of this, the system is far stronger in relation to self-employed rural people than it was a decade ago. But we need to continue to learn from this experience and work towards more fundamental and enduring changes so that all Australians are guaranteed the right of access to the same income security safety net.

Housing

As with income security, detailed systematic research has not been conducted on rural housing policy in Australia. Rural social care housing issues are different to urban because low-income residents are usually confined to a single locality and cannot easily move to more affordable or suitable accommodation in other places. Consequently, local factors such as housing supply and demand, property values, economic conditions and demographic changes have major impacts on the standard and cost of accommodation. This section discusses housing issues faced by disadvantaged rural people and implications of these for policy and programs. Issues are grouped according to whether they concern entrapment, access and affordability, quality, appropriateness, information or representation. Some issues facing people living in caravan parks are also discussed. The chapter concludes with some principles to guide future rural housing policy.

Entrapment

Many rural people, such as struggling private entrepreneurs, unemployed families and the aged find themselves trapped in poverty in country towns (Department of Prime Minister and Cabinet - DPMC, 1992). Their properties may be unsaleable, or so undervalued, that they cannot afford to sell and move closer to regular employment and support services, or they would suffer an unacceptable financial loss if they did so. The core problem here is falling real estate values. Social and legal justice requires that people, especially those on low incomes, should be compensated for property depreciation and income losses resulting from state and state-approved private actions, such as road investment decisions which change traffic flows and economic decisions which divert profits to other centres. These people currently bear an unfair burden in relation to the costs of development. Those trapped in poverty in rural communities because of falling property values should be provided with financial assistance to help them relocate elsewhere.

Access and Affordability

Private rental accommodation and public housing are in short supply in many rural communities. Where there is limited rental stock, owners and real estate agents have the power to discriminate against what they regard as high-risk tenants and frequently do so (DPMC, 1992, p.100). The housing situation is especially severe for Aborigines and Torres Strait Islanders, people on fixed and low incomes, female-headed households, the aged, people with disabilities, de-institutionalised people, unemployed workers, displaced farmers moving to towns, and for women separating from their partners, especially in mining towns where most housing is company-owned (Cass, 1991, p.74; DPMC, 1992, p.100;

OND, 1994, pp.24-5). It can also be particularly severe in remote communities with unusually low home ownership rates (OND, 1994, p.25) and in rapidly-growing communities with rising rents and property values where some residents can be excluded from the housing market altogether (DPMC, 1992, p.9; Bone, Cheers and Hil, 1993, p.110).

Housing availability is often compounded by affordability issues. On the one hand, because of reduced land values, rural housing can be less expensive than urban with regard to rents, purchase prices and mortgage repayments. But, on the other hand, new houses, renovations and repairs cost more in rural areas because of the additional expense associated with importing goods, materials and, in smaller communities, skilled labour. There are some pockets of extremely high housing costs, especially in the more remote areas of Northern Australia and in high-growth towns (Bone, Cheers and Hil, 1993). Furthermore, mortgage interest rates and repayments are much higher for people living on farms and large properties compared to those on the usual single-dwelling block in towns and cities (DPMC, 1992; OND, 1994, p.25).

Housing access and affordability are closely related to availability. Availability can be increased by either raising the level of total housing stock in a given community or by increasing the pool of social care housing stock. Increasing total stock might release some more affordable properties to residents on low incomes and reduce rental and property values in communities experiencing minor housing shortages. But it is a blunt instrument for dealing with the housing problems of financially-disadvantaged people. For this reason, it is usually more effective to increase social care housing stock by building new dwellings, purchasing existing open market housing stock and transferring it to the social care sector, or by providing money to people so they can rent or purchase in the open market. However, regardless of the method used, social care housing should be targeted towards people on low incomes and other 'special needs' groups such as Aborigines, Torres Strait Islanders, sole-parent families, the aged, people with disabilities, dislocated farm families, and young people and women requiring emergency or transitional accommodation.

Providing money to people may help in communities with a housing surplus. However, it can be pointless in towns with housing shortages or with high rents and property values, and in mining towns where most accommodation is restricted to company employees. New social care sector dwellings are required in these communities. Programs aimed directly at increasing social care housing stock can either operate directly through state authorities or provide funds to community-based organisations (including local government) to build, purchase or modify existing housing for rent by people in need. Those requiring community organisations to contribute land or buildings can be especially useful where rural local governments or other organisations own suitable properties. Some rental schemes provide funds for tenant cooperatives to build, acquire or modify dwellings and to manage rental properties. These can be especially important in rural communities because they have the potential to empower and unite marginalised and disempowered residents and to help them integrate into the life of the community. Unfortunately, because of small populations, many rural communities have a limited number of local people available to provide leadership in community-based housing projects (DPMC, 1992, p.9; Williams and McMahon, 1995, p.36).

One way of transferring housing stock to the social care sector is to give people money to rent accommodation on the open market or to meet current rental obligations. In addition, some transitional programs help people move from one living situation, such as crisis accommodation or violent domestic situations, into long-term rental premises. Such programs usually provide temporary rental assistance and/or bond payments. These direct forms of assistance are particularly helpful in communities with a housing surplus and in those where sponsoring organisations are poorly supported or do not give priority to housing issues. However, in communities where demand exceeds supply, owners and real estate agents can raise rents so that in effect they, and not tenants, receive the assistance. Where this is the case, it is preferable to increase social care housing stock and place control of rental accommodation in the hands of publicly-accountable, community-based organisations.

Rental programs tend to be more useful for low-income rural people than home purchase schemes given the high mobility of the rural population, the volatility of many rural economies, and uncertainties about future property values in many communities. Furthermore, home purchase schemes are frequently not available to people most in need, they deplete social care housing resources by transferring them to the open market, and they increase total social care housing costs for governments. However, they may have some value in economically and socially stable communities with low home ownership rates and an excess of supply over demand. Long-term home purchase schemes through, for example, reduced interest rates can be supported by more temporary assistance for people experiencing difficulties in meeting their mortgage costs because of unanticipated changes in their circumstances. This help can be especially useful for people affected by temporary economic slumps, unemployment, illness and natural disasters.

One way to obtain affordable accommodation is to live on the fringe, or outside, of town (DPMC, 1992, p.100). Usually, this solution involves trading accommodation savings off against the additional social and financial costs involved in accessing employment, services, transportation and social networks. These costs are especially high for people who require access to health services, for example the aged and people with disabilities (Williams and McMahon, 1995, p.42), and to support services and informal supports, such as sole parents and women in violent relationships. They are also high for those who need access to recreational facilities and social networks, such as young people (Bone, Cheers and Hil, 1993).

Australia's network of transitional, short-term and emergency accommodation facilities has expanded over the last decade, especially for women escaping from violent situations and for young people. These are provided directly by the state or through funding to community-based organisations to purchase, construct, upgrade, maintain or lease accommodation for people in crisis or who need transitional support to establish their independence.

In many communities, pre-existing housing access and availability problems have been aggravated by what the DPMC (1992, p.10) identified as:

> ... substantial increases in the number of people choosing to opt out of the metropolitan job and house market and establish themselves in towns and communities with lower housing costs and very limited economic futures.

Where poor urban people move to rural communities in search of low-cost accommodation, local residents must be prioritised in social care housing programs and this must be widely publicised. But, in the final analysis, this issue is best handled by introducing and improving urban programs so they don't have to migrate to rural communities at all (DPMC, 1992, pp.118-9).

The final access issue concerns low-income rural people who are forced to live away from home temporarily in order to access health or education services (OND, 1994, p.42). We appear to have no information whatsoever about where they stay or what they need in relation to accommodation, finance and other support services. The situation is especially severe for Aborigines and Torres Strait Islanders who find themselves in foreign ecological and cultural environments (ATSIC, 1993, p.35).

Quality

Some rural poor people attempt to overcome access and affordability problems by accepting low-quality accommodation. As discussed in Chapter 2, low-cost housing quality is generally poorer in rural than urban areas (DPMC, 1992, p.xv; OND, 1994, p.25). Especially in declining communities, low incomes, low rental values, poor capital gains expectations and high building maintenance costs mean that many rental properties are allowed to run down (DPMC, 1992, p.43). Furthermore, because of low incomes many primary producers are forced to live in dilapidated houses and sheds, and business people in cramped sub-standard accommodation attached to their business premises (DPMC, 1992). Many Aboriginal and Torres Strait Islander people in remote communities are also forced to live in poor-quality dwellings which receive sub-standard essential services such as power, water and sewerage or which aren't serviced by these at all. In these ways, monetary savings from living in sub-standard premises are often paid out through health care costs and social problems.

All Australian communities should be fully serviced with uncontaminated water, a reliable power supply, and quality garbage and sewerage disposal services. Funding programs, such as low-interest loans, are also needed to help low-income people maintain their dwellings to acceptable community standards. Furthermore, recalcitrant rental property owners should be forced to comply with legislated building standards and strong tenant representation organisations are required to ensure that they do so.

Appropriateness

Some rural accommodation is inappropriate to the needs, cultures and lifestyles of residents and to the natural environments of their communities (DPMC, 1992, p.xv). We saw in Chapter 2 how overcrowding occurs frequently in rural areas, especially amongst Aboriginal and Torres Strait Islander people (DPMC, 1992, pp.100-2; OND, 1994, p.25) and others on low incomes, such as youth in high economic growth communities (Bone, Cheers and Hil, 1993, p.110).

Although there have been some improvements in recent years, special purpose accommodation is lacking in many rural communities for people with special needs such as the frail aged, people with disabilities, indigenous Australians, and those in need of emergency and short-term accommodation such as women escaping domestic violence and homeless young people (DPMC, 1992, p.xv; Bone, Cheers and Hil, 1993; Williams and McMahon, 1995).

Women's shelters do not exist in most rural communities. Where they do exist, they face special problems (DPMC, 1992, p.59). In her study of domestic violence in rural areas, Coorey (1988, pp.114-5) reported that because their location was common knowledge, shelters in country towns were under-utilised by women living in those towns because they were concerned that their violent partners could easily find them. Consequently, women from neighbouring towns were far more likely to use rural shelters than local women. Other kinds of accommodation are also problematic for women escaping from domestic violence in country towns because they are so easy to find in small communities and because of discrimination by owners and real estate agents who know of the situation and wish to avoid property damage and difficult situations caused by violent partners.

More rural communities now have hostel and nursing home accommodation than was the case a decade ago. However, given the high *per capita* costs involved in providing residential care in areas of low demand combined with contemporary aged and disabilities care ideology, most communities do not have these facilities now and will not have them in the foreseeable future. In any case, institutional care tends to remove them from the many social provisions of their communities discussed in Chapter 3. The evidence at hand indicates that clients, carers, service providers and other stakeholders agree that it is preferable for aged and infirm people to remain in their own homes provided that appropriate community support services are available (Williams and McMahon, 1995, pp.43-4). Unfortunately, given low levels of local demand and decades of neglect, support services are often in short supply in rural communities. The situation is particularly severe both in declining communities because of closures to support services and in rapidly-expanding communities, such as retirement centres, where demand for services is outpacing supply. Additional programs are needed which provide flexible budgets to individualised case managers to purchase services which are not normally available through mainstream social care agencies. Financial assistance is also needed for people remaining in their own homes who cannot afford the high costs associated with renovations in rural areas to help them cope with their disabilities.

Low-cost rural dwellings, including public housing, are often not designed for specific climates such as the tropics or natural hazards including cyclones, floods, bushfires, dust and health-threatening insects, and are usually situated in the most vulnerable areas (DPMC, 1992; OND, 1992, p.41; Australian Science and Technology Council - ASTEC, 1993, p.140). Nor are they always equipped with climate-control devices such as heaters and air-conditioners. Further research is needed to establish how to provide environmentally-appropriate social care housing in a cost-effective way in rural and remote areas (ASTEC, 1993, p.140). Moreover, public housing is still being built for nuclear families with at least one parent and two or three younger children. Consequently, it is often unsuitable for youth, for cultural and ethnic groups who prefer to live in extended kinship arrangements and for people who are strongly embedded in their natural environments. Two major Commonwealth studies (DPMC, 1992; OND, 1994, p.41) have suggested that housing design issues will only be solved in relation to specific communities and special needs groups if people from the target groups participate fully in planning processes and if advice is provided by relevant experts such as engineers and architects. Local governments should be centrally involved in design issues because they determine building and land zoning regulations.

Information

Housing availability and access problems are frequently aggravated by the lack of information which rural people have about government-funded housing programs (DPMC, 1992, p.9; Williams and McMahon, 1995, p.36). Improvements in rural access to information have been made over the last decade (see Chapter 7), although there are still problems. Uninformed communities and misguided assessments of local needs by government departments frequently result in service deficiencies. For example, housing authorities recently concluded that there was no need for public housing in a rural community because there was no waiting list. What they did not realise was that no-one ever registered for public housing because there was none available in that community and because the relevant department did not have a local office to provide information.

Representation

Information about social care housing programs is not enough. Low-income rural people also need advocacy services. Over recent years, increased funding has been made available for non-government organisations and State-wide tenants' unions to provide advice and advocacy for low-income tenants in the private housing market. Unfortunately, influential advocacy organisations are yet to extend their services beyond the capital cities and major regional centres in which they are located. Where they become more involved in community housing projects, shire councils can provide a powerful, locally-based surveillance point for unscrupulous and prejudiced rental property owners and real estate agents.

People in Caravan Parks

Many rural people, especially low-income transients and newcomers, are forced to live in caravan parks which are not as inexpensive as they may at first appear (DPMC, 1992, p.21). Caravan park rental costs are high in remote communities with housing shortages and residents pay additional costs for power and gas. Furthermore, because many caravan parks are on the fringes of towns and are poorly serviced by public transport, many residents are forced to pay higher prices in nearby shops. Consequently, even when rental costs are lower than for other types of accommodation, the savings are frequently paid out in the higher costs associated with purchasing supplies, service access and transportation. Caravan parks can also be unsuitable for children who need space to run around in, youth who need privacy and access to peer groups, families with young children, the frail aged and people with disabilities.

Research is urgently needed on the social, emotional, material, transportation, communication and social support problems of people living in caravan parks and mobile homes in rural areas. Increased social care housing stock and financial assistance packages will provide alternatives for low-income people. However, if people in caravan parks do, indeed, pay more for their accommodation than people in regular housing, then perhaps those on low incomes need additional rental assistance. Those without private transport should have access to public transportation, which is notoriously deficient in most rural communities. And we need to think seriously about caravan park designs, especially in relation to the needs of young people, children and sole parents. Supervised open spaces where children can play, special private study facilities for young people, places where youth can be together away from adult intrusions, and on-site respite care arrangements for parents with young children come readily to mind.

Principles

The foregoing review supports a number of general principles for rural housing policy, programs and services. Most of these have also been recommended by one or more of three major Commonwealth reports, all of which were based on wide consultation with rural people, human services managers and practitioners, researchers and government officials (DPMC, 1992; National Housing Strategy (NHST), 1992; OND, 1994).

- The relationship between housing and other social care issues should be recognised, as should their interrelationship with economic and infrastructure issues. Furthermore, acknowledging the contributions made by social care housing programs to local employment, economic performance and human well-being will help raise the profile of rural housing issues (OND, 1994, p.42).
- Disadvantaged people in rural communities need greater access to affordable, quality housing. In most communities, emphasis should be given to increasing social care, rather than total, housing stock and on providing funds for rental arrangements rather than for home purchase.
- Rural housing issues are unique and should not be treated simply as a sub-set of general housing policy. For this reason, specifically rural and remote area housing programs should be developed at Commonwealth and State levels. Increased flexibility and rural relevance should also be built into mainstream national housing policies such as the *Commonwealth State Housing Agreement* (DPMC, 1992, p.xvi; NHST, 1992, p.116-7).
- Rural housing issues should be addressed in the context of the particular combination of demographic, social, cultural, economic and ecological circumstances of each community and each special needs group. This requires a high degree of

innovation in designing facilities and services (DPMC, 1992, pp.xv-xvii).
- Housing policies and programs should recognise that issues and needs can change rapidly in rural communities and that other problems of disadvantaged people are closely related to the location, provision, accessibility, affordability and relevance of housing and housing support services (DPMC, 1992, p.118).
- Planning and providing rural housing should involve residents, target groups and the three levels of government, and be more effectively coordinated at national, State and local levels (DPMC, 1992, p.xvii). It should also be linked with local area planning and, for Aboriginal and Torres Strait Islander communities, with ATSIC regional plans (OND, 1994, p.42). Because thoroughly localised services require local leadership, two major Commonwealth reports have recommended that local government should play a major role in coordinating, facilitating and resourcing housing initiatives (DPMC, 1992, p.118; OND, 1994, p.42). Coordination will also be enhanced where rural communities are provided with pooled funding and the power to allocate resources according to locally-determined priorities. This would also help to ensure that social care housing is accurately targeted towards those within the community who need it most.
- Provision of social care housing in rural areas should be controlled by or, at the very least, involve meaningful participation of local people, organisations and users in planning, designing and providing facilities and services. Tenant control of residential facilities should be encouraged.
- Rural housing issues and needs should be addressed in the context of present and projected future developments in relation to government policy and social care, health and education programs (OND, 1994, p.42). They should also be addressed in relation to the state of the local economy and labour market, local transportation and communication systems, and local community services and social care arrangements (DPMC, 1992, pp.xv-xvii).
- Provision of rural social care housing should be based on actual needs assessments rather than proximate measures such as public housing waiting lists (NHST, 1992, p.9).
- Strong advocacy is needed for rural housing interests generally and the needs of specific groups and individuals.

- Rural people should have direct access to information concerning housing policies, programs and services. Furthermore, government and non-government organisations providing housing to rural regions should have some form of local presence.
- As far as possible, rural social care housing arrangements should enable people to remain fully embedded in their communities; and home care services in relation to individual users should be coordinated locally and on a case-by-case basis.

As with income security policy, we urgently need detailed, systematic research into housing issues and policy in rural Australia.

6 Social Care Development

Social care development aims at improving people's lives through processes in which they are key participants. It involves them in identifying and working out how to meet their collective social needs and aspirations, and helps them to secure the resources, facilities and services required to do so. It also aims at building people's capacities to do these things themselves. Social care development is based on the belief that, in a truly human society, people - individuals, families, groups and entire communities - should determine their destiny rather than be forced to dance to an elite tune. It has two facets, social planning and community development, and is driven by participation.

After critically reviewing some of what we know about rural social planning, community development and community participation, this chapter concludes with a set of social care development functions and tasks for rural practitioners.

Social Planning

Social planning involves assessing and anticipating present and projected needs of residents with respect to their social, emotional, material and informational well-being and their human rights, and developing policies, services, facilities and resources to provide for these. It is a collective responsibility shared by all sectors of society - the state, government departments, non-government organisations, industry, community groups, and ordinary people. Rural social planning should be congruent with local demographic, cultural, social, spiritual, geographic and climatic realities and with residents' lifestyles, resources, knowledge and skills.

Social planning is most clearly portrayed as a linear, rational, data-driven process although, in reality, it is far more messy than this.

> It is complicated and can be a confusing process. It is not a series of discrete steps but an integrative process where intuition and judgement and a willingness to relate each part of the process constantly to every other part are just as important as technical competence and a systematic approach. (Lea and Wolfe, 1993, pp.9-11)

This is why social planning usually occurs incrementally through specific concrete projects rather than as a distinct integrated change process in itself.

We need not dwell for too long on social planning frameworks because they are readily available elsewhere, they are fairly obvious and most are more or less interchangeable. Figure 6.1 presents Lea and Wolfe's (1993) conceptualisation. Social planning can start anywhere and frequently backtracks and leaps ahead. It can focus on a specific need or service, a bundle of needs or services, or all social needs and service areas in a given community.

Let us assume, for example, that we want to plan for youth needs in a country town. First of all, someone, perhaps in a local community services coordinating committee, decides to do so. The committee then establishes planning structures, such as a youth services steering group comprising representatives of relevant non-government organisations, local government, Commonwealth and State government departments, industry and, of course, young people themselves. In the process, relevant stakeholders and the wider community are informed that the process is under way. Through youth and community forums, meetings, submissions and the like, a vision is formulated and planning goals and objectives are established.

Next, relevant information is obtained, perhaps through further forums, surveys, interviews and case studies, and from documented sources such as consultant reports, media presentations and census data. Table 6.1 identifies the range of information which could be collected in planning processes in a rural community, depending on the project at hand. In our 'youth needs' example, relevant information might include an audit of existing services, resources and facilities; a variety of local perspectives on youth needs, problems and priorities; and regional demographic information.

Once the information is assembled and analysed, priorities are established and a number of alternative plans are generated and compared through committee processes and community consultation. In the process, environmental opportunities and constraints are identified. A preferred option is then chosen. Further discussions now focus on how the preferred plan can be implemented and, eventually, a course of action is chosen which identifies strategies, tasks and time schedules. Who will do what to implement the plan is also decided at this point. This is where many planning frameworks stop. But the process has not been completed until the plan is implemented, services, facilities and resources are established and their success in meeting identified needs has been evaluated. This evaluation should feed into further planning and may result in anything from minor modifications to a major overhaul.

Although this kind of conceptualisation might be neat, social planning rarely seems to occur in such a self-contained way. Increasingly, rural social care practitioners are required to contribute their expertise to broader planning processes conducted by local, State and/or Commonwealth governments. In these situations, no one person, committee or organisation 'does' social planning in structural isolation from planning in other sectors such as economic and infrastructure development.

Figure 6.1: Social Planning Process

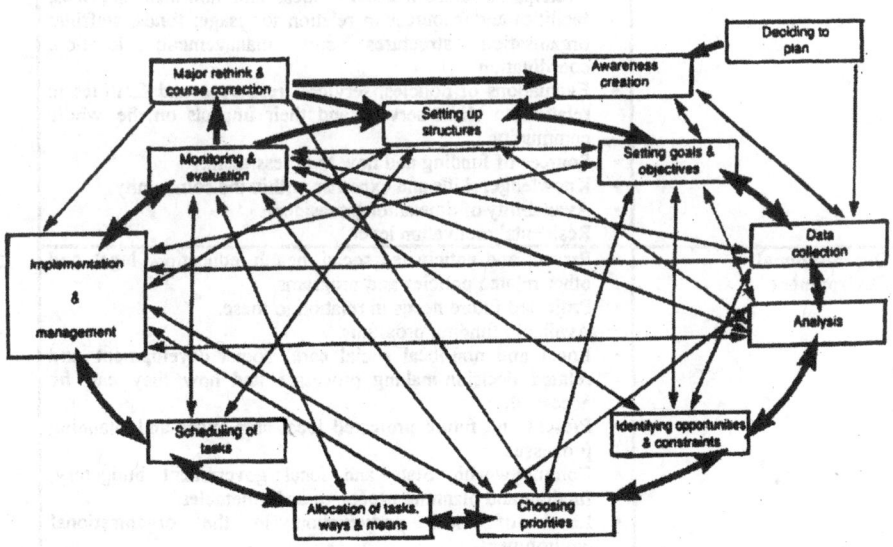

Source: Lea and Wolfe (1993, p.10)

Table 6.1: Information Relevant to Rural Social Planning

INFORMATION DOMAIN	INFORMATION REQUIRED
Disadvantage, Disempowerment and Marginalisation	• Who is disadvantaged, disempowered and/or marginalised and in what ways? Identification of individuals and groups according to: culture; ethnicity; gender; age; income; employment; health; education; housing cost, quality and location; social and geographic isolation; residential length and permanence; structural disadvantage, disempowerment and marginalisation; needs, problems and issues. • What they need and their extent of need in relation to: services; facilities and physical infrastructure; financial and other resources. • Relative disadvantage, disempowerment and marginalisation of the community as a whole in relation to: social and economic indices; income; living costs; employment and unemployment; poverty; housing affordability and quality; health; education; social problems; human services; other essential services. • What the community needs in the way of: services; facilities; physical infrastructure; financial and other resources; cohesion and integration; leadership and development; social, economic and political change.
Resources	• Currently available, and anticipated, local and non-local services, facilities and resources in relation to: utilisation capacity; available funds; staffing; organisation management and structure; location; coordination. • Anticipated future needs for local and non-local services, facilities and resources in relation to: usage; funds; staffing; organisation structures and management; location; coordination. • Evaluations of policies, services, resources and facilities in relation to client service and their impacts on the whole community. • Sources of funding and how to access them. • Knowledge, skills and expertise within the community. • Availability of time amongst residents. • Residents' motivation level.
Organisational Environment	• Present and anticipated social, health, education, legal and other related policies and programs. • Projected future needs in relation to these. • Available funding programs. • Local and non-local social care, social development and related decision-making processes and how they can be accessed. • Present and future projected local area plans and planning processes. • Commonwealth, State and local government budgetary, funding and planning processes and timetables. • Level of local participation in the organisational environment. • Impacts of the organisational environment on the community and on individuals and groups within it.

Table 6.1: Information Relevant to Rural Social Planning (continued)

INFORMATION DOMAIN	INFORMATION REQUIRED
Community Life	• Past, current and projected future social and demographic patterns and trends in relation to: cultural and ethnic groups; gender distribution; age distribution; income and wealth distribution; employment and unemployment patterns; distribution of occupations and industries; health status; education levels; housing affordability and quality; settlement patterns; population mobility. • Local cultural ideologies and aspirations. • Local spirituality. • Relationships of residents with the natural environment. • Leisure and recreation facilities and resources, and access to these. • Leisure and recreation preferences and practices. • Future needs in relation to leisure and recreation facilities and resources. • Local social, demographic, political and economic history. • Media outlets and processes, and knowledge of how to use them. • Relationships between local cultural and ethnic groups and those in the wider world.
Social and Power Structures	• Local social and cultural groupings. • Structure and composition of local power. • Local political structures and processes. • Relationships between local and non-local political, social and power structures and relationships.
Economy	• Current and future projected trends and developments. • Economic, social and environmental impacts of anticipated trends and developments. • Population according to occupation and industry. • Main industries and commercial enterprises. • Opportunities for diversification and 'uncoupling' from major local industries. • Relationships between local economic activity and State, national and international market processes.
Infrastructure	• Currently available and anticipated essential services including: power, water, sewerage and emergency services. • Availability, accessibility and affordability of communication technology. • Transportation systems and affordability. • Road access.
Natural Environment	• Information about facets of residents' natural worlds and their relationships with these, including: land, sea, air, flora, fauna, climate and seasonal variations, and natural hazards.

For this reason, it is important that the rural practitioner knows what these broader planning processes entail. In Australian rural communities, development is increasingly occurring at the local government level through a set of planning processes called *local area planning*.

Local Area Planning

Although detailed analysis is beyond the focus of this book, some introduction to planning at the local level might be useful for practitioners. (For further information see Dale, undated; ORA, 1991, pp.39-49; Jones, 1993, pp.14-7,71.) The aim of *local area planning* is to coordinate planned regional change in one or more local government areas by developing an integrated regional plan encompassing community services, industry development, ecological sustainability, physical infrastructure and land use. Local area planning is implemented through *strategic planning* which coordinates planning at the local level through a number of related *planning schemes*, each of which incorporates a set of controls aimed at regulating development.

> [A strategic plan] ... sets out the vision for the area and establishes a number of medium to long term objectives for development. [It] ... then states how it envisages these objectives will be achieved through implementation statements. (Dale, undated, p.4)

Strategic plans are intended to coordinate the activities of a wide range of players across all sectors, such as residential and commercial developers, Commonwealth, State and local governments, and non-government organisations (Crofts, 1992, p.5). They are now required and approved by State governments after their implications for State-wide or regional issues are reviewed. In Queensland, they last for seven years. Strategic plans always contain a *corporate plan* which specifies priorities, how the strategic plan will be implemented by local government, resources required, and how performance will be assessed. Social care practitioners should be involved in developing these because, as Dale (undated, p.11) pointed out, corporate plans provide:

> ... a prime opportunity for a local government to establish social objectives which will be reflected in its planning schemes, and ... [to set] ... a broad policy direction which will influence the way they are developed.

An example of a strategic plan comes from South Townsville in North Queensland (Harris, Cheers and Hatte, 1993). In this project a social development team comprising a social worker, an anthropologist/archaeologist and a psychologist contributed to a comprehensive planning process involving officials from local, State and Commonwealth governments as well as other consulting groups including town planners, architects, landscape specialists, traffic flow experts, surveyors and sound engineers. The social developers conducted research and generated recommendations concerning, amongst other things, future social objectives, development of community services, maintenance of the suburb's demographic composition, residents' preferences in relation to alternative development scenarios, and the likely social impacts of these scenarios.

Regional planning is strategic planning across a wider geographic area. It involves a number of adjacent local governments in planning their region's future. Commonwealth and State governments are also involved. Regional planning facilitates agreement across a region in relation to objectives and priorities and provides clarity about State and Commonwealth government plans. Regional planning is important for social care development because, in rural Australia, most formal services span more than one local government area and because it increases the collective power of local authorities vis-a-vis Commonwealth and State governments.

Whether it focuses on one, or a group of adjacent local government areas, local area planning encompasses a number of sectors. First, *community services planning* involves assessing current and projected social, cultural and recreational needs, auditing and evaluating what is currently available, and recommending resources, facilities and services to meet them. In government and town planning circles 'community services' normally include:

- human services such as health, education, social care, libraries, social and sporting clubs, voluntary associations, churches and the like; and
- cultural services such as formal clubs and voluntary associations based on ethnicity, culture or a shared interest in the arts.

An example of community services planning comes from the Whitsunday Shire in North Queensland where social researchers from the

Centre for Social and Welfare Research have conducted studies addressing the needs of young people, the aged and people with disabilities (Bone, Cheers and Hil, 1993; Williams and McMahon, 1995; Hil, Wilkinson and McMahon, 1996). These have invariably included audits of services, facilities and resources; surveys of target populations, human services providers and other key local informants; and analyses of statistical, archival, historical and economic information. Recommendations from these studies have resulted in many concrete resources, services and facilities being established in the Shire.

The second sector encompassed by local area planning, 'economic development', is regulated by *industry development planning* which determines directions for industries in the area. It is mostly the province of local and State governments, with some Commonwealth government involvement. Social care practitioners can contribute to this process in a number of ways, most importantly by conducting social impact assessments. These are discussed later.

Third, *environmental planning* generates objectives and strategies which are designed to ensure the future sustainability and development of the natural environment. This usually involves conducting environmental impact assessments which analyse and predict environmental problems, conflicts or natural resource constraints affecting the viability and likely success of an industry development project. Environmental impact assessments also identify measures to resolve or minimise these problems and recommend ways of improving a project's suitability for its proposed natural environment (Dale, undated, p.6). They are increasingly required by law. Responsibilities for environmental planning vary from State to State. In Queensland, for instance, local and State governments increasingly require environmental impact assessments for all major development proposals.

On a national level, the Commonwealth government has embarked on a major locally-based *Landcare* program. This is a Commonwealth funded program in which voluntary groups of farmers work together to identify environmental sustainability problems within their region, and to generate and implement environmental development plans. Government officials connect local people with funding bodies and sources of expert advice. With almost 30 per cent of Australia's farming community involved in around 1,900 *Landcare* groups across the country, this is probably the most dynamic and widespread rural grass roots participation program in Australia (Mues, Roper and Ockerby, 1994; Curtis, Birckhead and De Lacy, 1995).

Effective strategic development in all sectors must be supported by relevant infrastructure and land use planning. *Infrastructure planning* refers to improvements in facilities such as buildings, public transportation, lighting of public areas, traffic flow systems and services such as power, water and sewerage. In Australia, most infrastructure is the responsibility of local government although some public transportation and roads are State or Commonwealth responsibilities. The impacts of physical infrastructure on human well-being are clearly demonstrated by the many health problems suffered by people in remote indigenous communities as a result of contaminated water and inadequate garbage and sewerage disposal facilities. Another example comes from the South Townsville project mentioned earlier where the social development team made a number of recommendations concerning, for example, new buildings and traffic flow systems which would ensure preservation of local 'interaction centres' (see Chapter 3), easy access to public parks, and pedestrian access to shopping centres.

Finally, *land use planning* involves "... guiding and controlling the efficient use of land and infrastructure and ... creating environments that engender community health and well-being" (Dale, undated, p.6). It involves establishing zoning regulations specifying where, for instance, industry, private residences, shopping precincts and office blocks can be built and where public parks are to be located. In Australia, land use planning is the responsibility and a primary focus of local government activity. It has major ramifications for social care. For example, if new low-cost housing sub-divisions are built on the edge of town without adequate public transport, low-income families, especially women and young children, will be physically isolated from their social and support networks, public services and recreation facilities.

Social Impact Assessment (SIA)

Social impact assessment is a form of social planning (Dale, 1995):

> (It) is the process by which the social consequences of public or private actions are assessed and mitigated. SIA has been applied to date to resource use and development planning decisions although it can also be applied to policy formulation or program development and implementation. (Benzaken, 1995, p.9)

Social impacts can be positive and/or negative. They are:

> ... consequences to human populations of any private and public action that alters the way in which people live, work, play, relate to one another, organise to meet their needs and cope as a member of society. ... It includes cultural impacts involving changes in norms, values and beliefs that guide and rationalise their cognition of themselves and their society. (Interorganizational Committee on Guidelines and Principles for Social Impact Assessment, 1993)

Social impacts can include demographic, financial, cultural, social, psychological, political, institutional and aesthetic changes in relation to individuals, groups and whole communities.

The overall aim of SIA is to influence decisions about whether a project will proceed and, if so, how (Dale, undated). SIA involves describing existing social conditions, predicting changes likely to arise from alternative project strategies, assessing their significance for the people affected, and identifying strategies for maximising positive impacts and mitigating those which are negative. The South Townsville project is a good example of a comprehensive social impact assessment. Here, the social development consultants:

- developed a demographic profile of the suburb;
- conducted an audit of all community services;
- conducted an oral history of the area to identify culturally-significant themes, characteristics, events and physical features to be preserved and, where necessary, restored;
- surveyed human service workers about future facilities, resources and services which would be needed in their sector;
- surveyed residents and local businesses about issues, problems and their reactions to a number of development scenarios; and
- generated recommendations for social care development within the area in the context of a number of broader development options.

Table 6.2 presents core SIA principles and strategies.

Social impact assessment is especially important in rural areas because of the comprehensive long-term effects which decisions made by government and private interests can have on community and cultural identity, lifestyles, values and well-being. As the violence in the Gulf of

Table 6.2: Principles and Strategies of Social Impact Assessment

PRINCIPLE	STRATEGY
Involve the diverse public.	Identify and involve all potentially affected groups and individuals.
Analyse impact equity.	Clearly identify who will win and who will lose and emphasise the vulnerability of under-represented groups.
Focus the assessment.	Deal with issues and public concerns that really count, not those that are just easy to count.
Identify methods and assumptions and define the significance of impacts.	Describe how the SIA is conducted, assumptions used and how significance is determined.
Provide feedback on social impacts to project planners.	Identify problems that could be solved by changing the proposed action or alternative strategies and recommend solutions for these.
Use professional SIA practitioners and sound research methodologies.	Use trained social scientists employing social science methods.
Establish monitoring, evaluation and mitigation programs.	Manage uncertainty by monitoring and mitigating adverse impacts.
Identify data sources.	Use published scientific literature, and secondary and primary data for the affected area.
Plan for gaps in information.	Identify and evaluate information gaps and develop a strategy for proceeding.

Source: Benzaken (1995, p.12), adapted from the Interorganizational Committee on Guidelines and Principles for Social Impact Assessment (1993).

Carpentaria in 1996 demonstrates, a single development decision can have overwhelming ramifications for whole communities and for local cultural groups and their relationships. Dale (1995, pp.6-7) suggested that poor social impact assessment practice exacerbates the negative effects of development and pre-existing conflicts between local interests; increases development costs and, consequently, the commercial viability of proposed projects; and increases the vulnerability of development decision makers to legal action and administrative review instigated by disaffected community interests.

As with local area planning, social impact assessment has been neglected by social care practitioners and, perhaps more significantly, by those who contribute to their education. Despite being constantly called upon to contribute to the process, practitioners have little relevant training to draw on. This probably reflects the urban base of social care in Australia, its separation from other sectors, the focus of social care education on individuals and families rather than whole communities and regions, and the current rhetoric which falsely polarises 'qualitative' and 'quantitative' research methods while exalting the former.

Community Development

Community development is a participatory people-driven process which generates and influences policies, planning and services, builds residents' personal and collective capacities to do this themselves, and enhances community cohesion (Cheers, 1995, p.3). It is based on a clear set of values including the following:

- the pursuit of social justice;
- the belief that people should control their own destinies as communities, groups and individuals;
- collective action, or the intrinsic importance of people working together to address common problems and issues;
- participation, or the right of people to be involved in planning and decision making which affects their lives;
- open, democratic decision making; and
- partnership, or the importance of residents and relevant communities of interest being involved in the development, management and provision of human services (see Ernst, undated, pp.5-6; Kenny, 1994, pp.18-22).

Different community development projects place varying degrees of emphasis on resident participation or on more aggressive political action which mobilises local people to change social, political and economic structures and processes (Ernst, undated, p.6). MacPherson (1982, p.177) suggested that community development should always include the latter.

> Whatever the specific focus of particular programmes, development is more than the provision of funds or the establishment of services. In all areas of social policy it is about the mobilisation of people. Such mobilisation ...

means the progressive attainment by people themselves of control over the conditions in which they live. Not only must mobilisation entail broadly-defined educational programmes which give people awareness, knowledge and self-confidence but it must, if it is to be successful in the longer term, be concerned with the power which people have to translate ideas into action.

Community development always involves extensive interaction and, more often than not, conflict, confrontation and hard negotiation amongst competing interests. It is about local people controlling service programs, managing organisations and securing resources. Community development also means intervening in local and non-local social, organisational and institutional processes and value systems, maximising the positive contributions to human well-being of both horizontal and vertical structures, minimising their negative impacts, and facilitating cooperativeness where it exists and hard negotiation where it doesn't.

Sufficient time must be left for a process which can frequently be slow, gradual and complex (MacPherson, 1982, p.177). Community development often fails because the pressure for rapid change creates unrealistic expectations (Mushi, 1981, p.240). In this respect, experiences from rural Tanzania seem to have much in common with those of many Northern Australian indigenous communities. In Tanzania, pressures for rapid change have meant the introduction of:

> too many projects, programmes, operations and campaigns at the same time, often without elaborate implementation guidelines or timetables. Although this impatience is really the result of a genuine desire by the central leadership to improve the lot of the peasants (sic), it has led to a number of problems. The main ones include: unfinished projects; little attention paid to the utility and maintenance of projects after completion; little time left to the peasants (sic) and local leaders to do feasibility studies or to evaluate their own successes and failures and draw appropriate lessons; and premature winding up of projects and programmes without examining the reasons for poor outcome. (Mushi, 1981, p.240)

On the basis of a number of predominantly rural case studies from developing countries[1] MacPherson (1982, pp.173-5) identified two dominant approaches to community development. *Improvement*, he suggested, involves incremental improvement of services, resources and facilities and does not challenge the basic structures and the values upon which they are based. An example of this approach is the development of a youth drop-in centre in a country town which provides services such as counselling, referral, information and recreational activities. Long's (1977, pp.156-7) review of a number of community development projects in Tanzania concluded that *Improvement* maintains existing economic inequalities and patterns of social stratification and does little to change socio-economic and power structures in rural communities. It is similar to Mushi's *Liberal-incremental* model which is "... rooted in the basic values of Western liberal democracy", and which measures progress by:

> ... economic growth - with little concern with the distribution of the proceeds of growth - and stability of the polity and the class structure upon which it rests. (Mushi, 1981, pp.151-2)

While *Improvement* approaches can be criticised for failing to attack the local and broader structural foundations of inequality, disadvantage and human rights abuses they should not be rejected outright. Given the complexity and power of external constraints on structural change, small incremental achievements may be all that can be achieved in a given situation at a particular point in history (MacPherson, 1982, p.174). After all, many such changes are valuable in themselves. It is good to establish a youth drop-in centre in a community where young people are marginalised and have no place which they feel is 'theirs'. And a rural mental health service can prevent youth suicide, even though it probably doesn't do much to change fundamental social and economic structures.

However, our social justice mandate does require us to work towards more fundamental change, at least in the long term. MacPherson's (1982, pp.177-8) other approach, *Transformation*, mobilises whole groups and communities with the aim of redistributing power. This is how one Aboriginal leader in the Gulf of Carpentaria recently managed to re-open negotiations between government, company executives, ATSIC and the indigenous peoples in the region when his community was threatened by the development of the Century Zinc Mine.

MacPherson's *Transformation* approach encompasses Mushi's *Revolutionary-change* and *Guided-evolutionary* models. *Revolutionary-change* is based on the belief that:

> ... a fundamental revolutionary change of the pre-existing socio-political and socio-economic system, not just change within the system ... [is] ... necessary for development. (Mushi, 1981, p.152)

Mushi's third model, *Guided-evolution* blends his *Liberal-incremental* and *Revolutionary-change* strategies. Although it is dependent on mobilising group and individual action, this model seeks a balance between:

> ... material and normative goals, and a redistribution of wealth consonant with political stability and continued economic growth. Planning, an essential feature of this model, seeks to achieve a balance between bureaucratic action and mass or popular action. (Mushi, 1981, pp.152-3)

On the basis of his review of a number of rural community development projects, Mushi (1981) found that *Guided-evolution* is inherently unstable in that it tends to slide either into *Liberal-incrementalism* or *Revolutionary Change*, most often the former as members of the local power elite find ways to divert the process to their own ends.

After reviewing programs in a large number of Third World countries, MacPherson (1982, pp.164-81) concluded that social development can retain a vigorous commitment to social justice aims whether it be revolutionary or incremental, conflict- or consensus-oriented, or focused on one program or on the full spectrum of human needs in a given locality. In rural Australia, community development usually involves some combination of all these with the balance being determined by the situation in which participants, including social care practitioners, find themselves. In MacPherson's (1982, p.181) words:

> Community organisation can be, and has been in very many cases, crucial in the emergence of movements for radical change. Even the smallest, seemingly most insignificant local programme which involves the people in controlling their own development may increase the solidarity and self-confidence of the mass of people, and contribute to the emergence of those pressures which will achieve development from below.

For example, a youth drop-in centre might initially be established in a rural community to provide a 'space' for local young people, recreational opportunities, and a door into the wider human services network. However, the youth who gather there will inevitably discuss feelings and perceptions about their shared situation, which can lead to assertive collective action resulting in changes to the local employment market, increased responsiveness of local government to their needs, and their inclusion in influential local organisations.

Leadership

Community development is not the sole province of social workers, welfare practitioners and community developers. It is also useful for local government officials, town planners, economists and even private entrepreneurs. But more than this, the philosophy and ideology of community development means that it is truly an expression of community, a process for ordinary people.

There is overwhelming evidence from Australian and overseas studies that effective local leadership is a crucial ingredient in rural community and economic development (e.g., Luloff, 1990; Rural Industries Research and Development Corporation (RIRDC), 1992; Humphrey and Wilkinson, 1993, p.185; Department of Housing and Regional Development, 1994; Epps, 1994; Sorensen, 1994). But while some talented and skilled local leaders are necessary, development also requires 'community-wide leadership' - that is, a community which is responsive to the idea of development, to development opportunities and to leadership initiatives (RIRDC, 1992, p.10; Epps, 1994, p.14). And this, we know, is the product of a strong shared sense of community identity and commitment amongst local residents to furthering the well-being of the community as a whole (RIRDC, 1992, p.12).

Effective rural leadership harnesses local and non-local resources, energy and motivation through both horizontal and vertical ties (Humphrey and Wilkinson, 1993, p.185; DeSantis, Stough, De Frank and Kulkarni, 1994, pp.15-7; Epps, 1994, p.14). Recent evidence suggests that community leadership is more effective when horizontal and vertical functions are divided amongst different leaders who work together (O'Brien and Hassinger, 1992, pp.531-2). This is because the background, attitudes, skills and networks which equip leaders well for one sphere can reduce their effectiveness in the other. This fits with the discussion in Chapter 3 which suggested that many rural communities have two kinds of leaders: *locals*, who focus on horizontal ties; and *cosmopolitans*, who are more involved in vertical ties. Whereas local leaders must be highly committed to their communities to invest the time and energy needed for development (Cottrell, 1983; Ayres and Potter, 1989), cosmopolitan leaders must be equally well connected to networks, resources and power centres outside the community (McGranahan, 1984; O'Brien, Hassinger, Brown and Pinkerton, 1991). The issue of community leadership will be taken up again in Chapter 8 when we discuss the contributions which social care practitioners can make to leadership processes.

Participation

Participation lies at the heart of social care development. Views about what participation is range all the way from involving local residents in decision making, though in a subordinate position, to effective devolution to them of the power to control and decide on matters affecting their welfare and prosperity (Midgley, 1986b, p.150). A community participates in development if:

> ... the poorest groups in that community have an effective role in choosing social development programmes; if they contribute together with the rest of the community in the implementation of decisions; and if they derive equitable benefits from these programmes. (Midgley, 1986a, p.26)

Arnstein (1969) proposed a continuum, or 'ladder', of social care processes differentiated according to the extent to which they involve citizen participation and power (see Table 6.3).

Table 6.3: Ladder of Participation[2]

SOCIAL CARE PROCESS	DEGREE OF CITIZEN POWER/PARTICIPATION
Citizen control	Maximum citizen power
Delegated power	High citizen power
Partnership	Shared citizen power
Placation	Token participation
Consultation	Token participation
Informing	Non-participation
Manipulation	Non-participation

Source: Arnstein (1969)

All these processes are used in Australian rural social care development, although 'delegated power', 'partnership', 'consultation' and 'informing' are probably the most common. Genuine *delegated power* has been adopted in experimental multi-function service programs in remote communities such as Cooktown where the Queensland

Department of Families, Youth and Community Care delegates the power to decide local needs and service priorities to a community-based organisational management committee, albeit in consultation with the Department. However, *partnership* arrangements, such as 'service agreements', are far more common. In a service agreement, the relevant government authority and a community organisation negotiate and sign an agreement requiring the organisation to provide specified services under agreed conditions and the funding body to provide specified resources and support. Unfortunately, though, *consultation* is more often the rule (ORA, 1991, pp.41-4; Cox and Veteri, 1992, p.6). Rural Australians continue to be inundated by government officials, consultants, researchers, politicians, workshops and seminars ostensibly trying to find out what their problems are and what they need. And Australian literature is equally inundated with reports from local people that they are tired of saying the same things time and again for little observable benefit.

In relation to indigenous communities, Coombs (1993, p.15) suggested that consultation should be replaced with *negotiation*. He described this as:

> ... a process in which both parties can contribute proposals and seek modification or amendments. It is a process in which positions are explained and the justification for them more likely to be understood ... [than in consultation]. It is a process in which both parties have an incentive to achieve success or at least to avoid responsibility for failure. Above all, it can make possible the reservation from debate of some issues of principle while accepting, at least for the present, compromise action.

Arnstein's sixth process, *informing*, is also frequently used in Australia, often in the guise of 'consultation'. As with consultation, people in rural communities are tired of being 'informed' and prefer to see more action and greater local control.

There are many reasons why participation is important in rural areas (see, e.g., Australian Council of Social Service - ACOSS, 1993a, pp.viii-ix; OND, 1994). One of these is that the motivation of many rural people to participate in mainstream political processes has been eroded over the years by increasing centralisation, continuing neglect by governments, token participation strategies, political powerlessness, increasing dependence on the state, resource withdrawals, population decline, and the recent recessions and droughts.

At a general level, participation furthers our social justice ideals. It also fills the participatory gaps left by more conventional methods of citizen involvement such as elections and participation in political parties. Each elector, whether rural or urban, exerts only minimal influence over government decision making through democratic elections, and then only in relation to the most general election platforms. But rural voters have even less influence than their urban counterparts because there are far more urban than rural seats in Commonwealth and State parliaments. Furthermore, within rural localities, it is the most powerful people, not the disadvantaged, who exert most influence on mainstream political processes through shaping party policies, through party pre-selection procedures and through their use of the media (Wild, 1983).

Community participation is also important because, as discussed in Chapter 3, many rural people identify strongly with their communities (Cox and Veteri, 1992, p.26). Consequently, the effectiveness of many rural social care programs will be influenced by the extent to which local residents feel that the service belongs to the community. For instance, Manning and Cheers (1995) found that residents of a country town in Queensland preferred to notify suspected cases of child abuse to the local hospital social worker rather than directly to the relevant State Department because she was based in town, because she had good local credibility and because she was viewed as a member of the community. By going through the social worker the community continued to 'own' the problem. Residents even preferred to notify her despite the fact that officers of the Department visited the town regularly and even though they knew that she would refer the situation to them anyway. Similarly, in another study Cheers (1992b) found that residents of remote communities in North Queensland had more confidence that locally-based organisations which they felt were 'owned' by the community - such as schools, hospitals and residents organisations - would respond more positively to their grievances than external agencies such as State and Commonwealth government departments. This trend was so strong that residents in towns which were not seats of local government preferred to take shared community issues to local residents' associations, rather than to shire councils which were based in, and, they felt, were 'owned' by other communities. In contrast, residents' associations were rarely used in towns which were seats of local government.

If community ownership is important, and if each rural community is unique, then local perspectives are required in the planning, management and implementation of programs and services. These can come from either the community as a whole or a particular target group. When we deal with whole communities we tend to deal with locally powerful people because it is they who are most strongly represented in mainstream community structures such as local government, parents' and citizens' associations and hospital boards. Positively, these have the resources and influence to coordinate broad community input and to make local programs work. But in the process, the views of the disempowered - the users of most social care policies and services - are frequently overlooked. Furthermore, because our formal social care arrangements are so highly programatic, participation by whole rural communities is less common in Australia than selective participation by particular disadvantaged groups (Midgley, 1986c, p.9). This 'programatic' approach can divide a community and runs the risk of challenging the interests of, and consequently being undermined by the powerful. The solution to the dilemma - harnessing the resources and power of the local elite while deliberately maximising the contributions of disempowered groups - is far more difficult to achieve in reality than in theory and requires skilled rural community development workers (Midgley, 1986c, p.9). Herein lies another dilemma: participation may now be taken over by outside professionals who cannot represent local perspectives because they are not imbued with them. We will return to this issue in Chapter 8.

Participation serves both instrumental and developmental ends (United Nations - UN, 1975, 1981; Midgley, 1986a, p.26, 1986c, p.9; Putman, 1993; Braglio Luther, 1994). Instrumental goals include accurately identifying local needs; mobilising local resources, skills, knowledge and energies; assuring the relevance of services to local needs and conditions and, hence, higher utilisation rates and greater effectiveness; improving residents' material circumstances; and attracting resources - services, facilities and skilled staff - to the locality. Developmental goals include stimulating local involvement in decision making; creating 'social capital' by increasing the knowledge, skills, confidence and motivation of local people; engendering a sense of fulfilment and self-confidence amongst ordinary residents; raising their awareness of democratic processes and their capacity to make choices and influence outcomes; heightening the sense of local community; and strengthening local bonds.

The extent and effectiveness of local participation has much to do with the relationship between horizontal and vertical ties. Midgley *et al.*'s (1986) review of rural development projects concluded that, for two reasons, the state is a necessary partner in social development. First, and most obviously, it can provide necessary resources and expertise. Second, government sets the policy framework within which the non-government sector must operate and the laws and regulations which govern social care. More negatively, however, government assistance is usually conditional, frequently externally imposed, and usually falls far short of participation ideals. The authors concluded that:

> In spite of the rhetoric of most state supported programmes, poor communities were not fully involved in decision making and they did not have final say over matters that affected their own welfare. Nor did these programmes always mobilize the poorest groups in the community or bring about significant changes in power or in social and economic conditions. (Midgley, 1986b, p.148)

To help conceptualise the interaction of horizontal and vertical sectors Midgley (1986a, pp.39-44) suggested that the state can respond to community participation in four ways. In the *anti-participatory mode*, the state is strongly opposed to, and actively suppresses participation. In the *manipulative mode*, the state supports participation because it can be exploited for political and social control and because devolving program implementation to local groups helps reduce costs while increasing program acceptability. In the *incremental mode*, governments officially support participation and devolve responsibility for program implementation, but fail to support local activities properly or to ensure that participative processes function effectively (see, also, Hardiman and Midgley, 1982).

> In this mode, state politics are usually vaguely formulated, poorly implemented and lacking in determination. ... Governments do not formulate comprehensive social policies preferring instead to 'muddle through' on an ad hoc basis towards the attainment of loosely formulated social development goals. (Midgley, 1986a, p.42)

Finally, in the *participatory mode*, the state properly supports and resources full community participation and ensures that participatory mechanisms are adequate and function effectively.

Midgley (1986b, p.148) concluded that the incremental mode was most common amongst the social development projects reviewed, although the manipulative mode was also apparent, particularly in education and housing programs. The most effective programs were formulated and implemented with high local participation and good government support in the form of resources, expertise, consultation and advice. Furthermore, residents wanted to participate and did so with intelligence, knowledge and skill. Even so, where incrementalism was the dominant mode, many difficulties remained. These included haphazard and *ad hoc* planning, inadequate resource allocations, and participation getting lost in government administrative inefficiencies, bureaucratic indifference and procedural delays (Midgley, 1986b, p.149).

Looking for a 'third force' to facilitate participation, Midgley (1986b, pp.154-7) suggested that non-government organisations have much to contribute (see, also, Clark, 1995). He was writing here primarily about international aid organisations in the context of developing countries. Midgley suggested that, compared with government departments, non-government organisations are more flexible, more responsive to local interests and to regional diversity, more capable of rapid responses to emerging needs, more innovative, more genuinely driven by social justice ideals, more free to challenge dominant ideologies and existing laws and regulations, and less constrained by competing agendas such as professional careers, political and electoral considerations and those of powerful interest groups (see, also, Marsden and Oakley, 1982). Although we should be careful not to transpose these comments uncritically to the more structurally developed Australia context, Walsh (1993, pp.9-10) arrived at similar conclusions following his review of local non-government human service organisations in rural areas of this country. He added that they have good local networks and good knowledge of local needs because of their daily contact with disadvantaged and disempowered people. Because of this, they are well placed to feed information into planning processes, facilitate the flow of information throughout the community, press the interests of marginalised groups, and remind decision makers of the heterogeneity of rural communities.

But as we shall see in the next chapter, they are not perfect. Like government departments, larger non-government organisations can be bureaucratic, inflexible, uncreative and unresponsive. Especially in rural areas, some are staffed and managed by paternalistic (and maternalistic) middle-class people who impose their own agendas on disadvantaged groups. Most are under-resourced and under-staffed and, in any case, are not funded for development activities, especially of the more radical kind. Moreover, rural community service organisations are frequently so focused on the immediate needs of their clients that they don't have the time, energy or resources to encourage community participation. And when they do, they are subjected to the conditions, accountability procedures, regulations and bureaucratic limitations imposed by government funding bodies.

Social Care Development

This chapter opened with the comment that rural social care development has two facets - social planning and community development. These are, indeed, two facets of the same process. They are united by their common philosophy, aims and values and by their mutual interdependence. Planning without community development works against the very aims of social justice in that people are not determining their own destiny. More pragmatically, it will also be less than effective, because it will not have their support and will not be entirely relevant to their circumstances. Just as clearly, community development without social planning can be aimless, uninformed, haphazard and so pluralistic that it lacks a consistent ideological basis.

Let us not deny, however, that the different emphases of social planning and community development can create strains within organisational structures and between organisations, groups and individuals. Essentially, the more mechanistic, linear, time-limited, data-driven and deliberative approach of social planning can clash with the more subjective, lateral, participative, negotiative and spontaneous processes of community development.

There are a number of other important lessons in this brief review of rural social planning, community development and participation literature. First, vertical and horizontal inputs are both required. Here, as always, the social care practitioner - the social planner, the community developer and the service manager - stands at the intersection of horizontal and vertical spheres. Social care development means changing things by maximising the contributions of local community structures and external stakeholders and by facilitating constructive interaction between the two. It also means minimising the constraints emanating from both spheres, for there is substantial evidence that external forces will virtually always contain what can be achieved locally and that local forces will create their own problems. Many of these constraints are identified in Table 6.4. Furthermore, in any given community at any single point in time the interplay of local, national and international forces is complex. For this reason, we should avoid sweeping deterministic prescriptions about how to achieve socio-economic change and assess this interplay afresh throughout the life of each project.

The second lesson is that governments are indispensable to effective development. From the state, rural communities need resources, funding, information, special expertise and a counterbalance to local power elites. Sometimes they need government personnel to kick start projects by organising, advising and motivating local people. On a more general level, working with governments is essential because they set the broad frameworks in which the rest of us must function, regardless of how vague, *ad hoc*, piecemeal or inconsistent they may be. Examples include the *Australian Assistance Plan* of the 1970s, Keating's (1994) regional development framework and the Industry Commission's (1995) recommendations in relation to 'charitable organisations'. In the final analysis, we must work within such frameworks although, of course, never uncritically. If we do not relate to these frameworks - as the social work profession in this country has so often failed to do - we will be left out in the cold with our influence diminished and our capacity to pursue social justice ideals severely curtailed.

Third, while continuing to pursue and advocate for the ideal we do have to be realistic about the limitations to full authentic participation in rural Australia. For, in a relatively wealthy nation such as ours, only some people will be sufficiently dissatisfied with their lot to become involved. But, having said this, there is substantial evidence that, even in some of the most impoverished regions in the world, rural people value and are motivated to actively participate in development provided that adequate resources are available and that they are genuinely supported and encouraged in their efforts by statutory authorities.

Fourth, participation is meaningless unless all potential participants, including ordinary people, are aware of the issues and can collectively marshal the necessary technical knowledge and skills (Elderton, 1992, p.34).

Fifth, non-government service organisations have a crucial role to play in advocating for local rights, in providing structure and organisation for participatory activities and in providing expertise, additional resources and credible, powerful allies. However they, too, need government support and resources, though this should be less encumbered than at present with complex regulations, unnecessary conditions and hidden central statutory agendas.

Table 6.4: Constraints on Social Care Development in Rural Communities

Horizontal Constraints
- The inability of some communities to generate the motivation, energy and resources necessary for participation. In indigenous communities, this can result from social and cultural anomie caused by a breakdown of the traditional social order, and social pathologies related to unemployment, alcohol, violence, vandalism, crime and suicide. In these, and other, communities lack of motivation for development can also be due to economic decline, population depletion, service withdrawals, the daily grind of poverty and/or past experiences of token participation, or of not being involved at all. (Midgley, 1986a, pp.28-36; Lea and Wolfe, 1993, pp.12-6).
- Disinterest in major social and political change amongst local people because of their values, their relatively comfortable lifestyles and/or the strength of local normative systems (Epps, 1994, p.13; Sorensen and Epps, 1994).
- Insufficient time and resources available to community-based service organisations which are not usually funded for developmental activities (Walsh, 1993, p.6).
- Lack of strong local leadership (Douglas, 1989, p.31; Lea and Wolfe, 1993, p.13).
- Inability to achieve some uniformity of interests at the local level because of social structural divisions, factional and personal antagonism and/or competition for scarce resources (Midgley, 1986a, p.35; Lea and Wolfe, 1993, pp.12-6).
- Inequitable distribution of power and resources within communities, resulting in manipulation of some groups by others and resistance to social change by powerful community members (Midgley, 1986a, p.28; Lea and Wolfe, 1993, pp.12-6).
- Domination of local planning by the economic sector, including developers and private businesses (Walsh, 1993, p.6).
- Ineffective negotiation and bargaining amongst local stakeholders.
- Lack of skills, knowledge and resources amongst local people, including their inexperience with service administration functions (Lea and Wolfe, 1993, pp.12-6; Walsh, 1993, p.6).
- Resentment from local politicians who believe that they have an electoral mandate to represent local interests, but are threatened by grass roots leaders who they fear will be rivals at future elections (Yap, 1990, p.62; Lea and Wolfe, 1993, pp.12-6).

Table 6.4: Constraints on Social Care Development in Rural Communities (continued)

Vertical Constraints
- The strength of broader political, social and economic forces, which requires more widespread and radical intervention than local action can provide (Midgley, 1986a, p.28).
- Obstacles from within government bureaucracies arising from frequent staff changes, inappropriate policies, and insufficient recognition of the need for communities to control their own destinies (Lea and Wolfe, 1993, pp.12-6).
- A programatic approach to service planning by government departments which divides local communities and fragments data collection (Walsh, 1993).
- The wrong belief amongst government departments and other external organisations that genuine social care development *"... is too cumbersome and takes too long, that communities do not have the technical expertise and knowledge, and that local people are not 'rational' (by 'mainstream' criteria)"* (Lea and Wolfe, 1993, p.16).
- Insufficient resources and support for local community action from government departments and other external organisations (Lea and Wolfe, 1993, pp.12-6).
- Domination of the community by outside 'patrons' who are determined to maintain community dependence in pursuit of their own agendas (Crittenden and Lea, 1989; Lea and Wolfe, 1993, pp.12-6).
- Outright discrimination against local cultures (Lea and Wolfe, 1993, pp.12-6).

Table 6.4: Constraints on Social Care Development in Rural Communities (continued)

Constraints Affecting both Horizontal and Vertical Ties • Insufficient information and/or too short a time frame for effective development (Lea and Wolfe, 1993, p.13; Madden, 1993, p.38). • Insufficient commitment from horizontal and vertical interests to open discussion, information dissemination and decision making (Lea and Wolfe, 1993, p.13). • Ineffective negotiation amongst stakeholders. • The complex uncoordinated involvement of different levels of government, resulting in poor coordination in relation to development (Callaghan, 1993, p.88; O'Toole, 1993, p.9). • Inconsistent regional boundaries set by different levels of government, government departments and non-government organisations, and their poor fit with local geographic identifications (Smith, 1993, p.13; Taskforce on Regional Development, 1993). • The relative powerlessness of rural people and structures, such as local government and community service organisations, in negotiations with Commonwealth and State governments (Lea and Wolfe, 1993, pp.12-3; Walsh, 1993, p.6). • Conflict between government accountability for public expenditure and autonomous local decision making. • Ignorance amongst rural people and community service organisations of Commonwealth and State budgetary submission and planning processes which are typically fragmented and have long lead times (Walsh, 1993, pp.11-2). • Residents' inexperience and their difficulties in communicating and negotiating with bureaucracies because of divergent frameworks, bureaucratic jargon and the lack of culturally appropriate participation mechanisms (Lea and Wolfe, 1993, pp.12-6; Walsh, 1993, p.6). • Excessive dependency of the community on external agents and institutions for basic support (Lea and Wolfe, 1993, pp.12-6).

Sixth, community participation usually doesn't just happen. It requires organisational structures at the regional level to kick start it, to keep it going, and to ensure that it influences policy and planning (Walsh, 1993, pp.12-6). This is where regional non-government organisations such as the Mackay Regional Council for Social Development and peak organisations such as the State Councils of Social Services can be useful (Cox and Veteri, 1992, p.107; Jones, 1993). Organisations such as these can also help to counteract the agendas of governments and other external stake-holders and those of powerful local interests. However, in rural Victoria, Cox and Veteri (1992, p.107) found that for a number of reasons the contributions of State-wide peak organisations to rural development are often limited. Most are centralised in capital cities and have insufficient resources to extend their services to rural areas. Most also have poor rural representation on their management committees, inadequate information about the issues and communities within their respective regions and poor connections with rural networks. They also found that most of these organisations focus on specific issues and programs rather than on whole communities and regions. On the basis of these findings, Cox and Veteri (1992, pp.109-10) suggested that State-wide peak and coordinating organisations can improve their services to rural communities by developing a rural knowledge base, by recognising and working through existing regional networks, by developing policies and protocols which ensure that they respond appropriately to rural issues, and by allocating adequate resources to do so.

The seventh lesson is that, in rural Australia, increased local power will come from neighbouring communities and regions forming larger groups or coalitions (Smith, 1993, p.13).

Finally, social care development often involves competing interests, and factional conflicts and disputes. Consequently, negotiation, bargaining, trade-offs and exchange amongst a variety of groups and organisations will inevitably be components of the process. Rarely is development an entirely friendly cooperative process of discussion and consensus. This is yet another set of functions for which Australian social care practitioners are poorly prepared.

Functions and Tasks

For two reasons, it would not help much to tell the reader how they should 'do' rural social care development. First, in rural Australia, the process usually does not proceed according to the dictates of any neat, self-contained model. It is more messy than this and intermingles with planning in other sectors. Second, few rural practitioners are employed exclusively as social planners, community workers or community activists. Rarely in rural work in Australia is it one practitioner's, one organisation's or one committee's job to do social planning or community development. Virtually all practitioners are required to contribute in some way - whether through conducting or commissioning social needs and social impact assessments, participating in social and economic development meetings, being involved in service coordinating committees, representing local interests in vertical structures, facilitating community participation, supporting self-help groups, participating in developing new services or in a variety of other ways. So instead of telling you how to do rural social care development, I have presented in Table 6.5 a number of functions and tasks which should be performed in any rural community, regardless of who, or which combination of players does them. They are derived from discussion throughout this book, primarily from the present chapter. Functions include:

- collecting and maintaining an information base;
- information dissemination;
- social planning;
- encouraging, supporting and ensuring wide participation;
- building and utilising the capacities of local people to contribute to, and take responsibility for, social development;
- dealing with power issues;
- relating with developments in sectors other than social care; and
- establishing and maintaining ongoing social development structures.

Tasks are grouped according to whether they relate primarily to the horizontal sphere, to both the horizontal and vertical spheres, or to interaction between the two.

Conclusion

Rural social care development happens within, and as part of broader social, cultural, political, economic, natural and spiritual worlds. In rural work we should think carefully about how current social care arrangements fit, and how well they fit, within this world. We need to continually ask ourselves whether they are enhancing or reducing whole community well-being. A community frame of reference has been adopted here because locality-based communities have reality. It makes little sense to most rural people for social care practitioners to spend all their time, as most do in cities, secluded in buildings and offices relating to people exclusively on a one-to-one (or one-to-family) basis. Our credibility is questioned if we are not moving around the community - going to meetings, developing networks, involving ourselves in political, economic and media processes, and generally joining in the life of the community. Rural people expect us to be trying to do what is best for the entire community - identifying local problems, mobilising local people to work out what they need, and battling at the front-line to influence central decisions and secure resources. Given their history of disenfranchisement, many rural people quickly lose faith in formal social care processes, and social care practitioners, who fail to focus on community-wide issues.

This does not mean that we aren't expected to give priority to the needs of disadvantaged, marginalised and disempowered groups. Nor does it mean that individuals and families with immediate needs should be confronted with a *'Sorry, Gone Community Working'* sign when they knock on our doors for immediate assistance. Nevertheless, whatever we do as social care practitioners we do as part of broader and, at times, quite intense community processes across a range of contexts. It is best that we acknowledge these, know about them and use them in our work.

However, we lack impact if we simply 'go local'. Rural communities are where horizontal and vertical processes meet. Vertical processes - government structures, non-government organisations, market dynamics and the like are crucial in understanding and responding to local needs. Both spheres have the potential to exacerbate people's problems and to help solve them. The simple horizontal-vertical dichotomy is one of the keys to understanding rural social care.

In rural areas, the social care sector cannot afford to cocoon itself away from the hard realities of economics, politics and the media. If we are to contribute to local well-being we have to climb into the arena with players from other sectors. We have to learn how economic, political and social decisions are made in our communities, believe in and market our own expertise, get our facts right, keep our social justice goals firmly in mind and play the game. Although we will not be in charge of decision-making processes in other sectors, we certainly have much to contribute.

Effective social care development combines the neat, linear, tough-minded, data-based approach of social planning with the process-oriented, participative artistry and messiness of community development. In essence, it involves maximising the positive contributions to social justice of horizontal and vertical ties and minimising their constraints. Too often, we lose sight of the long term in our haste to solve present day problems. As has happened with the natural world, we have often neglected the sustainability of rural social

Social Care Development 161

structures and cultural foundations and frequently introduced social programs which have weakened, rather than strengthened, these. While the part played by out-and-out racism and exploitation cannot be denied, this is what we did to indigenous communities in this country. In every social development process, in every social care program, in every intervention we must keep one eye on the immediate need and another on their long-term implications for social and cultural sustainability.

Table 6.5: Rural Social Care Development Functions and Tasks

FUNCTIONS	TASKS
Information Collection and Maintenance (Present and projected future conditions)	*Horizontal Arena* • Collect and maintain information concerning local: social needs, problems and issues; social, economic and other forms of disadvantage, disempowerment and marginalisation; demography; social structures; power structures; history; cultures; spirituality; economy; physical infrastructure, including transportation systems; natural environments and people's relationships with these; climate and seasonal variations; natural hazards. • Development and maintenance of locally-based information storage and retrieval systems. *Both Horizontal and Vertical Arenas* • Collect and maintain information concerning local and non-local: expertise and how it can be accessed; services; social and economic trends; policies; funding programs; social development decision-making processes and how they can be accessed; Commonwealth, State and local government budgetary, funding and planning protocols and timetables; developmental constraints and opportunities. *Horizontal-Vertical Interaction* • Collect and maintain information concerning interaction between the region and the outside world in relation to: relative disadvantage; culture; marginalisation; disempowerment; political, social and power structures and relationships; economy; access, including transportation and communication.

Table 6.5: Rural Social Care Development Functions and Tasks (continued)

FUNCTIONS	TASKS
Information Dissemination	*Horizontal Arena* • See 'Both Horizontal and Vertical Arenas'. *Both Horizontal and Vertical Arenas* • Actively distribute information to local and non-local people and organisations and facilitate their access to it. • Inject information into local and non-local policy, planning and service decision-making processes. *Horizontal-Vertical Interaction* • Build awareness amongst groups and organisations outside the region about local issues, problems, needs and conditions. • Facilitate open exchange of information between horizontal and vertical arenas.
Social Planning	*Horizontal Arena* • Establish and maintain local planning structures. • Ensure that planning occurs, priorities are established, and regional positions, action plans and strategies are developed. • Ensure that plans are implemented. • Prioritise local needs on the basis of research, participative processes and negotiation. • Develop, maintain and review services, facilities and resources. • Advocate for representation of disadvantaged groups in the management of community-based organisations. *Both Horizontal and Vertical Arenas* • Encourage 'whole community' perspectives at all levels. • Harness local and non-local planning expertise. • Attract external and internal funding, resources and facilities. • Ensure the relevance and target effectiveness of services to the region. • Advocate consistent regional boundaries for all government and non-government policy, planning, funding and service organisations.

Table 6.5: Rural Social Care Development Functions and Tasks (continued)

FUNCTIONS	TASKS
Social Planning (continued)	*Horizontal-Vertical Interaction* • Advocate devolution to the local level of control over regional planning, service provision and service management. • Facilitate joint planning between horizontal and vertical arenas. • Facilitate joint planning between Commonwealth, State and local government. • Facilitate coordinated planning. • Advocate rural interests in central social planning and policy formulation processes. • Facilitate local input to central planning, policy formulation and funding decisions according to government budgetary and planning timetables. • Prepare and facilitate the preparation of funding submissions. • Advocate and facilitate development of more locally available and community-based services. • Advocate accountability of externally-based organisations to the local community. • Advocate simple and relevant service accountability procedures. • Try to reduce central bureaucratic delays and inefficiencies.
Participation	*Horizontal Arena* • Enhance awareness amongst local people and organisations of intra-regional cultural and other differences. • Encourage acceptance of differences based on culture, gender, etc. • Stimulate local interest in social development and social care issues. • Facilitate, support and encourage wide participation of people, groups and organisations, especially disadvantaged and disempowered people. • Coordinate and provide structure and organisation to participative activities. • Develop, encourage and support leadership amongst local people and organisations.

Table 6.5: Rural Social Care Development Functions and Tasks (continued)

FUNCTIONS	TASKS
Participation (continued)	*Horizontal Arena (continued)* • Ensure that local representatives are chosen and representative structures are developed. • Generate supportive public opinion. • Strengthen and harness existing supportive structures, including local government. • Advise local people and organisations about participation and motivate them to contribute. • Ensure local participation in service management and service provision. *Both Horizontal and Vertical Arenas* • Advocate the importance of participation. • Advocate effective representation of residents and local organisations in decision-making processes which affect them. • Advocate and support culturally appropriate participation mechanisms. • Mobilise and encourage effective utilisation of local and non-local resources, skills, knowledge, advice and energy. • Obtain resources for effective participation. *Horizontal-Vertical Interaction* • Encourage and mediate clear communication and negotiation. • Encourage the establishment of multi-level participation mechanisms and ensure that they function effectively. • Develop procedures and protocols for consultation at all levels. • Expose, and challenge, exploitation of participative processes by government and by national and State-wide non-government organisations. • Advocate local participation in the management of local branches of externally-based organisations.

Table 6.5: Rural Social Care Development Functions and Tasks (continued)

FUNCTIONS	TASKS — HORIZONTAL ARENA; HORIZONTAL AND VERTICAL ARENAS; HORIZONTAL-VERTICAL INTERACTION
Capacity Building and Utilisation	*Horizontal Arena* • Develop pride of place, and a sense of community, amongst local people and organisations. • Strengthen positive local bonds and community cohesion. • Develop commitment to the principle of community responsibility for social development and social care. • Increase local awareness of policy and service neglect, especially in relation to disadvantaged groups. • Develop local awareness of democratic processes and the need for political action in pursuit of social justice. • Increase social development expertise amongst local people and organisations. • Enhance the confidence of local organisations and people, especially the disadvantaged, to pursue social development and provide social care. *Both Horizontal and Vertical Arenas* • Encourage local people to contribute their expertise and reward their contributions. • Encourage local and non-local organisations to access local knowledge and skills. *Horizontal-Vertical Interaction* • Develop and strengthen links between horizontal and vertical spheres.

Table 6.5: Rural Social Care Development Functions and Tasks (continued)

FUNCTIONS	TASKS
Dealing with Power Issues (Also see Chapter 8)	***Horizontal Arena*** • Develop and implement effective social change and social action strategies. • Generate as much cohesion and mutual support as possible amongst local interest groups which are sympathetic to social justice ideals. • Establish and support coalitions amongst local disadvantaged groups, other residents and local organisations. • Elicit as much support as possible from local power actors for social development, especially in relation to the interests of less powerful local groups. • Encourage and support coalitions between disadvantaged groups and local power structures. • Increase the confidence and skills of local disempowered people to negotiate with powerful horizontal and vertical structures. • Engage factions in positive social development activities. • Facilitate, mediate and encourage effective negotiation and bargaining amongst local interest groups. • Challenge and confront established local power structures obstructing social justice, and try to reduce their power in relation to social development and social care. • Establish coalitions between neighbouring communities and regions. ***Both Horizontal and Vertical Arenas*** • Advocate the region's needs at all levels. • Enhance the credibility of local social care structures with powerful horizontal and vertical players. • Generate, and where necessary, change public opinion by, for instance, utilising mass media. • Maximise positive, and minimise negative, impacts of existing power structures on social development and social care. • Lobby, secure the support of, and harness the contributions of powerful allies such as Commonwealth, State and local government officials, major social care agencies and peak non-government organisations. • Counter manipulation of local social development structures by powerful horizontal and vertical interests.

Table 6.5: Rural Social Care Development Functions and Tasks (continued)

FUNCTIONS	TASKS
Dealing with Power Issues (continued)	*Both Horizontal and Vertical Arenas (continued)* • Try to change policies, regulations and procedures working against local social development. *Horizontal-Vertical Interaction* • Facilitate access by local people and organisations to decision-making processes in relation to social development and social care. • Advocate for devolution of as much power as possible to the local level. • Increase the power of local players relative to non-local players. • Organise, mediate and encourage effective negotiation between horizontal and vertical structures. • Facilitate communication between horizontal and vertical arenas by, for example, interpreting frameworks, perspectives and bureaucratic jargon. • Harness powerful external organisations and individuals to counteract obstructive powerful local interests. • Where possible, foster and support rural-urban alliances.
Relating with other Sectors	*Horizontal Arena* • Generate and sustain local cross-sector structures and coalitions between social care, health care, education, and economic development. • Connect with participative community development structures and activities in other sectors such as *Landcare*. • Use economic development processes and environmental issues to generate community cohesion. • Contribute social care sector information to local area planning. • Conduct social impact assessments. • Encourage coordination of local data collection, data management and data utilisation within and between sectors. *Both Horizontal and Vertical Arenas* • Facilitate and mediate negotiation, bargaining and compromise between social care and other sectors. • Advocate social issues, and market the knowledge and expertise of the social care sector. • Inject information and recommendations from the social care sector into decision-making processes in other sectors.

Table 6.5: Rural Social Care Development Functions and Tasks (continued)

FUNCTIONS	TASKS
Relating with other Sectors (continued)	***Both Horizontal and Vertical Arena (continued)*** • Ensure that the results of social impact assessments are effectively disseminated and influence development decisions. • Obtain and maintain information about other sectors in the local and non-local spheres. • Challenge economic reductionism. ***Horizontal-Vertical Interaction*** • Advocate and lobby for social impact assessments. • Engage in social action to resist developments which are undesirable from social care perspectives. • Mediate interaction and encourage productive communication between developers and community groups.
Establishing ongoing Social Development Structures	***Horizontal Arena*** • Encourage the establishment of, and support for, ongoing local social development structures. These could include, for example, information storage and retrieval systems, local and cross-regional social development committees and local citizens' representation organisations. ***Both Horizontal and Vertical Arenas*** • Encourage and support the establishment of permanent social development structures at all levels, such as inter-government regional planning committees. ***Horizontal-Vertical Interaction*** • Encourage and support the establishment of permanent social development structures which link horizontal and vertical spheres, such as formal service agreements, joint service planning and coordination committees, and organisation policies which require local participation in organisation management.

Source: Developed from Cheers (1993a, p. 68).

Notes

1. This section draws substantially on research from developing countries because rural social care development has been studied most extensively in these contexts. Much of this material is supported by Australian experiences.
2. Arnstein's 'therapy' is not included here because it is not focused on whole communities and because I disagree with the contention that it is, by definition, a non-participative process.

7 Formal Personal Social Care

This chapter addresses issues involved in providing formal personal social care services, facilities and resources to rural Australians and examines how these can relate with informal, or natural, caring processes. Formal personal social care is provided by service organisations to people on an individualised basis through direct interaction, whether this be face-to-face or via electronic media. They include, for example, counselling, home care, child protection and child care. Service issues addressed in this chapter concern:

- availability, accessibility, relevance, focus, funding, accountability, staffing and designs;
- coordination and integration;
- providing information about services; and
- the localism-centralism debate, with special attention being given in this context to community-based organisations.

It can no longer be claimed that we know little about these issues. This chapter draws on 158 research reports, scholarly works, government reports, consultancies, policy documents and case studies; 124 of which focus on rural Australia. Nor is it true that our information is mostly speculative or anecdotal. Only nine documents could be described as such. Fifty-three research papers were reviewed, each of which is based on information obtained from interviews, questionnaires, workshops or submissions from rural residents, service providers and managers. Thirty-six of these are systematic empirical studies. Sixty-four documents are serious theoretical works and 16 are based on studies of actual service programs. The other 16 are policy documents. It should be noted at the outset that there is overwhelming consensus throughout this literature about the issues and solutions to the problems involved in providing formal social care to rural Australians.

Availability

Rural areas, especially smaller towns and the more remote places, do not receive the vast array of personal welfare services that are available to urban Australians (Centacare Australia and Australian Catholic Social Welfare Commission - Centacare, 1993, p.6). For instance, in 1987 Coleman (p.5) reported that remote areas had less than half the range of general community services that are available in urban areas. Even when they exist, services provided by small community-based organisations will often be poorer in quality than those of larger urban agencies which have the advantages of specialised staff, greater resources and access to nearby specialised services. In recent years, these deficiencies have been compounded by service withdrawals and increasing demand resulting from harsh economic times, rural restructuring and high unemployment levels. Many rural services have been withdrawn or reduced, or have been required by funding organisations to extend their catchment areas though with no additional resources (DPMC, 1992, p.31; Dale, 1994, p.331).

There are three main reasons for rural service disadvantages. First, the myth that rural people are so self-reliant, mutually supportive, contented and blissfully free of social problems that they do not need services has, no doubt, played a part in the past (Collingridge, 1991, p.5). Thankfully, this view may now be receding in the wake of prolonged rural recessions and droughts, and recent media publicity of issues such as rural suicide, rural poverty and farm closures.

Second, the *per capita* cost of providing most services is higher in rural than urban areas (Carter and Jones, 1989, p.209; Industry Commission, 1994a, pp.38-9). This is because of lower demand, inappropriate funding policies and service models, and the additional costs associated with overheads such as travel, telephones and staff support. However, as discussed in Chapter 2, pointing to higher costs as justification for providing a lower level of services is essentially a political, rather than a financial, argument and, in any case, reflects the urbo-centricity of our social care system.

The third reason why rural people are relatively deprived of formal services concerns funding formulae. In a highly-fragmented service system such as we have in Australia, funding formulae based on 'critical mass', or how many people in a region need a particular service, inevitably favours larger population centres (Australian Catholic Social Welfare Commission - ACSWC, undated, p.33; Cox and Veteri, 1992, p.43). To make matters worse, the problems faced by rural organisations in establishing a critical mass have been compounded over the last decade by funding bodies requiring ever-increasing thresholds for target populations (DPMC, 1992, p.31). Programs which require matching funds from community organisations also discriminate against rural communities because they have fewer resources than urban areas. So, too, do those which provide seed funding for a limited period, because rural communities are less able than urban areas to attract additional continuing resources (Cox and Veteri, 1992, p.47). Rural communities also often lack the infrastructure needed to compile competitive funding submissions and the power to compete for resources against high-profile urban organisations (Industry Commission, 1994a, p.39). Finally, funding problems are compounded by the difficulties which regional managers in government departments frequently experience while trying to represent the needs of rural community organisations in competition with their counterparts in central office.

Suggestions made throughout this chapter will help to increase the availability of services to rural people. At a general level, rural areas should be given higher weighting in mainstream *per capita* funding formulae so that they receive additional, and more equitable, funding (Centacare, 1993, p.ii). Funds should also be more precisely targeted at disadvantaged regions and groups (DPMC, 1992, p.31). But this is mere tinkering. Other, more powerful, measures are required. Nationally-agreed realistic minimum standards for formal social care provisions should be developed and enforced throughout the nation (OND, 1994, p.6). Furthermore, innovative, cost-effective and relevant funding and service models recently developed for rural areas should be implemented more widely. These are reviewed later. We also urgently need a national database of rural community services which can be cross-tabulated with existing indices of relative disadvantage (Industry Commission, 1994b, p.XLVII). This would provide a more coherent rationale for allocating resources across regions.

Accessibility

Service access issues can be grouped into those concerning physical accessibility, factors connected with the service itself, socio-cultural barriers, and other user-related difficulties.

Physical access problems include user travel, telephone and accommodation costs, especially for services which require users to come to them rather than vice-versa (Centacare, 1993; Sorensen, 1993a, p.287). Recent service 'rationalisation' and cost cutting by government departments have only exacerbated these problems, in the process shifting service costs from taxpayers to users as the latter are forced to seek assistance over greater distances (Dunn and Williams, 1992, p.10; Rolley and Humphreys, 1993, p.253). Climatic conditions, such as the northern Wet season, can increase access difficulties as can geographic factors when, for example, potential users are deterred by difficult road conditions (Cheers, 1992b, p.479; OND, 1994, p.91). Settlement patterns within regions also affect access. For example, young people living in the rapidly-growing Airlie Beach/Cannonvale township in the Whitsunday Shire find it difficult to access services, recreational facilities and training programs, most of which are located in Proserpine which is some 30km away (Bone, Cheers and Hil, 1993, p.116). Furthermore, the problems of physical isolation are particularly severe in emergencies, such as when a woman on a property cannot access protective services located in town (Coorey, 1988, pp.122-3). As we shall see later, these physical access problems are compounded in rural areas by poor publicity about where, when and how services can be obtained.

Prospective users can also experience a service as unapproachable because of staff values, their lack of understanding of rural life, their language, the organisation's physical environment, its location, the image which workers present and other components of organisational culture. For example, in one study, two young sole parents spoke of:

> ... welfare workers ... who wear expensive looking clothes and jewellery and inadvertently make us feel poor and marginalised ... the people [at the welfare agency] are stuck up, with rings and posh clothes; they look down on us and our kids.

In some places, the service network is structured so that marginalised groups cannot find a comfortable entry point. Rural youth, for instance, often experience the world of formal social care as foreign 'adult territory' which they are reluctant to access and, in any case, would not know how to do so (Bone, Cheers and Hil, 1993, p.121; Cheers and Yip, 1994, p.108).

In small communities, a number of social factors can also hinder access. It is well known, for instance, that people's informal supports sometimes question the value of formal social care services, advise users to ignore expert advice or not go for help at all, and suggest alternative explanations for, and solutions to their problems (Poole and Daley,

1985, p.338). As with abusive men, they can even actively stop people, in this case abused women, from seeking help (Coorey, 1988, p.117).

Community processes also influence access. Local social structures may divert provisions away from intended recipients, as when income security payments do not reach women in remote communities (Breed, 1987, p.149). They can also bar access to resources. For example, in one town in North Queensland, members of one faction could not access the *Royal Flying Doctor* kit because the rival faction controlled the key to the room in which it was stored. Community processes can also result in serious local issues such as child abuse and domestic violence being denied by residents (IINA Torres Strait Islander Corporation - IINA, 1996, pp.24-5). People can be deterred from seeking help, such as counselling, because of the risk of stigma, negative stereotyping and gossip, especially when services are located in publicly visible places (Taylor, 1987, p.3). Furthermore, local structures, such as domestic violence perpetrators' relationships with local power elites and negative social attitudes, can make it difficult for abused women to obtain protection from police, the judiciary and even local women's services (Samyia, 1987, p.117). In this context, negative social attitudes include stigmatisation, blaming victims rather than perpetrators, the belief that domestic issues should remain private, and the importance attached to protecting the good family name in small communities (Coorey, 1988, pp.107-31).

A number of United States studies have shown that fear of stigmatisation is a primary reason why rural people are less likely than urban residents to access formal social care services and more likely to withdraw from them prematurely (e.g., Osgood, 1977; Keith, 1980; Camasso and Moore, 1985). Similarly, Rank and Hirschl (1988) found that withdrawal rates were higher for rural people because they had less opportunity to manage feelings of stigmatisation and alienation by interacting with other users. Focusing specifically on poor farmers, Sundet and Mermelstein (1987) found that they did not apply for assistance because of 'traditional' rural values, fear of stigmatisation, lack of information, and fear of embarrassment at being unable to negotiate the application process. Other studies have found that general rural attitudes also affect service utilisation (Camasso and Moore, 1985). These include the view that users are responsible for their problems rather than structural factors, a preference for private rather than public solutions to personal problems, and the belief that formal social care is a 'charity' rather than a right.

However, in the absence of equivalent Australian research, we should be cautious about generalising from studies of rural social attitudes in other countries. First, and overriding all else, a large proportion of people living in rural Australia are not traditionally rural at all. Many are urban itinerants and refugees. Second, even the United States evidence is inconclusive (Melton, 1983, p.5). Although some studies have found that rural people have more traditional values than their urban counterparts (Miller and Luloff, 1981; Willits, Bealer and Crider, 1982), others have found no such differences (Wellman, 1979; Christenson, 1984). Third, Australians may be more accepting of government assistance than United States residents. For instance, as we saw in Chapter 2, Australian farmers have a long history of accepting help in the form of tariff protection, export subsidies and other economic measures. Fourth, Australian society has become more homogeneous over time through urban dominance, the lack of natural geographic barriers to travel and communication, and the recent rapid development of transport and communication technology (Collingridge, 1991, p.4).

A number of suggestions are made throughout this book which are designed to improve access to services. They include implementing more widely a number of recent successful experimental service and funding models (reviewed later), improving rural public transportation systems, locating services so that they are on main regional transport routes, and integrating formal services more thoroughly with informal support processes. Reducing the barriers presented by local social structures is more difficult. As a start, practitioners and service managers should develop a detailed understanding of the social dynamics of their regions, intervene where necessary and generate local support for social justice principles. Furthermore, external authorities such as government funding bodies must take a more prominent role in supporting local organisations in their efforts to maximise access through clear program guidelines and effective consultation about service development.

Relevance

Service models designed for urban environments often have trouble responding to rural realities. For instance, community-based models assume that there are sufficient local resources, people and skills to support the management and provision of independent services. This does not hold for many rural communities, especially those with small and declining populations (Edgerton, 1983, p.275; Schindeler, 1993, p.9).

In Australia, most formal social care services are specialised in that they derive from vertically-segregated programs rather than local needs and conditions (Centacare, 1993, p.ii; Dale, 1994, p.331). Most are also provided from regional centres or State capitals. Consequently, when they eventually reach rural communities they are, or from the user's perspective seem to be, fragmented, poorly coordinated, duplicative and permeated with service gaps (ACSWC, undated, p.33; Madden, 1993, p.59). Moreover, specialised services usually rely on other related services being available, which is frequently not the case in rural communities (ACSWC, undated, p.33). Thus, for example, it doesn't help much to provide a visiting mental health service when ongoing counselling and home care services are not available locally. This was the conclusion reached by Poole and Daley (1985) in rural Arizona when they found that there was little point in providing a sophisticated mental health diagnostic service when there were no locally-accessible treatment facilities to which people could be referred.

Urban service models are frequently too standardised to respond to the diversity to be found within and between rural localities (Cox and Veteri, 1992, p.48; Madden, 1993, p.61). Many services fail to mesh with local cultures, values and social care wisdom concerning causes of, and solutions to human problems, especially in indigenous communities (Cox and Veteri, 1992, p.26; IINA, 1996, pp.24-5). Services also frequently fail to take account of local lifestyles. For example, a counselling service which relies on weekly contact will find it difficult to relate to beef cattle producers and truck drivers in Northern Australia because they are so often away from home. Centrally-designed services can also fail to relate to local expectations. For instance, practitioners in the Arizona mental health diagnostic program mentioned earlier had no choice but to comply with local expectations that they would help solve clients' problems, not merely diagnose them as was initially intended (Poole and Daley, 1985).

The high level of professionalisation of Australian social care can also reduce the relevance of services to rural life. The assumption that 'experts know best' devalues, and often dismisses, the contribution of local people to service provision and organisational management. Professionalism is convenient for planners, managers and educators in that it lends itself to uniformity of practice across regions and groups (Poole and Daley, 1985, p.342). However, because most professionals in Australia are city people who are trained in urban institutions according to urban frameworks, the resulting uniformity is urban uniformity which dismisses rural-urban differences. For instance, because Australian social work training emphasises face-to-face casework and group work, many social workers are ill-equipped to contribute to regional planning, social planning or community development. Furthermore, professionals trained according to Fabian socialist frameworks frequently have difficulty relating to traditional rural values, rigid social structures, conservative power brokers, economic developers and development-oriented shire councils (Cheers, 1992a, p.19; O'Toole, 1993, p.11).

Implications for enhancing service relevance are obvious. As will be discussed later, funding and service models should respond to the realities of rural Australia. Services should be regionally- rather than program-based, and responsive to local conditions including cultures, values, lifestyles, service expectations and the availability of other resources and infrastructure. They should also draw more extensively on the local 'social care wisdom' which abounds in all rural communities. Services, in other words, should be more embedded in horizontal ties and less demarcated by vertical structures.

Information

For services to be relevant, planners, practitioners and managers need access to accurate information about local needs, values, priorities and conditions (Coleman, 1987, p.5; OND, 1994, p.93). However, we still know relatively little about most rural regions in Australia. While electronic databases drawing on national census information such as *CDATA with MapInfo* (ABS, 1991c) and indices of regional socio-economic disadvantage such as the *Socio-economic Index for Areas (SEIFA)* (ABS, 1994) are useful, access to them can be expensive for smaller communities and interpreting data can be difficult where local personnel lack the relevant skills and equipment. In any case, quantitative demographic measures are crude indicators of social need (Centacare, 1993, p.ii). Service organisations, funding bodies and local organisations also need qualitative information concerning local lifestyles, values, needs and priorities which can only be obtained from detailed participative research involving local people (see Table 6.1 for information relevant to rural social planning).

For their part, people in rural communities need information about how policy is formulated in central offices and how services are developed and funded (Cheers, 1993a, p.67). They cannot influence policy and services unless they know which decisions are being made, by whom, where, how and with whose involvement. They need to know how to join the game, what the rules are, and how to influence the other players. They also need information about funding programs, their guidelines and conditions, who provides them, application procedures, key contact people, who to lobby and how to get their support.

Many reports have commented on how poorly informed rural Australians are about services, resources and facilities, even local ones (e.g., Dunn, 1990, p.121; IINA, 1996, p.5). For instance, Radford (1981, p.121) found that 20 per cent of a sample of rural aged people did not know how to seek information about accommodation and 33 per cent were unaware of how information about home support services could be obtained. In the Whitsunday Shire, Williams and McMahon (1995, p.24) found that only 50.6 per cent of their sample of aged people knew about *Blue Nurses*, 30.0 per cent about *Meals on Wheels* and only 9.0 per cent about home help services. Those in the outlying areas were least well informed. In the same Shire, Bone, Cheers and Hil (1993, p.105) found that only 20.4 per cent of their sample of 108 young people knew of the local *Neighbourhood Centre*, 13.9 per cent about *Kids Helpline* and 10.2 per cent about the *Cannonvale Crisis Care* service. Similarly, in their study of a sugar community in the depths of recession Foley, Fyffe and Grichting (1986, p.47) found that 33 per cent of their 296 respondents had heard of only up to eight of the 24 local services presented to them. The situation is much the same in the United States where Sundet and Mermelstein (1987, p.17) found that 25.7 per cent of eligible poor farm families reported that they had not sought assistance because they did not know what was available or how to approach service organisations.

Clearly, we have been doing a poor job of informing rural Australians about services. But we are learning how to do it better. Studies of how to present information to rural people (Dunn, 1990, p.121; ORA, 1991, pp.75-88) have shown that it should be:

- carefully targeted towards those who need it;
- timed when services are most likely to be needed;
- framed within specific regional contexts;
- presented in appropriate language; and

- as far as possible, produced and disseminated by local people through face-to-face contact.

The Office of Rural Affairs (1991, pp.75-88) also recommended that information dissemination and referral functions should be integral components of all rural services.

Rural people now have far greater access to information about social care services than they did a decade ago and a number of information dissemination strategies have been tried with varying degrees of success. In general, information emanating from distant centres through impersonal processes has proven least popular. For instance, a study reported by Coleman (1987, p.5) found that rural people prefer personal rather than impersonal methods such as toll free *008* telephone numbers. Morton Consulting Services Pty. Ltd. (Morton) (1990, p.37) also found *008* numbers to be unpopular with rural practitioners who saw them as just another instance of trying to fit people to services rather than the other way round. However, submissions to the Office of Rural Affairs in Victoria (1991) supported *008* lines as an effective and inexpensive way of providing community-based organisations with access to government departments (p.78). In line with this, the Office of Northern Development (1994, p.66) recommended that all government departments should have *008* numbers and that there should be one central office which distributes calls to the appropriate department. The *COUNTRYLINK* program (DPIE, 1995, p.iv) does this, but only for Commonwealth services and programs. Far better, it would seem, to have a central office which services all departments, whether Commonwealth or State, as well as all non-government organisations.

Mobile information vans were tried by the Victorian Government but they proved to be expensive and poorly utilised (ORA, 1991, p.83). Residents failed to use them because they were publicly visible and hence stigmatising, physically uncomfortable, and lacked important auxiliary facilities such as child care.

Printed information packages encompassing all programs, services and provisions of all organisations are well received provided that they are widely distributed and carefully targeted to reach those who need the information at the time they need it. *The Rural Book* (DPIE, 1995) is a good innovation although it is limited to Commonwealth programs and access tends to be restricted to those who have already entered the service network. Comprehensive regionally-focused service directories such as we find in cities, are useful supplements to *The Rural Book* (Clark, 1994, p.28).

Rightly, the trend is toward locally-based information dissemination strategies. It is common, for example, for centralised organisations to provide information through local agencies and groups such as shire offices, police stations, hospitals, schools, welfare organisations and the *Country Women's Association* (ORA, 1991, p.82; DPMC, 1992, p.32). Local *One Stop Shops* staffed by multi-skilled information and referral staff are provided as part of the *COUNTRYLINK* package (DPIE, 1995, p.iv). Similarly, Queensland's *Rural Agents* program provides information about, and access to a range of government services. Strategies such as these are useful for people living close to the towns in which they are located although they are probably less effective for those in outlying areas (OND, 1994, p.65). This problem is addressed through *Shopfronts* and *Community Information Stands* at various rural shows and field days. *One Stop Shops* embrace sound principles in that they are staffed and managed by trained local people, provide a face-to-face service based on an electronic database and are embedded in their respective communities (OND, 1994, p.65). *Information and Access Centres* targeted at specific marginalised and isolated groups such as youth, the aged and people with disabilities also provide a useful doorway into the total service network (Cheers and Yip, 1994, p.108; DPIE, 1995, p.170). Finally, *telecottages* provide access to non-local services for those who know how to use the technology in towns where they have been established (ORA, 1991, p.78). However, we are yet to provide people in need with access to existing public equipment such as computers, telephones, faxes, emails and video communication facilities in schools, hospitals and local government offices.

Mass media outlets are an especially powerful way of disseminating information. The Office of Rural Affairs found that a number of media strategies had been effective in rural Victoria (ORA, 1991, pp.83-4). These included press releases about local initiatives, projects and grants but emanating from central government offices, regular local newspaper articles, and frequent regional television and radio news releases and interviews with wide public appeal. Newsletters and other material distributed through regionally-based networks such as *Women's Info-net* also appear to be effective (Clark, 1994, p.28). On the other hand, simple newspaper, radio and television advertisements and pamphlets dropped in letter boxes are largely unsuccessful (ORA, 1991, pp.83-4).

Because most information dissemination strategies reach only a limited section of the population, a mix of strategies seems best. A multi-strategy approach also helps to penetrate the private informal social networks which can be so important in disseminating information to socially-marginalised and geographically-isolated people.

Focus

It was suggested in Chapter 3 that fragmenting people's lives and providing a service which responds to one or only a few parts violates the integrity of human living. As will be discussed in Chapter 8, it also bears little relationship to the realities of rural practice. Lacking a range of specialised services, rural people expect their practitioners to do something about whichever problems they have regardless of their agency's or funding program's official focus. They also expect practitioners to understand their problems within the context of their total lives. For their part, as a member of the same community the rural practitioner cannot but see people within broader community and family contexts. In brief, rural practice involves dealing with whole people living in whole communities and within social groupings such as families and kin networks.

As Martinez-Brawley (1989, p.6) commented, the trend in Western 'welfare' has been in precisely the opposite direction.

> We have moved from a **craft** social service paradigm in which we were interested in global results to a highly bureaucratic and industrial model in which we focus on partialized well-being. ... What do I mean by a craft social service paradigm? Remember the craftsperson? The cabinet-maker who cared about the quality and beauty of the total product rather than about the successful assembly of various bits into a perfectly symmetrical but boring structure? Remember the social worker who cared about the whole family in the community milieu, not just his or her client? They are nowhere to be found in our current system. The child welfare worker cares about the children; the area agency on aging worker looks after grandmother and the mental health office is concerned about mother's depression. Perhaps the unemployment office is working with dad, but no one is really looking at or serving the whole family in the context of its own networks in the local town. We are doing assembly line social work. (Original author's emphasis)

Similarly, regardless of their official charter, rural social care organisations cannot avoid addressing broader community issues. Most are expected to provide some leadership in relation to local social development and to contribute information, advice and time to planning in related sectors such as health, education and economic development.

Having said this, though, a community focus is difficult to maintain for most agencies, even those which are locally based. This is because they are embedded in wider structures which emphasise specialised rather than generalist practice, programatic rather than integrated funding, vertical rather than horizontal accountability, client-focused rather than community-based training, and a career reward system based on direct client work (Martinez-Brawley, 1990a, pp.7-8).

Localism

The localism-centralism debate concerns whether, and to what extent, service planning, service management and service provision should emanate from the *centre* or the *periphery*. In the present context, the *periphery* refers to people and organisations in rural places and the *centre* to organisational structures located in national and State capitals and larger provincial cities. To put the conclusion first: both have a role; the challenge is to maximise the positive and minimise the negative contributions of each.

Centralisation has the potential to provide a universal safety net, similar service standards for all organisations no matter where they are located, and an equitable distribution of resources across regions, groups and individuals according to relative need. Central organisations can also provide agencies at the periphery with access to funding and other resources, including specialised expertise. But because they are urban based, staff of centralised structures generally have little understanding of specific rural contexts and, consequently, can experience difficulties fitting services with needs and adequately representing rural interests (Centacare, 1993, p.i). Nor are they in a position to respond effectively to diversity between and within regions (McKenzie, 1987, p.80).

The centre's limitations are the periphery's strengths. People in local organisations know more about local conditions, needs and priorities. With this knowledge, and because they have more flexible structures, they are usually better placed to tailor services to their community and connect with residents through formal and informal networks. Because they are embedded in local structures they are also well placed to involve local people in management and service provision. Less tangibly, local organisations convey a sense of 'ownership' to the community which enhances access and makes it easier to harness local resources and skills. Negatively, they often have a limited pool of resources, facilities, personnel and expertise, and usually find it difficult to participate in central planning processes (Munn, 1993; Dale, 1994, p.331). They are also susceptible to exploitation by powerful local interests which have agendas other than social justice (Munn, 1993).

Centre-Periphery Relationships

In the organisational environment, centre-periphery relationships exist between:

- central and local offices of government departments;
- central and local offices of non-government organisations; and
- central government funding structures and local community-based organisations.

Central and Local Offices of Government Departments   Three major government reports have made the same general recommendations about relationships between central and local offices of government departments (ORA, 1991, pp.5-6; ACOSS, 1993a, p.vi; OND, 1994, p.82). These are that:

- central management should work with regional managers to decide the broad parameters of policies and programs, preferred outcomes and accountability processes;
- regional managers should be key players in central decision making concerning budget priorities and cross-regional equity; and
- regional offices of government departments should be provided with the managerial and financial autonomy and flexibility to decide how services should be provided locally and to work collaboratively with horizontal structures.

Central and Local Offices of Non-government Organisations   Local branches of non-government organisations usually enjoy greater autonomy from their parent structures than do regional government offices. Some non-government organisations provide an umbrella structure with local branches operating more as community-based organisations in their own right than as components of line management hierarchies. In this role, central offices secure funds for new programs, make initial staff appointments, provide administrative support and professional consultation for local organisations, help them with accountability procedures and lobby government funding bodies on their behalf. Ideally, the local office has its own management committee and works with the community to identify needs and priorities and to design, manage and provide services.

Central Government Funding Structures and Community-based Organisations Relationships between community-based organisations and government funding bodies are more complex. Funding bodies provide financial resources and ensure vertical accountability. Some also provide administrative support and consultation concerning service delivery and organisational management. As discussed in Chapter 6, they might also be required in some communities to act as a catalyst for local services development. At least in theory, community-based organisations:

- identify local needs and priorities;
- design, manage and provide services;
- apply for funding from governments;
- comply with vertical accountability requirements;
- ensure horizontal accountability to users and the community more generally; and
- harness local skills, knowledge, energy and creativity.

Ideally, relationships between funding bodies and community-based organisations are ongoing and mutually consultative, as with the Division of Community Services Development of the Queensland Department of Families, Youth and Community Care (DFYCC). At the time of writing, the Division has regional managers in major regional centres throughout the State and 'resource officers' in smaller centres (DFACS, 1995). Main functions of resource officers are to:

- develop a good understanding of communities within their respective regions;
- establish close working relationships with them;
- help local people identify needs, determine priorities and develop proposals for services, resources and facilities; and
- provide consultation and advice to community organisations on management, service provision and accountability requirements.

Regional managers also have a role in representing local community interests in central decision making concerning funding. They meet regularly as a group to determine funding allocations, review existing programs, develop policy and undertake new program initiatives. The Division's work is based on the belief that local communities should decide what is needed and how it should be provided, although it is also recognised that residents sometimes lack the necessary skills, knowledge and experience to do this. For this reason, resource officers often act as catalysts and consultants for local initiatives. The Division also accepts the reality that community initiatives sometimes need to be protected by Divisional officers from obstructive tendencies within their own communities, special interest groups, government policies and profit-driven media agendas.

Queensland's *Remote Area Aboriginal and Torres Strait Islander Child Care Program (RAATSICCP)* illustrates this relationship[1] (Dale, 1994; Hays, 1996). This program aims to improve the well-being of Aboriginal and Torres Strait Islander children living in remote communities in Queensland. It began because it was acknowledged by DFYCC that these children could not access child care services (long day care, occasional care and family day care) under existing arrangements as there were too few children in each community. Tricia Hays, Senior Resource Officer with the Department, in association with women she knew from her community services development work in these communities, met in Cairns in 1991 to discuss the kinds of child care services which the women wanted. Women and, in some cases, men from the communities controlled decision making about the kinds of services required and made recommendations about resources to the funding body. At the time of writing there are 43 services in remote communities on the mainland and on the Torres Strait Islands. Amongst them are some of Australia's most innovative and responsive child care services (DFACS, 1993, 1994).

There are two networks within the *RAATSICCP* - one for the mainland and one for the Torres Strait Islands. Each has an advisory group comprising the people who are running the services. Advisory groups discuss service development and management, provide training to service workers, make recommendations to the Minister about funding, discuss and share information about service models, and monitor the performance of each other's services. The Department's Resource Officers help facilitate the networks and provide assistance to managers and staff. But policy, program and service directions are set by the communities themselves. Network members provide holistic services within a philosophy which sees the community's children as its future (DFYCC, 1997). These have recently been extended to include child protection services to children and families.

Community-based Organisations

Community-based organisations are a key component of rural social care. Unfortunately, many have recently experienced serious problems in maintaining adequate service levels (Cox and Veteri, 1992, p.3, 47-56; Industry Commission, 1994b, p.11). As funding falls further behind and demand increases because of rural recessions, droughts and unemployment, many have been forced to curtail services, especially to outlying areas. Functions not associated with direct client work have also been reduced, including advocacy, social development, coordination, community needs assessment and service evaluation.

Many community-based organisations are experiencing staffing problems resulting from high workloads, low salaries, poor employment conditions, lack of viable career paths, and poor access to training and other supports such as professional and administrative supervision (Walsh, 1993, pp.7-8; Industry Commission, 1994a, p.39). Staffing problems include difficulties in attracting qualified personnel, low levels of experience and expertise, high turnover and disruptions to service continuity. With low staffing levels, many rural organisations have been forced to rely increasingly on volunteers to do the work (Queensland Community Services and Health Industries Training Council, Inc., 1996, p.58). These, however, can be in short supply in rural communities, especially where populations are declining and where more women are seeking paid employment. Award restructuring is adding to staffing costs thereby forcing some organisations to reduce services still further, withdraw them from outlying areas, reduce the working hours of paid staff, and increase the use and, consequently, the risk of exploitation of volunteers (Queensland Community Services and Health Industries Training Council, Inc., 1996, pp.57-9).

Virtually all community-based organisations are administered by management committees. Theoretically, these ensure local ownership of services although, for a number of reasons, the extent to which they can do so is currently under threat (Dixon, 1987). The responsibilities, demands and frustrations of members have increased because of resource cutbacks, service fragmentation, increasing use of limited-term funding arrangements, proliferating government regulations, and the complexity and changeability of funding policies and requirements. Many are becoming disillusioned as committees increasingly focus on tedious paperwork and procedural matters rather than the issues which had initially motivated them to participate such as the aims, methods and significance of services (Lipsky and Lounds, 1976; Dixon, 1987, p.178).

Management committees face a number of additional issues (Dixon, 1987, pp.176-82). Tensions frequently arise from clashes between management's concern with vertical accountability to funding bodies and the focus of staff on horizontal accountability to clients and other local organisations. Disagreements can also arise from committee members' claims to authority based on local knowledge and community support and staff's appeal to their professional expertise. Representatives of different local groups with competing agendas often clash and committees can be taken over by powerful local interests driven by agendas other than social justice. All this adds to the difficulties involved in trying to reach decisions through consensus while maintaining sufficient cohesion for a committee to accomplish its tasks.

The representativeness of management committees is open to question on a number of grounds (Dixon, 1987, pp.178-85). Given the tensions involved in membership, it is hardly surprising that simply finding enough people in a small community with the time, motivation, energy and skills to fill positions is difficult enough, let alone ensuring that they are representative. Representativeness is further reduced by irregular attendance of members at meetings.

We also know that people are not usually elected to management committees of rural organisations because they represent one or more local groups and that many committee members do not share the social, cultural and economic backgrounds of service users. As attendance at most annual general meetings confirms, people volunteer for membership for other reasons including their personal views, their availability, their ability to attend meetings at the scheduled times, their status and power, and the fact that they feel comfortable in what is essentially a middle-class professional group (Parkum, 1983; Dixon, 1987, p.180). Sometimes, funding bodies encourage people from particular local groups to stand for election because they believe, rightly or wrongly, that they are the most responsive to local needs (Bates, 1983, pp.16-22; Dixon, 1987, p.183). Or agency staff will encourage colleagues in other organisations to fill vacancies. The end result of either strategy is that committees can be dominated by professionals who share the values and views of staff rather than by people who represent a cross-section of the local community (Sharp and Inwald,

1986, p.7). This was confirmed by Cox and Veteri (1992, p.50) who found that management committees in rural Victoria were frequently dominated by local professional social care practitioners, mostly staff of Commonwealth, State and local governments. This not only biases committee decisions towards professional and government perspectives, it can also reduce managerial effectiveness. As Dixon (1987, p.184) pointed out, an aptitude for non-directive counselling, for collegial rather than hierarchical functioning, for social action, for attending to the details of government paperwork or for surviving the politics of large government bureaucracies does not necessarily make for an effective manager.

Despite their shortcomings, rural community-based organisations remain an important avenue through which services can be a genuine expression of community. The task is to make them more effective and more representative and, towards this end, some concrete suggestions have been made in a number of reports (Dixon, 1987, pp.185-6; Cox and Veteri, 1992, pp.47-56; Walsh, 1993; Industry Commission, 1994a, p.39; Queensland Community Services and Health Industries Training Council, Inc., 1996, pp.57-9). These can be summarised as follows.

- Community-based organisations need adequate resources which are not attached to specific services.
- Organisations in the same region could share costs and management structures. However, we should be careful because 'umbrella' administrative structures can develop a life of their own and divert significant funds away from direct service provision.
- Funding bodies have an important role to play in supporting more representative management committees by minimising funding uncertainties, by providing clear funding and accountability guidelines, by more clearly delineating the respective roles of agency staff and management, and by providing the kinds of consultative and support services discussed earlier in relation to community services development.
- Adequate resources should be provided so that staff and management can access training programs to prepare for their respective functions, including working with each other within a community framework.

188 Welfare Bushed

- The roles of volunteers should be clearly delineated and they should be protected from exploitation arising from staffing shortfalls.

Funding and Accountability

Funding

Many funding issues were addressed in earlier sections, including high rural service costs, program fragmentation, and inequitable funding principles such as matched, short-term, specific purpose and fixed *per capita* funding formulae. We have also discussed the lack of discretionary power available to rural communities to allocate funds. In addition, McDonald and Bullis (1991, p.6) pointed out that different funding programs have different cycles. Earlier discussion of these issues suggests that rural social care funding should:

- allow for the additional costs involved in providing rural services;
- replace fixed *per capita* formulae with more innovative funding methods which allow for smaller populations;
- recognise the difficulties which rural communities face in raising funds;
- be more long term than it is at present;
- be provided in a holistic, rather than a fragmented way;
- provide greater flexibility for communities to allocate funds according to their own assessment of local needs and priorities; and
- be provided according to a model which uses both subjective and objective indicators of need, and which involves the active participation of local people with the support, but not the domination, of regionally-based staff of funding organisations.

Substantial progress has been made by Commonwealth and State government departments over recent years in developing funding models based on these principles. An early attempt involved Commonwealth Government funding of rural multi-purpose centres (McDonald and Bullis, 1991, pp.7-9). Although funding for these was still tied to specific programs, additional allocations were made to meet shared infrastructure costs. The Commonwealth has also developed *cross-*

program approaches such as the *Remote Areas Children's Funding Package* based on 'pooled' funding arrangements (McDonald and Bullis, 1991, pp.2-3). In this program, allocations from a number of related programs were pooled into a fund to provide a package of services to a given region. The fund was administered from one unit according to a single set of contractual and reporting obligations (OND, 1994, p.96). Regional priorities were determined jointly by Commonwealth and State funding bodies in consultation with local organisations. However, the program encountered a number of difficulties associated with the joint funding arrangements, including competitive relationships between the various funding bodies and the degree of control retained by government administrators who continued to interpret guidelines in a programatic way. Queensland's *Rural Agents* program also involves a number of government departments contributing funds for multi-skilled rural agents to provide information about, and referral to all State programs (OND, 1994, p.98).

Despite some teething problems, pooled funding arrangements are rightly viewed as an approach which incorporates many of the principles listed earlier and, therefore, they have been recommended in a number of government reports (McDonald and Bullis, 1991; Rural and Remote Areas Unit, 1991; DPMC, 1992, pp.32-3). More recent pilot projects, such as the Queensland Government's *Cross Program Funding Initiative*, have taken the idea further by encompassing a broader range of programs and providing the opportunity for communities themselves to determine local needs, priorities and service designs (Dale, 1994, p.332). Under this program, communities can use funds to establish a local coordinated human services infrastructure which can attract and integrate other government initiatives. In addition, resource officers from the Department of Families, Youth and Community Care provide ongoing consultation to community groups. Dale's (1994, p.332) assessment of this program is that it results in strong local ownership, high service utilisation, stronger community networks and referral processes, and regional diversity in relation to priorities, projects, service designs and infrastructures.

Even so, the *Cross Program Funding Initiative* is restricted to one State department. Centacare Australia and the Australian Catholic Social Welfare Commission (1993, pp.16-7) have attempted to overcome this limitation with their recommendation that Commonwealth and all State governments should establish a single funding pool for all community-based rural social care services in Australia to be administered by one joint unit. Rural non-government organisations would apply to this unit for funds. However, the proposal seems unrealistic given the present level of fragmentation and competition between Commonwealth and State governments and even between departments at the same level. It also seems ironic and counter-productive to centralise community-based rural services.

Accountability

A number of reports have reached similar conclusions concerning present accountability arrangements in relation to rural social care organisations. The Industry Commission (1994a) suggested that, too often, they do not relate closely to local needs and socio-cultural contexts, or even to the grant guidelines themselves. ACOSS (1994, p.10) commented that there is too much emphasis on inputs and throughputs - such as resource acquittals, user numbers and management processes - rather than the quality and effectiveness of services. Concern has also been expressed about the lack of recognition given in current accountability requirements to activities such as advocacy, community development, community participation, social planning and horizontal coordination which are so essential in rural communities (Poole and Daley, 1985, p.342). Staff seem to either do these in their own time or not at all.

Horizontal accountability is absolutely essential although it is ignored by most government funding bodies. If we are serious about communities 'owning' services then community organisations need the freedom to be responsive and accountable to local as well as vertical demands. The degree of control which central funding bodies have in relation to rural organisations is limited anyway. They are usually too far away to know the details of what is happening at the periphery and too under-resourced themselves to enforce strict adherence to accountability procedures. Moreover, threats of funding withdrawals can sound hollow in relation to relatively minor inefficiencies and misdemeanours in a community organisation which is providing services that the community simply cannot do without.

Accountability requirements are frequently too complex and too demanding for small community-based organisations (ACOSS, 1994, p.10; OND, 1994, p.6). Stipulating the same reporting requirements, regardless of the size and conditions of the grant or the level of agency resources, is unfair to small agencies (Industry Commission, 1994a, p.176). As ACOSS (1994, p.10) commented, "... the same reporting requirements can apply to a one-off $5,000 grant and an ongoing grant of $400,000 a year". Small rural organisations lack the time and resources, and frequently also the skills, to devote to complex accountability requirements. For instance, Collingridge (1991, p.4) cited the example of the funding body which required monthly returns from a small rural agency thereby forcing it to redirect limited resources away from direct client services in order to employ a book-keeper.

The Industry Commission (1994a, p.31) has called for accountability rules to be simplified and for funding bodies to provide staff of community-based organisations with adequate resources, training and consultation so that they are better equipped to properly account for funds. The Commission also noted that requirements are often inconsistent between, and even within, the same government departments. They frequently overlap, are ill-defined and require unnecessary and incompatible detail, much of which is not used by the funding body anyway (ACOSS, 1994, p.10). Accountability rules are also frequently inconsistent with other statutory reporting requirements such as those associated with being a registered charitable organisation (Industry Commission, 1994a, p.31).

To summarise, we need simple, clear, streamlined and less frequent reporting requirements which relate directly to funding guidelines, to the socio-cultural contexts and expectations of communities being served, and to the functions which rural organisations actually have to perform. They should be focused on outcomes and recognise accountability of services to users and their communities. There should also be greater consistency amongst programs and funding bodies, although this should not result in increased standardisation or inflexibility. Furthermore, smaller organisations and smaller grants should not be subjected to the same reporting requirements as larger ones, and staff of small organisations should be provided with the necessary training and resources to fulfil accountability requirements. Above all else, the importance of horizontal accountability must be affirmed in funding rules, accountability requirements and organisational structures and policies.

Staffing

A number of studies have reported that rural human service organisations frequently suffer staff recruitment and retention difficulties resulting in high turnover, interruptions to service continuity and reduced effectiveness (e.g., Morton, 1990, p.37; Dale, 1994, p.331). Reasons for recruitment difficulties identified by the ACSWC (undated, pp.53-61) include:

- the urban orientation and preferred lifestyles of most Australians;
- professionalisation of services, which limits the recruitment pool;
- until recently, the inaccessibility of social care training to rural people;
- funding uncertainties for community-based organisations and their inability to provide viable career paths for staff; and
- especially in government departments, career disadvantages associated with rural practice.

Reports also suggest that it is often difficult to retain practitioners in rural areas, although empirical evidence is hard to find. In a study currently in progress, Lonne (1996) has found that 39 per cent of his sample of almost 200 social workers who had commenced a new rural position within the previous two years had left within the first 12 months. 67 per cent of these had left earlier than they had intended when they first took up the position. Of those who had anticipated staying longer than 12 months, 40 per cent had stayed for a shorter period than they had originally intended. Clearly, according to these data, turnover of social workers is high.

There are a number of reasons for high staff turnover in rural human service organisations. Many rural practitioners work in unsatisfactory conditions due to large and increasing workloads, limited budgets, unavailability of relief staff, infrequent administrative supervision, lack of access to professional consultation and continuing education opportunities, and demanding travel requirements (ACSWC, undated, pp.53-61). Some find their careers languishing in government departments which provide greater opportunities for advancement in central offices. It certainly does not help staff retention or morale when local personnel are overlooked for supervisory and management positions in regional offices which are used as 'testing grounds' for promising central staff or as 'dumps' for those no longer required in head offices. As we shall see in Chapter 8, some practitioners find it difficult to cope with the special demands of generalist practice and the stresses associated with living and working in the same community (Cheers, 1991; Munn, 1993). Some leave for personal reasons including their wish to be closer to family and friends, their children's educational and other interests, their partner's employment and career prospects, and lifestyle preferences such as access to quality theatres and restaurants (ACSWC, undated, p.53). Furthermore, some practitioners in community-based organisations find themselves unable to work with managers and management committees whose values are different from their own and which may even be at odds with the fundamental aims and values of their profession.

Service Designs

Experimentation with rural service designs over the last fifteen years has yielded a surprisingly large number of viable models, each of which is suited to different situations[2]. Table 7.1 presents the models addressed in the following discussion. The fundamental distinction is between *central point* services which emanate from a specific geographic location and *network* services which are not fixed in space.

Central Point Services

Central point services can adopt an *out-reach* model where services go to users or an *in-reach* approach where users go to services. *Out-reach* services reduce access costs and inconvenience for users but increase expenses and travelling for the service organisation. *In-reach* services do the opposite, in the process transferring financial and other costs from the service organisation to users. Consequently, *in-reach* services work well in larger towns located in densely-populated hinterlands but are usually only available to town residents and people living close by. On the other hand, *out-reach* approaches are a more effective way of extending services to smaller and more remote population centres and scattered populations.

Out-reach Services Out-reach services can either be provided by service personnel *visiting* clients where they live, such as mobile counselling for farmers (Lifeline, 1992), or through a *satellite* outpost in a small town which, in theory, is more accessible to people in outlying areas than a central office in a regional centre (Poole and Daley, 1985). For example, a *satellite* child protection service could be made available once each fortnight at the local hospital. The further a service travels to get to users, the less costly and time consuming it is for them and the more so it is for the provider. However, given equal resources, fewer clients can be serviced as more staff time is devoted to travelling. Thus, while mobile services have the advantage of providing a full face-to-face service, satellite offices can probably assist more people given the same resources.

As with all approaches, *visiting* services can either be *specialised* or *multi-purpose*. Whereas the *specialist* provides a single service such as psychological assessment, *multi-purpose* programs provide a range of services including, for example, financial, personal and family counselling, organising home care for aged family members, and assistance with applying for income security benefits. *Multi-purpose* services extend the widest possible range of assistance to users in the most cost-effective way, thereby reducing service gaps. By providing a range of services in one visit they can also reduce costs for the overall service network. Furthermore, because they relate to a number of different social care sectors, *multi-purpose* services are well placed to link users with a wide range of more *specialised* services. The main weakness of *multi-purpose* services is that they lack advanced expertise in specialised areas, although this can be obtained through other support services (Martinez-Brawley and Delevan, 1991). For this reason, *visiting multi-purpose* services are usually provided either in relation to issues which do not require highly specialised skills or through teams of *visiting specialists*. As the latter is an expensive option it is usually reserved for *satellite* rather than *visiting* services. Most *visiting multi-purpose* services in Australia either provide information and referral exclusively or in combination with brief general counselling for issues which can be handled in one or two visits. These are described as *generic* services in Table 7.1. The other kind of *visiting multi-purpose* service provides a *brokerage* function which, in Australia, usually means that the practitioner actively organises services for the client, frequently in relation to home and community care (Williams and McMahon, 1995, p.36). *Brokerage* is especially useful for isolated people who live fairly close to, but not in, towns which have the required services.

Satellite services are located in smaller outlying settlements. They go some way towards reducing access costs for users and service providers while providing a personalised face-to-face service. They can be provided either *occasionally* by visiting central office staff or on an *ongoing* basis by staff who live locally. For reasons which will be discussed in Chapter 8, the latter is usually preferable. Because of low local demand and the high costs associated with *specialised satellite* services, these are usually provided on an *occasional* basis. Research has shown that *occasional satellite* services are most effective when they link with an existing ongoing front-line service which can provide a certain level of help when required and which links clients with *visiting specialists* (Blacksell, Clark, Economides and Watkins, 1988). The relationship between the *Royal Flying Doctor Service* and remote area hospitals is a good example of this arrangement. Whilst the remote area nurse provides an ongoing local health care service, the Flying Doctor visits most hospitals on a regular basis to provide more advanced diagnosis and treatment. Furthermore, the doctor is always available for consultation by the nurse who remains the key access point to the health care system for residents. *Occasional multi-purpose satellite* services are also frequently used in Australia. For the most part, they provide information, referral, advice and community education.

There are two kinds of *ongoing specialised satellite services - integrated* and *unintegrated*. An *integrated* service is provided as part of the usual services of another local organisation and, ideally, is supported by visiting back-up specialists. For example, school teachers in a small country town might receive special training so that they are equipped to advise parents on child development difficulties. In smaller towns, specialised functions such as these are frequently performed by front-line professionals anyway, even though they don't have the required expertise, simply because *specialised* services are not available. This suggestion was supported in a recent study of informal social support in remote areas of Queensland where I found that, because they could not access specialised services, many parents chose to discuss child development problems with local school teachers and remote area nurses rather than other residents or even child development specialists located in regional centres (Cheers, 1992b, pp.516-8). In contrast with *integrated* services, *unintegrated ongoing specialised satellite* services stand alone. They are relatively rare in the more remote regions because of high *per capita* service costs.

Ongoing specialised satellite services are rare because of high service costs, low levels of local demand and, as discussed earlier, community expectations that practitioners will provide generalist services regardless of what their duty statements stipulate. *Ongoing multi-purpose satellite* services, on the other hand, are an important component of rural, especially remote area, personal social care service networks. *One-stop*

Table 7.1: Service Designs

Central Point Models:	Out-reach:	Visiting:	Specialised Multi-purpose	Generic Broker
		Satellite:	Occasional:	Specialised Multi-purpose
			Ongoing:	Specialised: Integrated Unintegrated Co-location Service hubs Combined services funding Generic services
				Multi-purpose:
	In-reach:	Face-to-face:	Specialised Multi-purpose	Co-location Service hubs Pooled funding Generic services

Formal Personal Social Care 197

Table 7.1: Service Designs (continued)

Electronic:	Specialised	
	Multi-purpose	
Network Models:	Created relationships:	Mutual aid networks
		Volunteers
	Embedded relationships:	Key helpers: Role-related
		Natural
		Personal networks: Direct intervention
		Resourcing
Circuit		
Facilitating informal support		

Shops, *Rural Agents* and *Rural Youth Access Centres* are examples of these.

There are four kinds of multi-purpose arrangements. At the lowest level of integration, *co-location* occurs when a number of human services are placed in the same building or in close physical proximity to each other (ACSWC, undated, p.33). *Co-location* provides the opportunity to increase inter-service coordination, strengthen cross referral processes and reduce overheads. Another multi-purpose arrangement, *service hubs*, was recommended by Morton (1990, p.39). This entails attaching small services to larger locally-based infrastructures such as hospitals and schools. For example, community health, counselling, disability, rehabilitation and home care services could be attached to a country hospital. Because they are attached to larger infrastructures which are owned by the community *service hubs* have the potential to enhance coordination and cross-referral and to increase community acceptance and the credibility of small scale services. More thoroughly integrated *multi-purpose* services were discussed earlier in relation to *combined services funding* models. In these, an organisation is funded to provide a variety of services according to client needs and local priorities. Finally, in a truly *generic* service, practitioners provide a holistic service to individuals and families.

In-reach Services In-reach services require users to go to the service, either through travelling or through various electronic media. Given Australia's rural settlement patterns, the term should be reserved for services which are located in major regional or urban centres. They can be either *specialised* or *multi-purpose*. The four kinds of *multi-purpose* service models - co-location, service hubs, pooled funding and generic services - were discussed earlier in relation to *out-reach* services. Advantages of *face-to-face in-reach* services include cost savings for service organisations and funding bodies and the fact that they can develop close working relationships with other organisations in the same place. Because of their location, they can also have more success than *satellite* services in attracting appropriately qualified staff. Their main weakness is that access is costly and difficult for people in outlying areas. Despite this, people in some remote places actually prefer going to services in regional rather than satellite centres when, from their perspective, both are more or less equally distant. For instance, in one study, people in a remote town in North Queensland said that they preferred to go to Cairns for many services rather than *satellite* offices in Atherton because: they go there every so often anyway; they can avoid accommodation costs by staying with friends; they would rather deal directly with the decision makers rather than go through subordinate satellite staff; and the extra hardships and costs involved in travelling the extra distance are minimal (Cheers, 1992b, pp.478-9). From their perspective, having got to the *satellite* centre over 400km of tough roads, the additional 100km on a good sealed road seemed trivial.

However, *in-reach* services are not a solution in emergency situations, such as youth suicide or domestic violence, where a rapid response and the physical presence of a skilled practitioner are required. For these, services need to link with rural people through various *out-reach* programs.

Rural people can access some *in-reach* services through *electronic media* such as telephones, video facilities and, more recently, computers (Clark, 1994, p.28; Lundin and Arger, 1994). In Australia, telephones, video conferencing and computer access are most commonly used for information, referral and emergency services. *008* numbers are now in wide use across Australia. They provide rural people with information and refer them to other sources of assistance. Despite the reservations of some rural practitioners they are better than nothing and can, in some situations, help them negotiate the government service maze. However *008* numbers can be frustrating when callers can't access services to which they are referred. Call-in services which provide counselling and referral have also been introduced in recent years. These, too, are useful although, as with *008* numbers, their existence should not be used as a rationale for withholding or withdrawing on-the-ground services. It is well established that crisis telephone counselling can help avert some personal tragedies such as youth suicide. But where there is no possibility of follow-up, as is the case in many rural areas, it is a temporary measure only. Most emergencies will re-occur unless more substantial assistance is available.

Video conferencing has recently opened up many possibilities in relation to *specialised* services such as counselling, psychological testing, psychiatric assessment and remedial education (Lundin and Arger, 1994). Unfortunately, though, the social care sector has been slow to take advantage of these facilities. Through video conferencing, more complex information can be provided to users, and specialised assessment and consultation can be made available to generalist out-reach practitioners. Video conferencing also provides the immediate, spontaneous face-to-face interaction with visual and auditory cues which is so essential in personal and family counselling.

The main barriers to the more widespread use of video conferencing are its cost and user access to facilities. Costs can be reduced by sharing equipment amongst service organisations and through pooled funding arrangements. In some places, telecentres are making the technology more available to users, although access is limited to people living nearby and to those who know how to use the equipment (Lawrence and Share, 1993, p.7). In other places, people in need of social care could be provided with access to equipment in government offices such as schools, hospitals and local government offices (Cheers, 1992b, p.565). Computer technology can also be used to reduce access difficulties. However, without the visual component, its use is restricted to information giving, education and interaction which does not require extensive dialogue or intensive personal interaction. It is also most efficient with simple content and where only two sites are required. On the other hand, because access via computer is not limited to times when the service is operating it is more responsive to user availability and, depending on how it is used, can be cheaper than telephone calls.

Network Care

Network care is not fixed in space. It can be provided in two ways: through *circuit* services and through *informal caring arrangements*.

Circuit Services These are more or less continually on the road. One example is George and Willi Smith's mobile counselling service in Western Australia (1987). Successful *circuit* services come to be accepted by residents as part of a region's infrastructure and, for this reason, are well utilised. They can provide people in isolated situations with an ongoing source of help and a doorway into the wider service network. In the process of providing assistance they accumulate a great deal of information about local conditions which is essential for effective service delivery and which can be fed back to organisations based in larger centres. However, *circuit* services have difficulty responding quickly to emergency situations and can be impeded by adverse climatic and geographic conditions. They must be supported by an efficient contact system for users and good publicity about the service, including emergency contact details and information about when it will be where.

Informal Care The other kind of *network care* involves formal service organisations activating, facilitating, supporting and utilising (or 'linking with') *informal* social care processes. *Informal* care is provided by private individuals such as relatives, friends and neighbours. It can also be provided by organisations, such as sporting clubs, which exist for reasons other than providing social care.

As with urban residents, we know that regardless of who they are, the social, emotional, material and physical well-being of rural people is closely related to the accessibility, availability and strength of their informal social care networks (e.g., Lorenz, Conger, Montague and Wickrama, 1993; Ganguli, Gilby, Deaberg and Belle, 1995; McCullough, 1995; Cheers, 1997). But generalisations such as this are not enough. To link services with informal supports we also need to know where different kinds of people living in various types of communities go for help with different kinds of problems and what the outcomes are. Unfortunately, there are very few studies which examine all these factors simultaneously (Cheers, 1997).

The following conclusions about the supports of rural people are based on two reviews of relevant research (Cheers, 1992b, pp.469-540, 1997). First, most people use both formal services and informal supports (Taylor, Chatters and Mays, 1988; Martinez-Brawley and Blundall, 1989). Indeed, the research indicates that the two sectors frequently support each other. While resources from the formal sector can help people take maximum advantage of their informal support networks, informal sources can provide a gateway into, and reinforce the work of the formal sector (Goodfellow, 1983; Scott and Roberto, 1985). Second, the natural support networks of rural residents tend to be larger and stronger than those of their urban counterparts (e.g., Kivett, 1985; Scott and Roberto, 1987; Mercier, Paulson and Morris, 1988; Romans, Walton, Herbison and Mullen, 1992). Third, amongst natural supports, rural people generally prefer to seek help from close friends and relatives rather than more superficial acquaintances (Goodfellow, 1983; Scott and Roberto, 1985; Taylor *et al.*, 1988). More specifically, for needs which are deeply personal and/or socially stigmatising, such as relationship, emotional and financial problems, people prefer to seek help from only their closest kin and friends in the first instance, regardless of how far away they may be (Kivett, 1983; Taylor *et al.*, 1988). They also prefer close kin and friends for more practical kinds of assistance which tend to create high dependency on the support, such as accommodation or full-time continuing child care. On the other hand, for needs which are minor and those requiring immediate physical accessibility to the support, such as watching over the home during vacations or borrowing minor household items, people will settle for help from others who live close by, but with whom they have more superficial relationships (Kivett, 1983; Taylor *et al.*, 1988).

The extent to which source proximity influences support seeking is an important issue for rural research, especially in the more remote areas. Most studies have concluded that proximity is a significant influence for rural people although, unfortunately, almost all of these have implied, rather than directly confirmed, the hypothesis (e.g., Bates, Clarke and Bertsche, 1980; Cotterell, 1984; Scott and Roberto, 1985; Kivett, 1988; Mercier *et al.*, 1988). In a more direct study, Fischer (1982) concluded that rural and urban Californians preferred natural supports who lived nearby when being close at hand was critical in the situation, and that they were more likely to turn to their closest intimates no matter where they live in "... situations involving the most intimacy, sacrifice and faith" (p.175).

Contrary to popular mythology, rural people do not generally prefer to seek help from other local people rather than non-local associates (e.g., Fischer, 1982, pp.56-61; Cheers, 1992b, pp. 469-540), they do not generally prefer informal to formal social care arrangements (Martinez-Brawley and Blundall, 1989; Cheers, 1992b, pp.469-540) and, as discussed below, local key helpers do not always exist in rural communities (Cheers, 1997).

Overall, then, informal social care is a highly complex and individual phenomenon. There is now a large body of evidence suggesting that where rural people go for help and how effective the help is depends on a combination of factors (e.g., Kelley and Kelley, 1985, p.363; Patterson, Germain, Brennan and Memmott, 1988, p.278; Cheers, 1992b, pp.535-40, 1997; Williams and McHugh, 1993, pp.2-4). These include:

- the nature of the problem;
- the type of help being sought;
- characteristics of the help seeker and the support source;
- the nature of their relationship;
- the relative accessibility of various potential supports;
- their availability at the time;
- whether direct physical accessibility is important for the need in question; and

- other environmental factors such as the availability of transportation, the cost of long-distance telephone calls and, in some places, geographic and climatic conditions.

The foregoing conclusions were supported and extended in a recent study of small remote towns in North Queensland (Cheers, 1992b, pp.534-40, 1997). What is significant about this study is that all respondents were living more than 500km from the nearest sizeable town, and most of them more than 500km from many or all of their informal supports. Overall, most people preferred to seek help from formal services for problems which are generally believed in Australian society to require specialised assistance such as health and education issues, those which are highly stigmatised such as destitution, and those for which they believed society has an obligation to provide assistance such as income security. Some residents were prepared to seek help for these kinds of problems over vast distances while for others, such as child development problems, they were prepared to make do with relevant local professionals such as school teachers, even though they did not have specialised training. For intimate personal issues such as social, emotional and family problems, respondents overwhelmingly preferred to seek help from close kin or friends. Where these did not live locally, they were prepared to traverse vast distances to seek their help either by travelling or through expensive telephone calls. Respondents also preferred to seek assistance from close kin and friends for needs which place large demands on supports, such as emergency accommodation and long-term child care. As with intimate problems, many were prepared to travel vast distances to seek this help or, alternatively, to meet the costs involved in bringing a support into their home. For example, couples would fly a grandmother to town to help look after the home and children for prolonged periods when the mother was too ill to do so. Finally, respondents who did not have close kin or friends living locally were prepared to seek help from other residents for minor impersonal issues, such as occasional child care, for which physical proximity is important and which are not demanding of supports.

The main lesson to be learned from studies such as this is that we cannot make assumptions about informal support processes in any rural community or in relation to specific individuals. We must assess each situation on its merits.

In relation to service models, the central question concerns how formal services can relate to informal social care. In this context, there are two kinds of informal support processes: those *created* by formal service organisations and those *embedded* in people's natural social environments[3]. *Created* relationships include *mutual aid networks* and client relationships with *volunteers*. In rural areas, *mutual aid networks* are useful for people who are socially and geographically isolated and for people at risk who need a lifeline to the outside world (Kelley and Kelley, 1985, p.358). The former includes parents of young children on remote properties, youth in small settlements who lack local peers, and geographically or socially isolated aged people. People who need a lifeline include those suffering serious ill-health, such as heart problems, or who face other dangers such as domestic violence. As indicated in Chapter 2, until recently the 'party line radio' provided a medium through which spontaneous *mutual aid networks* could operate throughout rural Australia. Its demise has meant that networks created by service organisations are now more necessary than ever before. Roles of formal service organisations in relation to *mutual aid networks* usually include initiating, facilitating and resourcing them.

In rural Australia, *volunteers* do a wide range of things for people who lack other supports such as providing company, transportation and meals; helping with home maintenance; and generally maintaining contact with those who are at social, emotional or physical risk. Formal services have a vital role to play in selecting, training, resourcing, supervising and allocating tasks to *volunteers*.

Embedded relationships occur within personal environments. *Key helpers* are people from whom a number of other community members seek help. They can be *role-related*, in the sense that they occupy a formal position which brings them into contact with people with problems, or *natural* in that the help they give is unrelated to any formal positions they occupy. Contrary to popular mythology, the evidence suggests that *key helpers* exist in some communities (e.g., Roberts and Thorsheim, 1982; Martinez-Brawley and Blundall, 1989, p.515) but not in others (e.g., Kelley and Kelley, 1985, pp.361-2; Cheers, 1992b, pp.484-8, 1997). In general terms, they seem to be important in communities which have existed for a long time, and in those which have low population turnover (Cheers, 1992b), strong and extensive local kin networks (Bates *et al.*, 1980; Martinez-Brawley and Blundall, 1989) and where the church is a key institution (Eakins and Kleven, 1988; Martinez-Brawley and Blundall, 1989). *Role-related key helpers* include, for example, school teachers, sports coaches and bar attendants. Formal organisations can support their social care functions by identifying who they are in a given community, training them, and providing specialised back-up through consultation and information about services and resources.

Natural key helpers simply help a lot of other people. For example, early in my social work career I met a woman in Woolloomooloo in Sydney who was an important source of help for other marginalised people in the area. Rita was a pensioner who helped others in her own home. She had excellent counselling skills and an extensive library of material relating to income security provisions, housing assistance and a variety of personal social care services. She asked me to act as a consultant for her casework and as an additional source of information for her 'clients'. Over time, we referred many people to each other. These are just some of the ways in which formal service personnel can support *natural key helpers*. They can also be provided with training and resources for their work. However, we have to be careful not to change or reconstruct their natural helping talents, understanding of community life or wisdom about how to help their neighbours so that they conform to prevailing bureaucratic or professional paradigms.

People also receive help from their *personal social networks* including kin, friends and neighbours. Formal services can facilitate these spontaneous caring processes by encouraging clients to use them and by participating in them directly as we often do in family therapy and traditional casework. However, we can also provide resources to facilitate them without ever becoming directly involved (Cheers, 1992b, pp.541-83). For example, social care organisations may subsidise telephone calls from a low-income depressed woman on an isolated property to her close friend in Perth 1,000km away. Or they might provide a stressed man with access to telephone or videophone facilities at a local school, hospital or shire council office so that he can talk to his mate in Cairns. Similarly, financial assistance could be provided so that a mother in Burketown can take her children to her own mother in Mt Isa while she recovers from illness. Or, alternatively, resources might be provided to help bring her mother to town to help look after the children. Furthermore, tax concessions or direct financial assistance could be made available for low-income private enterprise families to employ extra staff so that a husband is freed from business commitments to care for his children and his sick wife. Assistance such as this would be invaluable for low-income people in areas where it is not feasible to establish services and where visiting services either don't exist or are too infrequent to be useful. It helps to provide a measure of social justice to people who are deprived of public services which are normally available to urban people in similar situations.

Clearly, there are a number of strategies which formal organisations can use to support *informal* caring processes. Which to use when must be determined by an accurate assessment of the particular situation. While we should be cautious about reconstructing *informal* caring according to dominant professional ideologies and paradigms, these strategies can also help provide a socially just share of social care resources for people who live in areas which are rarely reached by formal services.

The most important lesson from this review of rural service designs is similar. Which strategies to use when, and in which combinations, should be based on a thorough understanding of the options available as well as precise information concerning the needs and characteristics of the particular community and target group being served. It should not be based upon popular mythology.

Coordination and Integration

Much of the discussion thus far relates to individual services, agencies and funding programs. A key strategy for improving rural social care is to bring some organisation into the currently chaotic and fragmented array of funding programs and services (Centacare, 1993, p.ii; Industry Commission, 1994a, pp.297-304; OND, 1994, p.92).

A number of factors have exacerbated the chaos over the last two decades. Government funding and service programs have proliferated because of the increasing dominance of programatic, rather than integrated, approaches to social care (Walsh, 1993, p.7). Programatic approaches have gathered momentum in response to the demands of an increasing number of special interest lobby groups and their growing political influence, and because more public attention is now being paid to social issues. Community-based organisations have also expanded dramatically in number and diversity, partly because of ideological shifts towards user participation, and increasing demands for local control over decision making and community involvement in service provision (Walsh, 1993, pp.7-8). The trend has been further influenced by some growing economic, political and public administration problems including the national fiscal crisis, problems which governments and government departments face in maintaining legitimacy, and the growing difficulties involved in governing in an increasingly complex world (Fine, 1995, p.144). Put simply, by devolving responsibility to communities and their organisations, governments can reduce social care expenditure, side-step the problem of statutory legitimacy and offload some of the responsibilities (and blame) associated with governing. Consequently, we now have many small, poorly-resourced and overloaded, single-purpose, community-based organisations, each providing partial services to a few people according to narrow and rigid guidelines in a financially insecure environment (OND, 1994, p.90; Fine, 1995, pp.144-5).

Confused geographic administrative boundaries complicate the picture still further. Government departments frequently use different regional boundaries, thereby exacerbating the difficulties associated with user access, service publicity, referral and coordination (DPMC, 1992, p.32). Furthermore, access costs increase for users and service providers alike when administrative boundaries do not coincide with regional telephone zonings or integrate with major transportation routes. Where they do not coincide with ABS statistical boundaries it can be impossible to obtain complete regional demographic profiles and cross-regional comparisons of relative disadvantage. What we need is a standard national grid of administrative regions which coincides with local government boundaries, ABS statistical divisions, major transportation routes, settlement patterns, existing communities of common interest between neighbouring local government areas, traditional social, political and economic connections, regions with which people identify and natural geographic formations, roughly in that order (Smith, 1993, p.13; OND, 1994, p.84). In the past, State boundaries were one barrier to developing such a grid (McDonald and Bullis, 1991, p.8). However, progress is now being made on this issue in places such as central Australia, north-west Australia and the Albury-Wodonga region.

One way to bring order into fragmented service networks is to improve the relationships between the pieces (Centacare, 1993, pp.16-7; Industry Commission, 1994a, pp.297-304; OND, 1994, pp.89-107; DPMC, 1995, p.31). They can be interrelated either through:

- *integration*, which involves amalgamating components into the one structure; or
- *coordination*, which involves interrelating the components more closely together.

Integration and coordination can be thought of as lying along an *interrelationship continuum* with fragmentation at one end, integration at the other and coordination somewhere around the middle. Furthermore, components of service networks can be interrelated in five domains:

- *direct service provision* by front-line practitioners;
- *infrastructure* - staff, funds, buildings, facilities, equipment, transport, management information systems and databases;
- *management structures* - organisational structures and management processes;
- *funding* - models, guidelines, regulations and accountability procedures; and
- *service planning*.

Each domain can be thought of at horizontal and vertical levels as these were defined in Chapter 3. Accordingly, components can be interrelated more closely:

- within each domain at each level, which gives us ten possible arenas; or
- through more comprehensive models which incorporate all domains and both levels.

Tables 7.2 and 7.3 present examples of coordination and integration mechanisms for each domain within the horizontal and vertical spheres. For three reasons, it is neither possible nor desirable to recommend generally preferred options. First, we know very little about how these mechanisms work under different conditions in rural Australia. Second, as argued throughout this book, coordination/integration packages should be determined in relation to each region. But this does not mean that they should be decided and imposed by government planners, no matter how regionally relevant they may be. In keeping with the theme of local ownership, the crucial questions which planners now face concern how to maximise participation rather than the design details of specific service packages. To this end, they should be ensuring that:

- local decisions about preferred packages are made;
- there is broad local participation;

- local people are in control of service planning and service provision;
- decision-making structures are put in place locally and within government; and
- decisions made locally are binding on all organisations servicing the region.

The third reason why generally preferred mechanisms cannot be recommended is that the structure of formal social care in Australia places limits on how much coordination/integration can be achieved and the feasibility of various mechanisms. There are many such constraints. For instance, Australia will continue to have three levels of government although there may be some scope for local government to increase its role in social care networks (ACOSS, 1993a, p.iv; Madden, 1993). At Commonwealth and State levels, a number of government departments will continue to be involved in social care and each will continue to compete with others for resources and jurisdictional power (McDonald and Bullis, 1991, p.6). Furthermore, our categorical service system will not suddenly disappear although it can be modified by strategies reviewed earlier such as pooled funding arrangements and multi-purpose organisations.

Analysing coordination and integration in relation to specific dimensions, as we have done thus far, fails to capture the big picture. It ignores the fact that fragmentation runs throughout the entire formal rural social care network. Although analysis might help to identify strategies in relation to discrete sections of the total network, a more holistic perspective is needed if we are to find comprehensive solutions for what is, after all, a comprehensive problem.

As usual, it helps to think at horizontal and vertical levels. For reasons given throughout this book, we should also adopt a community (or regional) perspective. All relevant reports - government and non-government alike - have recommended that in each region there should be some kind of recognised representational structure which is responsible for coordinating social development[4] and service provision (e.g., Morton, 1990, pp.v-vi; Industry Commission, 1994a, pp.297-304; OND, 1994, p.83; Cheers, 1995, pp.18-20). Some reports focus on the structure's role in funding, some on planning and some on coordination. Reports disagree about whether it should be wedded to local government (Reynolds, undated, pp.15-6; Morton, 1990, pp.v-vi) or independent of all government structures (Schindeler, 1993, p.11; OND, 1994, p.83).

Table 7.2: Examples of Horizontal Service Coordination and Integration Mechanisms

NETWORK DOMAIN	MECHANISMS
Direct Service Provision	*Coordination* • Ongoing interaction amongst practitioners. • Case coordination meetings. • Co-location of practitioners. • Service brokerage. • Shared, locally-based service publicity packages, and information dissemination mechanisms. • Locally-based single-point information, intake and referral processes. *Integration* • Generic (multi-skilled) front-line workers.
Infrastructure	*Coordination* • Co-locating local organisations and services. • Sharing databases and management information systems. *Integration* • Multi-purpose services and organisations supported by single-point pooled funding arrangements. • A unified database and management information system at the local level.
Management Structures	*Coordination* • A local umbrella/sponsoring organisation for community-based services. • A local service coordinating committee. • A regional managers committee or forum. *Integration* • Community-based management committees shared by a number of organisations.

Table 7.2: Examples of Horizontal Service Coordination and Integration Mechanisms (continued)

NETWORK DOMAIN	MECHANISMS
Funding	*Coordination* • A local representative peak organisation which receives and distributes funding through collective decision making. • Cooperative fund-raising. *Integration* • Block grants to local multi-purpose services and organisations through pooled or consolidated funding arrangements.
Service Planning	*Coordination* • A joint local planning committee. • A regional managers planning committee or forum. *Integration* • A unified and representative local planning organisation, such as a *Regional Council for Social Development* or a single umbrella/sponsoring organisation. Leadership could be provided either by local government or an autonomous representative organisation working in close partnership with local government.

Table 7.3: Examples of Vertical Service Coordination and Integration Mechanisms

NETWORK DOMAIN	MECHANISMS
Direct Service Provision	*Coordination* • A single-point telephone information and referral service. • A regionally-focused cross-service, cross-organisation publicity package. • Externally-based specialists visiting as a team. • Visiting practitioners participating in horizontal coordination strategies listed in Table 7.2. *Integration* • Visiting practitioners working closely with generic front-line workers to provide more integrated services.
Infrastructure	*Coordination* • Shared, regionally-focused databases. • Visiting practitioners participating in local co-location, resource-sharing and database arrangements. *Integration* • Visiting services participating in, and sharing the infrastructure costs of, local multi-purpose services.
Management Structures	*Coordination* • State-wide peak agencies coordinating local community-based organisations on a regional basis. • 'Lead' social care departments at State and Commonwealth levels. • A single agency covering both levels of government to provide regionally-focused leadership and coordination in the social care sector. • 'Clearing-house' offices at State and Commonwealth levels to coordinate rural social care across departments and review policies from all portfolios at that level. Conceivably, one national office could relate to both levels. • Externally-based organisations participating in local service coordinating committees and regional managers forums. *Integration* • Amalgamating rural social care functions into a single department or section at Commonwealth and State levels respectively. Theoretically, the one department could be established to cover both levels.

Table 7.3: Examples of Vertical Service Coordination and Integration Mechanisms (continued)

NETWORK DOMAIN	MECHANISMS
Management Structures (continued)	*Integration (continued)* • Within departments, amalgamating cross-program rural social care responsibilities into one division. • At the Commonwealth and State levels, a cross-department *Regional Social Development Commission* to integrate rural social care services at that level (see text). Conceivably, a single inter-government commission could perform this function for both levels. Commissions would be regionally focused and involve representation from rural local government and non-government organisations. • Vertical structures taking responsibility for developing and maintaining unified databases and management information systems. • Externally-based organisations participating in the horizontal integration mechanisms listed in Table 7.2.
Funding	*Coordination* • Regionally-focused cross-program, cross-department and inter-government committees to coordinate funding. • 'Lead departments' coordinating funding at Commonwealth and State levels, or one agency to cover both. • Within regions, funding allocations of externally-based organisations complying with locally-developed regional plans. *Integration* • Block grants to local multi-purpose services and organisations or to single regional umbrella organisations, with local autonomy to determine regional priorities and funding allocations. • Regionally-focused pooled funding arrangements: across programs within a single Commonwealth or State portfolio; across departments; across government levels. • A single unit to administer regionally-focused pooled funding: across programs within a single portfolio; across departments; across government levels. This would involve participation by local governments and community-based organisations.

Table 7.3: Examples of Vertical Service Coordination and Integration Mechanisms (continued)

NETWORK DOMAIN	MECHANISMS
Service Planning	*Coordination* • Cross-program, cross-department and inter-government committees to coordinate planning (see 'Coordinated Funding' section). • 'Clearing-house' rural policy and planning offices (see 'Coordinated Management Structures' section). • Externally-based organisations participating in horizontal planning processes (see Table 7.2). *Integration* • A single regionally-focused rural social care planning unit: across portfolios; across departments; across government levels. • This would include local government authorities, local community-based organisations and externally-based non-government organisations. • Externally-based planning, funding and service organisations participating in local planning structures.

Opinions also differ about whether social and economic development should be integrated into the same regional organisation (Cheers, 1995, pp.18-20) or whether they should remain structurally separate (Morton, 1990, pp.v-vi; Industry Commission, 1994a, pp.297-304). However, all agree that, in Australia, the regional social development structure (or a *Regional Council for Social Development*) should span a number of neighbouring local government areas (Madden, 1993, p.48; Saw, 1994, p.38) and comprise representatives of the three levels of government, local non-government organisations, service users and local residents. Reports also agree that these *Regional Councils* should provide leadership in relation to:

- assessing social needs within the region;
- prioritising needs;
- proposing services, resources and facilities;
- developing and maintaining a regional social plan;
- facilitating submissions for funding in accordance with the regional plan;
- making recommendations to funding bodies about priorities; and

- coordinating formal social care service provision and management at the local level and representing it within vertical structures.

Morton (1990, p.vi) also recommended that *Regional Councils* should maintain regional databases of existing social and demographic characteristics and of services, resources and facilities; and, where appropriate, sponsor or provide particular services.

Although regional social plans sound good in theory they are impotent unless government departments and non-government organisations can be compelled to adhere to them. For government departments will continue to fund local services according to other programatic, bureaucratic and political agendas, and non-government organisations will continue to seek funding wherever it lies, regardless of local plans. Moreover, by themselves, regional social development councils and social plans do little to organise the chaos at Commonwealth and State levels. Thus, although wide representation at the local level maximises horizontal legitimacy and accountability, the legislative power of a vertical structure is required to enforce local plans.

To resolve these problems some reports have recommended establishing one or more joint regional social development authorities (*Regional Social Development Commissions*), comprising representatives of government departments involved in social care, regional local governments, national and State-wide non-government organisations, smaller local community-based organisations and rural people (Centacare, 1993, pp.16-7; Industry Commission, 1994a, pp.297-304; Cheers, 1995, pp.18-20). The ideal seems to be a single authority which is the collective responsibility of Commonwealth and State governments, although it may be more realistic to aim at one in each State and Territory. The most comprehensive proposals (e.g., Cheers, 1995, pp.18-20) have recommended that the Commission should have the power to recognise *Regional Councils for Social Development*, legitimate their respective social plans for a specified period (say three years), and compel government departments to allocate social care funding within a region according to the local plan. Centacare (1993, pp.16-7) took the idea further, suggesting that *Commissions* should allocate all rural social care funding from a common national pool. Although this seems unrealistic, perhaps a Commission could be responsible for pooled funding arrangements and for encouraging the development of local multi-purpose services throughout rural Australia.

Concluding Comments

We now know enough, and there is now sufficient agreement about what is required, to make firm recommendations about how to improve the contribution of the formal sector to rural social care. Many specific suggestions have been made throughout this chapter, the most important of which seem to be the following.

- A national set of minimum standards for services, facilities and resources is urgently required.
- A national database of social care services should be developed and cross-tabulated with indices of relative regional disadvantage.
- Rural policy formulation and service planning should be regionally focused and based on integrated quantitative and qualitative information generated in consultation with local people.
- A number of successful innovative rural service and funding models have been developed on an experimental basis. The time has now come to adopt these more widely as key strategies in formal social care networks throughout rural Australia.
- Rural services and funding guidelines should be responsive to rural realities both generally and in relation to specific regions and communities. Furthermore, different service packages which best meet local needs should be developed for each region. As far as possible, these should be regionally, rather than program, based.
- Far greater effort needs to be made to integrate formal services with informal social care processes.
- Policies and protocols are needed which maximise the respective contributions of, and the potential for mutual support between, central structures and peripheral organisations.
- Because community-based organisations are an important way of expressing community they should be preserved as the key component of formal rural social care. However, they require more resources and support from, and closer working relationships with, funding authorities.
- Rural service organisations should focus on whole communities and address broader community issues as well as the needs of specific clients. They should also be funded to do this.

- Although advances have been made in recent years, rural people need more information about what is available and how to access it. Service publicity should be based on principles recommended from existing Australian research.
- Coordination/integration of formal rural social care networks should be regionally based and extend from there to State and national levels, rather than the other way round. In each region, a local representational structure should be responsible for developing a regional social plan. Plans should be supported and legitimated by vertical structures which have the power to enforce adherence to them by government and non-government service and funding organisations.

Notes

1. I am indebted to Judy Taylor, formerly of the Department of Families, Youth and Community Care (Townsville), for this information.
2. Useful reviews will be found in ACSWC (undated, pp.33-4), Smith (1987, 1989), Cheers (1992b, pp.96-8), Centacare (1993, pp.19-20) and OND (1994, pp.96-8).
3. This discussion draws substantially on Froland, Pancoast, Chapman and Kimboko (1981) and Cheers (1992b, pp.50-79, pp.541-68).
4. The term 'social development' is used here rather than 'social care development' because, traditionally, Australian planning structures at local, State and Commonwealth levels incorporate all community services as these were defined in Chapter 6. In the interests of integration this seems to be good practice.

8 Practice

In this chapter we examine how rural contexts affect social care practice. All the knowledge, theory and skills documented in mainstream literature and taught in generic education programs are available for use in rural practice. These are not reviewed here because they are readily available elsewhere. Nor is this a 'how to' primer. For while we can discuss knowledge, theory, techniques and strategies as abstract concepts, they are real only as they exist within the individual practitioner. There they lie in waiting as 'potentialities' to be actualised only when they inform or are expressed directly in practice. When applied, the form they take is determined by the professional's judgement and behaviour on the basis of her or his understanding of the practice situation. Practitioners are not merely 'knowledge applicators'. They are aware, feeling, thinking, reacting and creating human beings who make conscious and unconscious decisions according to their ideological frameworks, their predictions about what will happen if they do this or that, and their understanding of the situation at hand (Cheers, 1980).

Is rural practice different from urban? While studies have shown some differences the evidence remains unconvincing. For example, in their widely cited survey of social workers in North Carolina, York, Denton and Moran (1989) reported only two weak, though significant, results. First, social workers practicing in more rural areas were slightly less likely to act in a 'broker' role, involving "... guiding client systems toward existing services, helping them to negotiate the service system and/or linking components of the service system together" (p.205). The researchers also found that practitioners in larger communities were slightly more likely to use clients' informal networks in their work. Though weak, these correlations were in the opposite directions to what had been predicted.

However, this study can be criticised on a number of grounds. First, the survey focused on practitioners' perceptions of current practice. Inevitably, these would reflect the broader social care system. Second, it is doubtful whether mailed questionnaires can penetrate the complex issues involved in practice. Third, the response rate was only 25 per cent. Fourth, neither the study design nor the analysis controlled a number of crucial variables such as the practitioner's organisation and position within it. Consequently, urban-rural differences which depended on other variables could not be identified.

In Australia, Puckett and Frederico (1992) more or less replicated this study. In brief, they found that rural practitioners were more likely than urban to be involved in social planning, community development, management, research and community consultation and in utilising, establishing and supporting informal helping processes. They were also less likely to adopt 'clinical' roles in relation to individuals, families and small groups or to perceive intrapersonal or interpersonal conflict, reactive emotional distress, conflicts with formal organisations or resource deficiencies amongst their clients. But, as the authors pointed out, these differences could have resulted from the fact that the urban practitioners were overwhelmingly qualified social workers whereas most rural practitioners were not. Certainly, most differences disappeared in analyses which focused exclusively on social workers. Nor were results presented after controlling variables such as the practitioner's position and organisation. Because of design similarities, the study also suffered from similar methodological difficulties as the York et al. (1989) work.

Descriptive comparative studies such as these are unlikely to show major rural-urban differences because they are based on current work practices which are largely determined by prevailing social care structures, practitioners' world views, and paradigms emphasised in mainstream professional literature and education programs. In Australia, these are predominantly urbo-centric and emphasise uniformity of practice across contexts. While it is important to know about current practices, we also need to identify how rural practice *should* be different from urban.

Descriptive studies miss the heart of the matter. True to Western ideology they treat practitioners as if they float free of their social contexts. This may work for much of urban practice where practitioners spend their working hours dealing with people who they will never come across in other roles. But the assumption does not hold where they live in the same small community as their clients. Social care practice is not merely *influenced* by the rural context - practice, and practitioners are integral parts of that context. Practitioners relate with people personally and professionally. What they do, personally and professionally, affects how people view and respond to them. Some practitioners have local histories which are inseparable from those of their ancestors, partners, children and other local personal associates.

All practitioners relate to community norms, embracing some and rejecting others. They have feelings and opinions about their communities; and other residents have feelings and opinions about them. They and their 'clients' do not leave these at the door when they walk into the social care office. Nor do they leave behind what has transpired there.

Community-oriented Practice

Community-oriented frameworks for rural practice have developed in response to concerns such as these. *Community-oriented practice* is not a method, a theory or even a model. It is a frame of reference based on rural experiences in a number of countries including the United States (Martinez-Brawley, 1990b), the United Kingdom (Hadley and McGrath, 1984), Canada (Collier, 1984), Spain (Martinez-Brawley, undated), the Hebrides (Martinez-Brawley, 1986) and Australia (Cheers, 1992a). Community-oriented practice is an attitude which a practitioner has towards living and working in a rural community. Social care is viewed as an expression of community. It is as much the responsibility of ordinary people which arises from the mutuality of community living as it is the responsibility of formal service organisations. And it is as much an expression of everyday human relationships as it is a manufactured provision of formal societal structures (Martinez-Brawley, 1989, pp.5-6).

In community-oriented practice, the practitioner is part of the comprehensive network of mutuality which binds a community together. She or he is not, as Jones (1980, p.16) put it, an "... anonymous person from county hall, dropping in from outer space". The framework does not share the traditional emphasis on professional distance and the steadfast, but bizarre, separation between professional and personal 'selves'.

> The sharing process involved in real community living can enhance the social worker's credibility as a human being. ... Being in community represents a modification, if not a curtailment, of the degree of freedom for both the social worker and the client. Yet, the understanding and sharing that both parties experience by their mutual communal experience can enhance the professional relationship and the degree of satisfaction the social worker and client derive from the contact. (Martinez-Brawley, 1990b, p.45)

Practitioners are proactive. They do not simply sit in an office waiting for clients to visit or call for an appointment. They are out in the community, being visible, becoming known, learning of people in need, helping them, working their way into social and political networks and connecting people with each other. They are finding out about current and emerging social issues, participating in regional development activities, working with power brokers, organising committees and so on. They are part of the ongoing fabric of community life.

The mutuality of the practitioner's community involvement touches her or his work in many ways. For instance, a resident may help a neighbour as a personal favour to the social worker, a debt which in some way may be called in at some future time. In rural practice, boundaries between practitioners and clients become blurred and even reversed. On Monday the practitioner may be counselling a school principal about emotional problems while on Tuesday the principal is advising the social worker about her or his child's education. In the process, the practitioner becomes a real, visible person to other residents. Fenby's (1980) experiences are common amongst rural practitioners.

> The face that the professional puts on in the office is difficult to sustain as a discrete image in the rural community. Certainly the well-dressed, poised Ms Fenby at work is very different from the distraught lady, shoeless and in cutoffs, who tries to recapture an impish dog on the town's main street while holding up three school buses of laughing children. Yet both images are public, and the non-professional, neighbor image is reflected into the professional setting. (pp.149-50).

In a small community the professional cannot remain a mysterious, omnipotent social care expert. Knowledge and skills take their place alongside the social care wisdom of other residents. The practitioner must now enter into and understand local cultures and linguistic frameworks which may well be at odds with those into which she or he has been socialised, both personally and professionally.

> Perhaps even more of a problem to young professionals is the stark awareness that they have been socialized to the language, norms, and values of their profession and the age-status cohort to the extent that they may have become blind and deaf to the rich, varied, and intricate cultural mosaic that characterizes daily life in the small community. (Martinez-Brawley, 1990b, p.84)

As we saw in Chapter 4, rural communities have political dimensions. They are the location of power struggles, factional disputes, status hierarchies and oppression. Rural practitioners cannot insulate themselves from these as easily as they might in a cosy city office. What they say and do as professionals and as residents occurs within a political context and could have repercussions for their work, whether it be direct practice, community development or social action.

By definition, community-oriented social care is *preventive*. For where the practitioner is strengthening local bonds and encouraging ordinary people to care for each other the community is well placed to anticipate and respond to personal and community issues before they become major problems. Other residents are, for example, more likely to provide support and child care relief for a low-income sole parent with pre-school children before the situation becomes overwhelming.

Principles of community-oriented practice have entered professional knowledge primarily as documented practice wisdom rather than as conclusions of systematic research. This does not make them any the less valid or useful. They are grouped here into issues concerning:

- generalism;
- localism;
- professional and personal boundaries;
- confidentiality;
- community energising, conscientisation and politicisation;
- working with community power structures; and
- joining.

Generalism

Whatever their official functions, most rural practitioners have to be *generalists* (Collier, 1984, pp.58-65; Martinez-Brawley, 1987, pp.526-7). Because they are one of few professionals in the community, most use all the traditional methods at some time or another, including casework, group work, community work, policy development, social planning, research, management and consultation. They are expected by their communities to respond to a wide range of issues across most fields of practice. For example, the same practitioner may be required to counsel a suicidal young man, organise home care for an aged woman, chair a group seeking funding for a new child care service, act as treasurer for a women's shelter, evaluate a service for young people, and develop a social plan as part of an integrated local area planning process.

Generalism fits well with rural cultures. Lacking qualified people, country folk develop a variety of skills.

> People in rural communities do not categorise their lives along rigid bureaucratic lines of task specialisation. Rural people are more likely to be generalists in their everyday lives. ... By extension, the rural social worker ... is ... expected to help out in a variety of areas, ... [to] ... bring into focus, arrange and tap various systems and resources to resolve a problem. (Martinez-Brawley, 1990a, p.4)

Community-oriented practitioners are constantly devising new solutions to problems and situations for which they have not been prepared by professional education or in-service training programs. As with generalism, this fits well with rural cultures which expect people to improvise (Collier, 1984, pp.60-2). In a rural community, if you don't know how to do something, and there is no-one else around who does, then you simply have to do your best. Just as the lack of local specialised expertise has bred many bush mechanics and lawyers so, too, has it bred many bush social workers and community developers. Furthermore, as generalists rural practitioners have more freedom than specialists to respond to situations as they are because they are less constrained by standardised bureaucratic expectations and general professional edicts.

Rural practice tends to be *practical*. Practitioners frequently do not have administrative officers, clerical assistants or case aides to do the concrete tasks such as taking a child to school, helping an aged person with their shopping, or arranging teleconference time for a mutual aid group. The community expects them to 'muck in' - to help organise the fete, work on a street stall and assist with fund-raising. These are not necessary evils taking up valuable time which would be better spent exercising more sophisticated skills. Through activities such as these, practitioners become involved in community life and gain credibility with other residents. They are gaining access to local networks, to information about the community, and to people who have much to contribute to service provision, agency management and genuinely participative social development. They are also developing important links with local influentials who could be useful supports for social change.

Because they are generalists rural practitioners require a diverse knowledge base. Not only do they need some psychology, sociology and anthropology, they also need some understanding of geography, political science, economics, management and human service organisations. But, because no-one can be expert in all disciplines they should also cultivate relationships with other local specialists such as medical practitioners, nurses, teachers, local government professionals, accountants and lawyers. They should also maintain comprehensive databases of services and resources relevant to their communities.

Community-oriented practice is not merely an unfortunate, though necessary, diluted, eclectic version of specialised work. It is qualitatively different and has an integrity of its own. The approach takes its social and political purpose from social justice principles and is informed by a philosophy of holism at individual and community levels. It is based on defensible assumptions about human living, empirical knowledge of rural life, and interventions developed from the realities of the situation at hand.

Localism

Localism was discussed in Chapters 6 and 7 in relation to social planning, community development and service issues. In direct practice, *localism* means that practitioners inevitably focus more on the community in which they are embedded than the vertical structures and programs which are the world of central managers and urban specialists (Martinez-Brawley, 1990a, pp.9-13). It can be as difficult for rural practitioners to fathom the administrative context of many central decisions as it is for managers to comprehend the world of direct practice. This underlines the importance of practitioners actively representing community perspectives to central management and for managers to strive to understand local realities.

Localised practice responds to local needs, priorities and circumstances. For example, home care services and recreational resources would receive higher priority than residential facilities in a community where most aged people want to remain in their own homes.

Rural practice should also be *indigenous*, or individualised to the cultural and linguistic characteristics of the person or people with whom the practitioner is working (Martinez-Brawley, undated, p.6). Practice takes place within cultural frameworks which provide meaning to social issues and which suggest how they should be handled. For example, incarceration in detention centres will not help young Aboriginal offenders whose cultures interpret their behaviour to be the result of alienation from their own communities. It would be more useful to reconnect them with their cultures through re-absorption into their communities, indigenous role models and participation in cultural activities.

Indigenous practice also relates to people in culturally appropriate ways. This is why social care agencies should employ indigenous people as practitioners for their own cultures. Where this is not possible, non-indigenous practitioners should work with indigenous cultural and linguistic interpreters. The importance of understanding and behaving congruently with non-indigenous rural cultures is perhaps less obvious. For instance, I once had a rather poetic conversation with a male pastoralist with both of us hanging over the back of a Toyota 'ute' staring into the tray. Early in the conversation he made the following comment:

> Look mate; when I have problems I ask a gum tree what it thinks. If I don't get the answer I want from the first one I go to the second. I just keep going down the line until I hear something that makes sense.

I suggested that he might try this in relation to his current problems. A few days later we continued the conversation after he had consulted his eucalypt counsellors. One of them had given him a clue which, after we discussed it for awhile, became a solution to his situation. Men in his sub-culture do not often talk about their personal issues directly and they avoid direct eye contact while doing so. To 'go bush' for awhile to try to resolve personal issues alone is quite common. And they do some of their 'serious' talking with each other while hanging over the back of a Toyota, a fence or something similar.

Although indigenisation is important, it is not a license to acquiesce to all cultural interpretations. For while regional, cultural and, for that matter, national diversity must be fully recognised we cannot afford to let our commitment to this principle become one of the "... special lies that people tell themselves and each other to justify doing unjustifiable things" (Midgley, 1989, p.98). As Warnock (1967, p.60) observed:

> That it is a bad thing to be tortured or starved, humiliated or hurt, is not an opinion: it is a fact. That it is better for people to be loved and attended to, rather than hated or neglected, is again a plain fact, not a matter of opinion.

There are times when rural practitioners must challenge dominant cultural norms in the interests of the whole community and disempowered individuals and groups. For instance, social care practitioners cannot support the view that domestic violence or child abuse is acceptable. Nor can they agree that poor families should be ostracised. In dominant and disempowered cultures alike, normative structures are frequently historical products of internal oppression and usually make some contribution to its continuation (Booth, 1995, pp.114-5).

The idea of localism focuses all rural practitioners on shared community issues, even those who are employed primarily to help individuals and families. This broader focus on the community as a whole is important for a number of reasons. First, the evidence of rural disadvantage presented in Chapter 2 compels all practitioners to use their strategic location at the intersection of horizontal and vertical ties to advocate and fight for a better deal for their communities. In this respect, community-oriented practice takes us back to our roots - where there is obvious social injustice, we are obliged by the very meaning of our profession to try to reduce it. The second reason for maintaining a community focus is that many individual and family problems are produced by community dynamics. Clearly, when community factors are the cause, changing them should help resolve the problem. For instance, in one town a young woman told me that she was miserable and had lost interest in school work because she felt ostracised by her peer group. I knew from other information that this was true and was related to her new step-father being regarded as deviant by other residents. I told her this and mentioned the problem to her school teacher and the remote area nurse, who was an informal adviser for some of the local young women. The teacher organised interaction at school so that she was included and the nurse told a couple of the young woman's former friends about her plight and encouraged them to resume their relationships with her. They did so and her grades subsequently improved. A number of community dynamics were involved in this situation including local norms and definitions of deviance, the step-father's position as 'deviant' according to this culture, the lack of alternative local peer groups for the young woman because of the town's small size, the position of the nurse in relation to the peer group, and interactional dynamics at the school.

This example illustrates the use of community dynamics to change an individual's situation. It also illustrates the importance of rural social care practitioners integrating their practice with the life of the town. In reality, the practitioner is one carer amongst many, both formal and informal. The community-oriented practitioner seeks to understand and connect residents with local caring processes. An example comes from 'patch' work in the Barra and Vatersay districts on the North-west Scottish Isles.

> It is the responsibility of the patch worker to coordinate and energise local community informal systems and resources. The idea is that the patch worker will become known to those she serves, will capitalize on their strengths and generally tailor services to needs in very personal ways. In the Barra "patch", the social worker employed local home helpers from the community. She had developed a cadre of workers whom she had trained. Because she knew the elderly and the home helpers, she was able to place them close to their homes and with compatible personalities. What the elderly got was someone who looked after them in a personal way, who stopped by their houses even when they were not scheduled to work, etc. The home helpers often coordinated with other neighbors. All this resulted in a close and very supportive network of care. The social worker knew the mothers of young children who were feeling overwhelmed. She knew who needed a break from children but might enjoy caring for an elderly person a few hours a week; she knew who could cope with young children and who couldn't, etc. She could arrange many creative "switches of care" or "bartering of resources". (Martinez-Brawley, 1989, p.12)

Because they are located at the intersection of horizontal and vertical ties, rural practitioners are ideally placed to coordinate local and non-local services to individual residents. This should be fairly straightforward within a rural community because practitioners interact with each other constantly in both formal and informal settings. It is in relation to non-local services that coordination problems usually arise. Theoretically, the rural practitioner is well placed to coordinate the contributions of outside organisations to the lives of individual residents by referring people to them, briefing outside specialists about their situations, providing a continuing local service in consultation with non-local specialists, and advising external organisations of service gaps and duplications. Unfortunately, this is uncommon in Australia's current social care system. Full localisation is really only possible in administratively decentralised service systems where generalist rural practitioners who are integrated into their communities have the authority to orchestrate services.

Boundary issues

The genericism of rural practice, and the practitioner's embeddedness in community life give rise to boundary issues concerning distinctions between members of different professions and client-practitioner interaction (Collier, 1984, p.60; Martinez-Brawley, 1986, pp.362-3).

In rural areas, inter-professional boundary blurring has a number of origins. First, small organisations providing generic services, either by mandate or because of community expectations, tend to be more flexible than larger more specialised agencies with more rigid management structures, more comprehensive policies and a pool of related services to which they can refer clients. Consequently, rural practitioners are more likely than their urban counterparts to go beyond traditional professional role definitions and to accept that their local colleagues will do likewise. Second, it is commonplace for non-local specialised organisations to ask local practitioners to provide a continuing service in their absence, even though it might not fall strictly within professional or organisational role definitions.

The third reason for inter-professional boundary blurring concerns the absence of local specialised services. Where practitioners have special expertise through training, experience or aptitude their local colleagues are usually keen to refer people to them regardless of traditional professional and organisational role definitions. In a rural community it makes no sense to residents or to the practitioners themselves when the latter fail to utilise each other's skills. Where relationships within the local service network are built on mutual trust and respect, practitioners are happy to refer clients on the basis of their respective skills as well as traditional role definitions. This is usually the case as most are aware of how important it is to maintain good relationships given that they are so few in number, because they can provide each other with support and refuge from the high visibility of rural practice and because, like most residents, they have a commitment to their community which tends to override professional and organisational loyalties. In any case, they usually know each other socially as well as professionally.

The other boundary issue concerns the informality of many interactions between practitioners and residents. Early in my career, I learned on the streets of inner-city Sydney that the content of interaction with 'clients' is more important than its location, whether the interaction is planned, or its degree of 'formality' with regard to language and behaviour. Much was accomplished while lying in a park with a skid-row alcoholic early one Sunday morning, through chance meetings under the Sydney Harbour Bridge with homeless men, and while watching a football game with a young offender. During more recent rural travels, opportunities to help people have arisen while fishing with a young Aborigine on Cape York Peninsula, panning for gold with a prospector, and helping a young man fix his car. The flexibility which is inherent in generic work, the many opportunities which rural practitioners have for chance meetings with other residents, and their general embeddedness in community life mean that rural practice often occurs through informal interaction. Returning to social work in the Barra and Vatersay 'patch', Martinez-Brawley (1986, p.362) observed that:

> Theoretically, all cases were supposed to be formalized through the intake process. Yet, the social worker found herself providing informal services to individuals, particularly elderly residents, who did not wish to become cases and for whom formalization of the help would have been detrimental. The informal tasks she performed were often sporadic but very important, and helped those individuals maintain their integrity and independence.

Like rural practitioners everywhere, this social worker was anxious about the legitimacy of these activities within her Department. They are usually neither supported by official policies, recognised in accountability requirements nor allowed for in workload calculations. Rural practitioners everywhere know that their freedom to help people in this way, as well as their level of integration within the community which it represents, depends on the whims of central administrators and, in an unsympathetic managerial environment, their ability to keep these services secret.

Confidentiality[1]

Their embeddedness in community life presents some confidentiality dilemmas for rural practitioners. Four traditional assumptions concerning confidentiality are not always congruent with the realities of rural practice. These are that:

- confidentiality is a strictly dyadic issue between practitioner and client;
- information exchanged between them is not known in the public arena;

- the practitioner is accountable only to the client and her or his organisation; and
- we need concern ourselves with breaches of good faith, or trust, only in relation to our clients.

The rural practitioner is also accountable to, and must maintain good faith with community members who are related to the client's situation. For example, Martinez-Brawley (1990b, p.232) reported a situation where a minister of religion had referred a woman to a local social care organisation. Later, he encountered a social worker from the organisation at the local markets and enquired as to whether the woman had actually followed through with the referral. The minister became sufficiently irate to lodge an official complaint after he was curtly told that the information was confidential. In this situation, the organisation lost good faith with an influential member of the community who could make a valuable contribution to its work and who believed that he had a right to the information.

Sometimes we assume that information is private when, in fact, it is shared by a number of people in the community (Martinez-Brawley, 1990b, pp.228-9). Although this does not, in itself, give practitioners permission to disclose confidential information, it does remind us that we are working in a public arena. This is especially clear when public information about a client is incorrect and potentially damaging. For example, during their temporary absence from town the rumour was circulating that a local man and woman had become lovers and that they were, in the local parlance, 'druggies'. Because of this, they and their respective children had been labelled as deviant. The rumours had particularly serious repercussions for the woman and her children because her ex-husband (who lived elsewhere) was seeking custody and he was being supported in this action by the town's police sergeant. I was aware from information they had given me in confidence that the rumours were false. I also knew that I had sufficient standing with local people to quash the rumours. However, I could not contact the people concerned because they were on his remote property which did not have a telephone. Should I adhere to the ethic or allow the gossip to continue? I chose to set the record straight and, for this, the couple later thanked me.

The inability to contact clients before having to decide about confidentiality issues often arises in rural work because of the distances involved. Some years ago a man I had seen once several weeks earlier in relation to his separation from his wife and children telephoned from his office to say that he was about to leave work, go into the bush and commit suicide. His place of work was a two hour drive from my rural office. He claimed to have written a note blaming his suicide on his son's refusal to speak with him when he telephoned the previous evening. He told me not to contact anyone at his workplace. Even though it could have been an attempt to force his wife to return to live with him, there remained the risk that he would commit suicide and that his son would be left with the guilt. Should I maintain confidentiality and risk the potential emotional consequences for the boy, or should I breach confidentiality and risk litigation by contacting someone at his workplace so they could try to stop him? I decided that the boy's long-term well-being was more important and called a senior executive who discussed work issues with the man for the next few hours. To complete the story, the man did not commit suicide, although he did call a few weeks later to challenge what he called my 'breach of professional ethics'. I gave him my reasons for doing so, after which I never heard from him again.

Practitioners, especially those who visit from out of town, should be suspicious of what they hear through the grape-vine (Fenby, 1980, p.152). For example, early in a research trip, a number of residents in one town referred me to a local woman who, they claimed, could tell me everything I needed to know about the community. Although I did speak with her I also persevered in my efforts to interview other residents. As she was quite garrulous I could well have come away convinced that she had given me a great deal of accurate information about community life. As it turned out, however, other residents hid much of the truth from her because she was prone to gossip. As some residents revealed later, they were trying to use her to avoid talking to me.

In all rural communities some people ask practitioners about their neighbours because they genuinely want to help (Martinez-Brawley, 1990b, p.230). This can pose a dilemma for the practitioner who is stopped on the street by a well-intentioned neighbour who asks after a client. Should the practitioner answer the enquiry or risk the person feeling snubbed? For, as was suggested earlier, rural practitioners should actively seek the involvement of local people in social care. Not responding can damage a practitioner's acceptance in the community and capacity to engage residents in social care practice, especially when the enquirer is a high-profile resident with a great deal of local influence.

Other confidentiality issues arise in rural practice. In stigmatised fields such as income assistance and counselling it is important that other residents do not know that someone is receiving assistance. In general, rural people will not access social care services or resources if there is any risk that this will become public knowledge. Privacy of contact can be maintained, for instance, by working from multi-function buildings, by designing offices and scheduling appointments so that people don't come across each other in the waiting room, and by not parking a marked car in front of clients' homes (Fenby, 1980, p.150). Furthermore, practitioners' families must be included in confidentiality undertakings because they will frequently be there when people telephone practitioners at home or talk to them in the street (Fenby, 1980, p.152).

There are no simple answers to the dilemmas posed by confidentiality issues in rural practice. Professions must have general rules. But it is equally important that the practitioner honestly confront the dilemmas. On the one hand, maintaining confidentiality is perhaps even more important in rural than urban communities because one unjustifiable slip by the practitioner can lead to widespread loss of trust throughout the community. But, on the other hand, the repercussions can be equally severe when a client is damaged because the practitioner withholds information from the public arena.

Clearly, maintaining strict confidentiality in relation to information given in confidence is the first rule and should be broken only for extremely good reasons. It is important that the practitioner informs the community about this when she or he first arrives, perhaps by discussing confidentiality with clients (and perhaps one or two nosy locals) and allowing the 'bush telegraph' to spread the word (Whittington, 1985, p.105). Whenever possible, information should be disclosed only with the client's permission, after the practitioner has provided alternative scenarios and different ways of handling the information. This is standard practice. However, in rural communities situations frequently arise when the client cannot be contacted and when an immediate judgement is required. Should the practitioner tell the minister that the client has come to the agency or risk breaching good faith with an influential member of the community? Should I have told residents that the couple did not have a sexual relationship and were not taking drugs? In situations such as these, practitioners should make considered responses according to what they anticipate might be the consequences of either disclosing or not disclosing the information.

Community Energising, Conscientisation and Politicisation

Community energising, conscientisation and *politicisation* are frequently mentioned in the literature as principles of community-oriented practice. They were addressed in different terms in Chapter 6. *Energising* involves encouraging local people to act on their commitment to their community by actively caring for each other, and by initiating and participating in social care development (Martinez-Brawley, undated, pp.16-7). It is especially important in communities where morale and cohesion are low because of recession, population depletion and service withdrawals. However, *energising* might also be necessary in rapidly-expanding communities where some groups are feeling alienated from local structures and institutions.

Conscientisation and *politicisation* go together. *Conscientisation* involves creating and increasing awareness amongst rural people of their oppressed and disadvantaged situation (Martinez-Brawley, 1990b, p.41). *Politicisation* builds on this, involving the practitioner in generating political action amongst residents (Martinez-Brawley, 1982). Although both principles are usually discussed in relation to community development and social action they also apply to practice with individuals and families. For example, through counselling, disempowered women in a patriarchal community can be freed from the shackles of their socialisation, become aware of their oppressed situation and encouraged to join together to challenge local community structures.

Conscientisation also involves generating pride amongst local people in their 'place' and culture and in the rural way of life more generally. Encouraging 'pride of place' can help to generate local cohesion, revitalise local cultures and provide "a positive, identity-enhancing force" for individuals (Martinez-Brawley, 1980, p.172). For example, when residents of Tumby Bay in South Australia felt insulted by reports in the *Adelaide Advertiser* suggesting that their town had no future, they were mobilised by their pride of place to generate and implement a successful integrated regional development plan.

The role of *animateur* brings together *community energising, conscientisation* and *politicisation* (Martinez-Brawley, 1986, p.365). Successful *animateurs* have high credibility with local disempowered people and the capacity to mobilise them into constructive action. Some may also manage to win the support of some local power actors although, more usually, they have to influence decisions through more strategic methods. To be effective, animateurs need support from their employing organisations, secure funding and good political and media skills. Practitioners located outside the community, employees of government organisations, and staff of community-based agencies whose management committees reflect local power structures face formidable obstacles in acting as animateurs (Martinez-Brawley, 1986, p.365). Martinez-Brawley's (1986, p.369) comments from the Hebrides are equally valid for many Australian rural practitioners.

> While community-oriented social work can apparently take place successfully under the aegis of the statutory sector, community work in the animateur tradition seems particularly hard to carry out by statutory workers. If animation work is expected from them, major philosophic, political and technical adjustments have to be made. Regardless of titles, job descriptions or intent of policies, social workers in the statutory sector are much blocked by a tradition of apolitical behaviour; they are also fearful of negative sanctions by the system and consequently do not readily embark on community work. ... The practice of community-oriented social work, while facilitating the advantageous use of existing community networks, will not necessarily supplant the work of animateurs in bringing about changes that have significant political dimensions.

Dealing with Community Power Structures

The rural practitioner's pursuit of social justice inevitably touches the interests of local power actors. Perhaps this is most obvious in relation to social planning, community development, social action and advocacy. However, in rural communities it can also be true of direct client work. For instance, supporting (or simply not challenging) a woman's decision to separate from her husband who is a powerful pastoralist might be challenged by his influential associates. At stake could be their support for the practitioner's employing organisation generally or the establishment of a new women's health centre.

How the practitioner relates to local power structures has repercussions for other aspects of rural practice. Conflicts with powerful individuals and groups, involvement in controversial or failed projects, and being seen by disempowered people as unwilling to tackle important but controversial issues will all affect a practitioner's credibility, ability to attract support for future projects and relationships with clients. However, awareness of this should not intimidate practitioners into inaction. On the contrary, it should encourage them to adopt a community perspective and a strategic approach to all their work.

Rural practitioners need to know about power in their communities (ACSWC, undated, p.58). They should find out how power is structured, how decisions are made, who is influential, and how much influence various power actors have in relation to particular kinds of issues. They need to know about local interest groups, factions and coalitions, who belongs to them, and their respective spheres of influence. It is also important to know which issues unite and which divide the community. Practitioners need to know where - socially and physically - power is played out and decisions are made. In one town, for example, many community decisions are made before, during and after meetings of the *Residents and Ratepayers Association*. And in many Australian communities, social and political business is frequently transacted at the pub or a social club. If practitioners do not know where power is exercised they cannot get involved.

Martinez-Brawley (1990b, pp.71-5) suggested three ways of identifying local power actors. In the *reputational* approach, the practitioner finds out who residents think is influential by asking the residents themselves. People who are strategically placed around community networks, such as long-term residents, journalists and clergy, can be especially useful sources of information. In the *positional* approach, the practitioner identifies people in influential formal positions such as bankers, shire councillors and presidents of local organisations. Those who hold multiple positions frequently have the most power. The *decisional* approach involves identifying key players by directly observing or studying records of decision-making processes such as media reports and minutes of meetings. Because each approach has different strengths and weaknesses, Martinez-Brawley (1990b, p.75) suggested that rural practitioners should use all three and compare the results.

The practitioner should also develop a profile of local interest groups, paying particular attention to their respective spheres of influence and the extent to which they are likely to support, resist or remain neutral in relation to various issues. For example, in many communities the *Country Women's Association* would expect to be involved in developing a women's shelter and, perhaps depending on the framework adopted, would be supportive. In contrast, although the local chamber of commerce might not take an active interest in women's issues, it would expect to be involved in developing local employment programs.

The level of support which a practitioner can anticipate from local power structures is related to the scope of the project, how controversial it is, the extent to which it serves the general public good, and the power and resources which can be marshalled (Martinez-Brawley, 1990b, p.69).

In general, projects which touch a wide cross-section of the community, such as establishing a residents action group, will attract either broad support or widespread resistance. For these, the practitioner needs the support of the most powerful local influentials and those who span a wide spectrum of local interests. Narrower issues, such as forming a domestic violence action group, require the support of power actors with more specialised interests and spheres of influence. Controversial issues require a higher level of support than those which are ideologically 'safe', although it will be more difficult to muster. On the other hand, issues which are clearly in the general public good, such as establishing a community health centre, will normally attract widespread support.

In developing new projects or initiating social action, rural practitioners should be aware of the pace of change that the community will accept (Heyman, 1983, pp.243-4). This varies from place to place and from time to time. Social change usually happens slowly and incrementally in traditional rural communities with stable populations, strong local kin networks and enduring structures and institutions. In these, a practitioner might first need to address a number of narrower issues and work towards small cumulative changes, postponing the more controversial and broader issues until later or dropping some altogether (ACSWC, undated, p.31). However, other kinds of communities may be open to more rapid and pervasive change in the form of new institutional structures, new industries and new leadership. These include places with unconsolidated social structures such as those experiencing rapid social change (e.g., tourist and retirement centres) and communities which are declining rapidly.

If they are to obtain support for new initiatives, practitioners will need to establish strong working relationships with key power actors and generate sympathy for social justice issues across a wide cross-section of residents (ACSWC, undated, p.31). They can do this by keeping issues in the public eye through media activities, through public meetings, and by getting them onto the agendas of various committees. Practitioners should also establish as broad a power base as possible across a variety of interest groups.

Practitioners should know whether they are *cosmopolitan* or *local influentials*, or some combination of the two, and be aware of the strengths and weaknesses of their position. Because Australia is so highly urbanised, most will be the former. Although *cosmopolitans* usually have good access to non-local resources and vertical structures they need to work hard at establishing alliances with local stakeholders. The professional who can cooperate with the less controversial and more palatable wishes of local power actors will be in a stronger position to secure their support for other social justice issues. On the other hand, practitioners who are *local influentials* will probably have good local networks but will have to build connections to, and obtain support from, vertical structures.

There are a number of strategies which rural practitioners can use to attract community support. In most towns, people will need some education about social justice issues. It is easy to forget that what the practitioner takes for granted might not be general public knowledge. For example, many residents simply may not know that respecting what they believe to be the right to family privacy can place women and children in physical danger. Local power actors will need to be briefed on specific issues and what can be done about them. For instance, in one tourist town some local influentials decided to support youth issues when we produced evidence indicating that under-age drinking and drug-taking was prevalent amongst local youth and resulted partly from the lack of local recreational opportunities other than hotels and nightclubs.

One way to educate people is to involve them in social care work (Buxton, 1976, p.37). For instance, a prominent business person may come to understand what it is like to be a poor young person in a high unemployment town without recreational and leisure activities by working as a volunteer in a youth centre or by employing young people in a job training program. Local influentials can also be invited to join management committees of community-based organisations, help with media work, act as political lobbyists, or provide consultation in relation to management, budgeting or strategic planning.

In different situations it will be more effective for rural practitioners to oppose, confront, collaborate with or attempt to persuade power actors (ACSWC, undated, p.31; Martinez-Brawley, 1990b, p.58). They might co-opt influentials into projects, or build coalitions with or amongst special interest groups (Cheers, 1992a, p.17). Especially in the more remote areas, it can be important to form coalitions between neighbouring towns and regions. Some issues will create or exacerbate pre-existing conflict between the practitioner and local power actors or amongst influentials themselves. When this happens, the professional might seek out areas of common ground and issues on which there is room for negotiation, bargaining and compromise (Buxton, 1976, p.36). For instance, a shire chair might agree to allocate a council property for an emergency accommodation program provided that the practitioner refrains from publicly supporting local opposition to a new mining development. At times, practitioners will initiate projects and then encourage other groups to provide the leadership necessary to see them through to completion. In these situations he or she might act as an energiser, an expediter, a mediator between various groups, or an expert consultant in relation to, for example, submission writing and service designs (Martinez-Brawley, 1990b, p.58). Clearly, there are many roles which the practitioner can play when working with community power processes.

Social change strategies should be chosen partly according to the type of power structure operating within the community (Martinez-Brawley, 1990b, pp.69-71). *Elite* power structures can be particularly resistant to change, although significant power actors within these can make powerful allies once they are on side. Where practitioners anticipate resistance in elite power structures, they should look for weak links and try to enlist their support. Where these do not exist, they might have to actively organise disempowered people and initiate more radical social action. Sometimes, sources outside the community, such as members of parliament and staff of government funding bodies, might be able to influence local power brokers. For example, rural shire chairs have been known to change their minds about new social care initiatives when a government funding body guarantees continued funding. In communities with *pluralistic* power structures, on the other hand, it can be useful to build coalitions with and between leaders of relevant interest groups and educate them about the issues. For example, sporting clubs, the police and local churches will probably be interested in a proposal to attract funding for recreational facilities for young people.

In communities with *elite* power structures, which strategies to use also depends upon the degree of compatibility between the practitioner's objectives and the interests of local power actors (Martinez-Brawley, 1990b, pp.70-1). Where there is substantial compatibility, collaborative strategies can be adopted, such as educating influentials about the issue, facilitating their involvement, and working cooperatively towards a successful outcome. But where the practitioner's objectives are incompatible with powerful local interests, he or she should first estimate the likelihood of success before initiating the project. This involves assessing how, and the extent to which, the proposal threatens local interests, and the resources and influence available to the practitioner compared with those at the disposal of oppositional groups and individuals. If the decision is made to run with the issue it will be important to activate disempowered people who stand to benefit from the proposal and obtain the support of sympathetic local and external interests. For example, opposing a mining development because of its social and cultural impacts will most likely conflict with local economic interests. In this situation, the practitioner may need to conduct a social impact assessment, energise, conscientise and politicise the people affected, lobby local and non-local interests and involve non-local organisations such as environmental action groups.

In a community with a *pluralist* power structure, the practitioner should assess the compatibility of the project with the interests of local influentials in sectors related to the issue. As with an elite power structure, where there is compatibility a collaborative approach can be undertaken. For example, the proposal to conduct a 'youth needs' study in the Hinchinbrook Shire was supported by the Shire Council, the *Community Neighbourhood Centre*, the police, local youth leaders, and a number of relevant State and Commonwealth government departments. This ensured the project's success and the subsequent implementation of many of its recommendations. However, where there is conflict between project aims and relevant dominant local interests the practitioner may have to use conflict resolution strategies, form coalitions between sympathetic leaders and groups in other sectors, and activate non-local interests. For example, a shire council which resists a public housing proposal might be persuaded to change its position by the chamber of commerce which supports the proposal because of the business it would provide for local tradespeople and the employment it would generate.

Joining

Practitioners need the confidence of the community if they are to influence local events, whether these concern individual clients or broader issues. One way to gain this confidence is to *join* with the community generally, with its various interest groups and with prominent residents (Cheers, 1992a, p.18). Many rural communities establish clear social boundaries between themselves and the outside world. They divide the social universe into 'us' and 'them'. In *joining*, the practitioner crosses this boundary to become 'one of us'. He or she ceases being an unknown 'foreigner' to be treated with caution and suspicion and becomes, within the systems of meaning provided by local cultures, a familiar, non-threatening person. However, having joined with a community, the practitioner is not necessarily accepted as a 'local'. He or she is simply experienced as more 'like us' than 'not like us', more 'with us' than 'against us'. The same general concept can be applied to:

- the community generally;
- local cultures, groups and organisations;
- individual community members;
- clients; and
- clients' associates.

The present discussion does not address joining with clients and their associates because this is covered in counselling and therapy literature (e.g., Minuchin, 1974, pp.123-9; Cheers, 1990a). It should be noted, however, that a practitioner who has joined with the community will find it easier to join with most of its members, including clients, than one who is regarded as 'foreign'.

Through joining, practitioners accumulate credits which they need if they are to enjoy the initial confidence of clients, gain support for their initiatives and successfully challenge local structures, processes and values. As credits accumulate, practitioners enjoy more, and more widespread, confidence and support. Armed with this they can take on more ambitious and controversial projects, and are better placed to challenge established community structures, processes and values. Beware though! Every time you take on a controversial issue or challenge local ways you cash in some credits. When credits are down, practitioners must accumulate some more to regain the level of support which they had previously enjoyed. Social workers in Tucson, Arizona, refer to this as a 'cistern' model - the water level rises until the cistern is full; then something happens to flush it away, at which point the cistern has to be filled up again.

Creative practitioners will find many ways to join with the community and its residents. Above all else, it is important to be patient as it takes time to join effectively. Inevitably, community gate-keepers will test the practitioner's values, priorities, interest in the community and willingness to conform to important local norms. The practitioner should show commitment to the community by being involved in committees, organisations and recreational activities; through participation in important social institutions; by attending major community events such as rodeos and fairs; and by shopping locally. The new practitioner should quickly identify local social customs and adopt those that feel comfortable. For example, in many small remote towns in North Queensland, most residents take a shower, dress up a little and go to the pub on Friday nights. Practitioners should also observe how local people relate to them and respond in kind - provided, of course, that they feel comfortable with the custom. If people are friendly, be friendly; if they behave somewhat reticently at first so, too, should the practitioner.

Although mimicking the speech, dress and appearance of local people will be viewed as patronising and ingratiating it is also important not to be too different (Ginsberg, 1977, p.1233). For example, many residents of hot, dry, dusty towns would be cautious about a practitioner who works in a pin-striped business suit. The practitioner should take note of the behaviour of local people and how they like to present themselves to the world and accentuate personal characteristics which are compatible with these. I like to go fishing, wear a cowboy hat, drive a four wheel drive vehicle, sleep in a swag and wear dirty blue overalls when on the road. No doubt, these aspects of my lifestyle have helped me join with many communities in Northern Australia. No-one seems to mind if I don't like most country music, can't ride a horse or if I am not much of a mechanic. Above all else, traditional rural folk like people who are proud of who they are and who don't pretend to be otherwise.

During the early period in a community, the practitioner should identify with locally-cohesive issues, the ones which bind the community together. For example, in Chapter 3, I mentioned an otherwise bitterly divided town which united around the primary school. In this town a new practitioner would gain credits by taking an interest in the school, commenting favourably on the community's commitment to its children's education, and attending some *Parents' and Citizens' Association* meetings. It would be equally important to stay away from divisive issues until gaining a greater understanding of community dynamics and accumulating a good stack of credits. For instance, it would have been risky for a new practitioner in this town to become involved in, or even comment on economic development issues for these were central to the factional disputes.

Similar principles apply to joining with local cultures, groups and power actors. The practitioner's aim is to cross over the 'us-them' boundary to be experienced as 'familiar' rather than 'foreign' and as more 'like us' than 'not like us'. To this end, the practitioner will: initially support issues which are important to the group, or at least show an interest in them; identify with issues which unite, and stay away from those which divide the group; adhere to important group norms; and accentuate aspects of his or her personality, lifestyle and appearance which are similar to those of the group or power actor. However, practitioners will be seen as phoney, and perhaps patronising, when supporting norms and values with which they clearly disagree or adopting behaviours, images and lifestyles which do not come naturally.

Visiting Practitioners

Clearly, community-oriented practice is most directly relevant to practitioners who live and work in the same community. However, most rural practitioners, even those based in genuinely rural areas, provide services to communities in which they don't live. Considering how commonplace this is in Australia and, for that matter, in most other countries it is remarkable how little has been written about visiting practice. Given this dearth of information, research on the issue is urgently required, including documentation of their experiences by visiting practitioners.

As with all frameworks, community-oriented practice provides a number of perspectives, concepts, ideas, methods and strategies which will be more or less useful for visiting practitioners depending on the situation at hand. These should not be ignored simply because the framework, as a whole, assumes that people live where they work.

While visiting practitioners cannot participate in community life to the same extent as their locally-based colleagues they should still try to do so as much as possible. This means timing visits and staying in town long enough to take part in significant community events such as fairs and celebrations, attend major community meetings, join in important social traditions such as the family night at the pub, and perhaps join a local committee. If only in a limited way, visiting practitioners can participate in local information networks, gain the trust of residents and establish their credibility with prominent people.

For the most part, visiting practitioners will have to rely on their links with locally-based colleagues, people in other key positions and informal carers to obtain information about the community, gain credibility and secure the trust of residents. By linking with people who are regarded by other residents as competent, credible and trustworthy visiting practitioners can also be seen in the same light. As one woman put it to me: "If you're okay with Barbara then you are okay with me". In this way, visiting practitioners can to some extent join with the community and its members. Try as they may, however, most will never earn the same degree of credit as successful locally-based practitioners.

Unless there are good reasons to become directly involved, it is probably best to leave the power processes to locally-based colleagues. They will usually have more of the necessary joining credits, a deeper and more accurate knowledge of the community, more direct and immediate access to power actors and the local presence required to implement power strategies. Having said this, externally-based professionals can still have many uses for local practitioners in relation to power issues. For instance, by publicly supporting a worker at a community services development meeting, a regional manager can enhance the former's credibility. This might also help to build hope within the community because the local practitioner is now viewed as having the support of, and consequently the ability to influence, vertical power structures. Sometimes, someone who is perceived as an 'outside expert' can sell ideas to residents more effectively than a practitioner who is regarded as 'one of us'. For example, community workers employed by a shire council recently asked me to speak at a council meeting about the importance of social development and its relationship to economic planning. Because I was perceived as an expert by councillors my presentation and subsequent discussions with local power brokers resulted in social development being given greater importance in local area planning.

Sometimes the sheer authority or power of someone from vertical structures is needed to resolve local issues. A dramatic example of this happened in relation to juvenile justice issues in one community when the government minister came to town and told residents which roles her department could and could not play in dealing with these. This helped to redirect discussion toward feasible solutions to the town's problems, something that the locally-based resource officer and the regional manager had been trying to do for some time.

Living and Working in a Rural Community

For practitioners who live in their community, rural practice is entwined with rural living. Before examining the stresses involved in living and working in rural areas, we should remind ourselves of the many advantages. Rural communities offer an excellent lifestyle for practitioners who enjoy a slower pace of living, direct experience of nature, the time and space to centre within themselves and a relaxing, relatively unpolluted environment. They can also provide the sense of identity, the feeling of belonging and the joys of community participation discussed in Chapter 3. Working close to home provides the opportunity to spend time on personal interests and with family and friends. Belonging to an interdependent professional network provides professional development experiences and a level of collegiality which is difficult to find in an urban environment. For independent spirits, rural practice provides relative freedom from organisational constraints, pressures to conform to established ways of working, and the dictates of various professional factions and their doctrines. It also provides the opportunity to work innovatively and to join with others to find creative solutions to local issues. Although, for some, a rural position represents a delay in career advancement, others relish the opportunity to develop a wide range of direct practice, supervisory, administrative and managerial skills. Those who wish to contribute on a broader scale through social planning, community development, social action and political involvement will find a plethora of opportunities to do so.

However, rural work also has many potential sources of stress, 'potential' because it depends on the practitioner's personality, personal circumstances and level of personal, professional and organisational support, as well as the nature of the community.

In Australia, many rural practitioners are isolated from managerial, supervisory and professional support and consultation, professional development opportunities, their intimate social networks and personal supports, and opportunities to pursue preferred leisure activities (ACSWC, undated, p.37; Sturmey and Edwards, 1991, p.15). They also frequently lack the human and financial resources available to their urban colleagues, such as support staff, relief workers and access to professional development opportunities (Sturmey and Edwards, 1991, p.15). Rural practitioners face a number of additional practical difficulties. Most spend a great deal of time travelling to people in outlying areas and to regional or central offices for supervision and in-service training, and to participate in decision making (ACSWC, undated, p.37; Sacco, 1994, p.100). This is time-consuming and energy-sapping. Many a practitioner spends nights and weekends catching up on reports, case notes and essential reading about new policies and procedures because of time lost through travelling. Compared with their urban colleagues, rural practitioners also lack support staff who can attend to the time-consuming, practical tasks such as organising appointments, answering enquiries, keeping accounts, servicing vehicles and purchasing stationery.

Rural social care practice involves some loss of anonymity (Martinez-Brawley, 1990b, pp.223-6). Practitioners who fail to establish boundaries between their personal and professional lives will be in constant demand through telephone calls at home, and on-the-spot interviews and meetings - at football games, in supermarkets or in restaurants. This becomes energy-draining and annoying for practitioners and their families. On the other hand, this lack of anonymity can also have positive implications. Being out and about in the community provides many opportunities to establish community acceptance, connect with a wide range of people and organisations, and establish relationships with local power actors. It can also yield information which is useful for direct client work and community development projects. In one town, for instance, 'pub talk' gave me the clues and the confidence to raise the issue of domestic violence with an abused woman.

Being involved in multiple roles can have both positive and negative implications for the practitioner's work. For example, serving as secretary to the *Parents' and Citizens' Association* will help establish credibility with local influentials which can be important for social action projects and direct client work alike. On the other hand, becoming embroiled in an ideological dispute with a respected school principal could well result in fewer referrals and increased resistance from clients. Being known around town as a private individual as well as a practitioner can also affect practice. Fenby (1980, p.150), for instance, tells of the difficulties she experienced joining with a client until she discovered that because her husband was on only a one-year employment contract, the client had assumed that the practitioner would soon leave town.

Although generalist practice has many delights it can also be demanding. It is not easy, for example, to move continually between the roles of therapist, child abuse investigator, social planner, office manager, community developer, politician and networker; to be interacting at one moment with a suicidal young man, the next with an abused woman and, after that, to play politics with a mayor. Furthermore, generalists cannot afford the luxury of doing only those things which they are good at. Many therapists do not make good social activists and many activists are terrible therapists, even though most rural practitioners must do their best with both roles.

While participation in community life brings many professional and personal rewards, it can also be another source of stress for practitioners. Professional values may conflict with dominant local values in communities where patriarchal structures and attitudes are at odds with social justice principles. Rural practitioners may need to form coalitions with, or refer clients to, people whose social attitudes are radically different from their own. Although opportunities to challenge dominant local values do arise, rural practitioners frequently must live with the frustration of not doing so in the immediate situation because open conflict would work against meaningful long-term change or have negative repercussions for their clients. Current professional education programs only exacerbate these difficulties when they portray traditional rural values and those who hold them as the enemy, either to be attacked, taught the error of their ways or simply avoided. We must develop more sophisticated ways of working with rural power actors who profess values which are different to our own.

Because they are unaccustomed to, or deprived of, social care services, rural people can be suspicious of new practitioners or hold unrealistic expectations of their ability to resolve local problems, influence central decisions and attract resources into the community (Heyman, 1983, p.239). Either attitude will become a source of stress for practitioners who share these inflated views of their power, their social development skills and their helping capabilities.

Commencing Rural Practice

A number of Australian studies have shown that, although successful rural practitioners have a variety of personalities and lifestyles, some characteristics are more helpful than others (ACSWC, undated; Lonne, 1990, p.38; Sturmey and Edwards, 1991). They should enjoy the rural environment and living close to nature. Good rural practitioners have a *sociological imagination* - when they look out at the world they see social processes, structures and institutions rather than aggregations of isolated individuals. They enjoy a socially-involved lifestyle, feel comfortable with their high visibility and do not need to hide behind professional roles and facades. They also have the capacity to understand and relate to a variety of people and cultures, including those with different values to their own. Good rural practitioners have the humility to acknowledge that they share the responsibility for social care with others and to respect and learn from the natural social care wisdom which abounds in all rural communities. They are personally flexible, adaptable, innovative and creative. They embrace, rather than cringe from, the freedom to deal with issues unencumbered by established practices and close supervision. Successful rural practitioners tend to be sensible and pragmatic people who see and respond to reality as it is, rather than how it appears when viewed through the conceptual prisms of mainstream professional paradigms and ideologies. Because they are so visible - warts and all - and because their most earnest social justice ideals will not always win out, they must also have a good sense of humour.

Many practitioners experience difficulties when they move into a rural community, especially those coming from urban backgrounds. Zapf (1993) studied the experiences of social workers commencing rural practice in the remote Yukon region in northern Canada. Those who had moved from urban areas or the more densely-settled southern rural regions of Canada experienced initial *culture shock* for up to six months followed by slow recovery for the next six months. In contrast, those with previous personal or professional experience in northern Canada experienced the same process but nowhere near to the same degree.

Whilst employment-related factors were associated with the depth and duration of culture shock, personal variables affected the recovery process. Culture shock was most severe for social workers without local colleagues and whose jobs had ambiguous or conflicting priorities and expectations. According to Zapf (1993), those reporting greatest recovery by the end of the first year were "... probably male, open-minded, and comfortable with social diversity and (had) a broad education and some understanding of the culture shock phenomenon" (p.701).

Zapf suggested that clashes between professional and community cultures may lie at the heart of the culture shock experience. He argued that practitioners typically arrive in remote northern communities viewing themselves as 'objective outsiders', a role which is acquired through professional training and supported by the employing organisation.

> The community is considered theoretically according to systems of attributes rather than as a place of immediate experience. ... The newly located worker attempts to understand the community using frameworks from his or her own familiar culture and profession. Applying metaphors from the South leads to a limited view of the northern community as a pathological variation of the southern experience. (Zapf, 1993, pp.701-2)

This initial framework gradually disintegrates in the face of contradictory experiences within the community. At first, this causes confusion and anxiety although most practitioners eventually enter into "... local systems of meaning and priorities" (Zapf, 1993, p.702). Zapf continues:

This shift will probably be accompanied by a stressful period of frustration and disorientation, giving way eventually to regained confidence and a sense of well being as the worker learns to operate within the new system of meanings. (p.702)

In Australia, Lonne (1990) proposed a more elaborate five-stage framework of the adjustment process which he is currently testing. He suggested that new rural social workers first go through a *Disorientation* period, lasting around one month, which is typified by confusion and uncertainty as they acclimatise to local conditions and learn about their position. They then enter a *Honeymoon* period for about four months, during which they are excited about their job, their surroundings and their new colleagues and friends. During this time, new practitioners are generally optimistic, energetic and enthusiastic about their work and about living in the community. Eventually, however, they miss familiar environments, their previous lifestyles, their personal social networks and support systems, and the security of being surrounded by colleagues, professional and organisational supports and more specialised services to which they can refer clients. According to Lonne, this process reaches a climax at around six months when they enter a *Grief and Loss* phase which lasts for approximately three months. Work performance plateaus or deteriorates during this period. For some, this leads into a *Withdrawal and Depression* stage during which performance and job satisfaction deteriorate further, resulting in feelings of inadequacy and some loss of confidence. Some practitioners distance themselves from personal and professional relationships. Somewhere between fifteen and eighteen months after arriving in the community those who have survived move through what Lonne calls a *Reorganisation and Adjustment* phase as they come to accept their environment, their community, and their lifestyle. During this time, they adjust to the realities of rural practice, become more realistic about the opportunities and limitations of their position and what they can achieve, and start to enjoy the community participation that their work brings.

The early period in a new community is crucial to the practitioner's subsequent adjustment and a number of strategies are available to help ease the transition. Hart (1995, pp.43-4) advised practitioners to acquaint themselves with the region's economic foundations, settlement patterns, geography, climate and cultures before they arrive to take up their position. Upon arrival, practitioners should allot time before commencing work to establish themselves in accommodation, become acquainted with their physical and social surroundings and attend to personal and family details such as enrolling children at school. Once they start work, practitioners should try to avoid becoming overloaded until they have had the opportunity to learn about their organisation, local services and resources, and the community's social and political life. One of their first tasks is to join with the community and with significant groups, organisations and individuals. However, practitioners should be careful initially not to join with a group if doing so means that they cannot join with a rival faction. They should avoid being stereotyped at the outset because, in rural communities, first impressions are circulated quickly and can take a long time to live down (ACSWC, undated, p.36). Because residents will gossip about new practitioners regardless of what they do, it is important to give them positive rather than negative things to talk about, as defined according to local cultural meanings. For personal satisfaction, and as a way of becoming established in the community, practitioners should connect with people who have interests similar to their own and seek opportunities to pursue preferred recreational activities (ACSWC, undated, p.25). However, it is important not to hide within professional, middle-class or intellectual networks because this will be interpreted as reluctance to associate with other local cultures (Hart, 1995, p.44).

In the early weeks following their arrival, practitioners should get to know their community through discussions with residents, professionals and key community informants. They should also review documented information in historical records, statistical profiles, research and consultancy reports and committee minutes. Table 8.1 lists some aspects of community life which should be included in this review. While they will inevitably update and add detail to their community profile as time goes by, practitioners should conduct a quick early review of the community's history, physical characteristics, demography, services and dominant social, political and economic issues. Information about systemic ties and social and cultural characteristics will take longer to accumulate and validate. Still, it is important for practitioners to take special note of their first impressions and 'feelings' about the community before they become acculturated and start to view it through the lens of local cultural meanings.

Rural practice is not inherently stressful. But it can be for practitioners accustomed to living and working in urban environments and whose training has not prepared them for rural work. A number of additional strategies are available for coping with the 'differentness' of rural practice. It is important to abandon any pre-conceived notions of

Table 8.1: Components of the Practitioner's Community Assessment

History
- The community and its people.
- The historical development, significance and meaning of community institutions, rituals, important social and recreational occasions, and symbols of community.

Physical Characteristics
- Geography.
- Climate.
- Settlement pattern.
- Transport systems.
- The social significance of forms of space, including buildings and architecture.
- Interaction centres.

Demography
- Demographic composition of the population.

Services
- Local and non-local services in the social care, education and health sectors.
- Potential sources of funding.

Systemic Ties
- Horizontal and vertical ties in relation to political, economic, education, health, social care and other service sectors.
- Horizontal and vertical ties associated with power structures and class hierarchies, and the strengths and weakness of these ties.
- Local informal support networks.

Social and Cultural Characteristics
- Local cultures.
- Social customs, rules, rituals, institutions, symbols, values and lifestyles; and the extent of uniformity and diversity of these throughout the community.
- Degree of '*communityness*' of communities within the region and the extent to which this is tied to locality.
- Symbols of community.
- Degree of local cohesiveness, mutuality and interdependence.
- The relative extent to which community relationships are holistic or partialised, *gemeinschaftlich* and *gesellschaftlich*.

Community Issues
- Unifying, divisive and neutral issues in political, social, economic and other sectors.
- Dominant current issues.

what makes for good and bad communities, and even good and bad practice, and to accept, rather than fight against, the realities of the community (Martinez-Brawley, 1990b, p.102). Rural practitioners work in places where real-life encounters occur, not in the detached, rarefied atmosphere of city government offices. Their professional relationships will be more personalised than in urban practice, they will be subjected to public scrutiny, their privacy will be invaded, and they may be living and working far away from their personal social networks and professional supports.

Rural practitioners should seek to establish professional support systems (Sturmey and Edwards, 1991, p.23; Sacco, 1994). This might involve creating local peer consultation groups, obtaining supervision from staff in other local organisations, taking the initiative in seeking supervision from their own organisations even though their supervisors may be some distance away, activating consultation links with respected colleagues in larger centres and, where they work in organisations with other practitioners, ensuring that space is created in busy work schedules for regular staff discussions. They should also actively seek professional development opportunities through attending conferences, workshops and in-service training programs.

On a personal level, practitioners will need to maintain links with their own social and support networks (ACSWC, undated, p.37), although they should also establish personal connections with other local people (Hart, 1995, p.44). Furthermore, although rural practice is embedded in community, practitioners will quickly lose their enthusiasm if they do not establish some boundaries between their private and professional lives, however minimal these may be. This involves placing some limits on their availability outside normal working hours and making sure that they include creative leisure activities in their private space (Hart, 1995, p.44). Although they will lose 'joining credits' if other residents see them escaping from the community at every opportunity, going somewhere else now and then helps to relieve the intensity of living and working in the same place.

Finally, even the practitioner who is the only one in town is not alone. The realisation that rural practice is an expression of community should immediately exorcise any feeling of responsibility for all local social care arrangements. Other residents want to share the responsibility, whether it be direct client work, social planning, community development or social action. For they are not only our neighbours and our friends, they are also our colleagues.

Note

1. This section builds on Emilia Martinez-Brawley's (1990b, pp.227-33) seminal work on confidentiality issues in rural practice.

Part 3
Threads

9 Threads

I wrote this book primarily to organise our collective thinking, research and practice in relation to rural social care and to suggest some possible future directions. Some key organising themes have emerged from this work - the threads which weave the myriad pieces together into a social care fabric.

Chapter 7 demonstrates that we have developed an impressive *service technology* - ideas about service models and designs and the organisational structures and administrative processes which are required to implement them. This is typically Australian - we are a nation of innovative doers. But we are yet to implement much of this technology on a comprehensive scale. Some other topics which require urgent attention include: income security policy in relation to farmers and other self-employed rural people; approaches to rural practice, especially for practitioners who don't live and work in the same place; and approaches to rural social care development, especially as it relates to the other sectors involved in managing regional change. And although a start has been made here, we still need to investigate more comprehensively and in greater detail the implications of what we know about rural life for policy, services, development and practice.

It is also typically Australian to develop useful technologies but fail to articulate the frameworks on which they are based. This is true of rural social care in this country. Three key concepts have evolved in the course of writing this book:

- *dialectic interaction*, or the interaction between dialectically-related concepts and systems of ideas;
- the *interrelatedness* of various structures and processes involved in social care and its relationship with other sectors; and
- *managed interaction*, or the structures, processes and strategies designed to manage interaction amongst the various components of social care and its relationships with other sectors.

The very notion of social care illustrates all three. As suggested in Chapter 1, we need to rediscover the meaning of social care. In essence, it comprises *all* those arrangements and processes through which people try to meet each other's social, emotional and material needs. Beneath all else, it is an expression or, if you will, a function of human society - of all the relationships and interaction between people, groups and organisations. This is the starting point, not the formal structures from within which so many of us peer out at the world. The capacities to cooperate with and care for each other are so deeply embedded in human society that, on the basis of recent archaeological evidence, some ecologists now claim that they may have evolved genetically through natural selection (Bookchin, 1995a, p.25). They also suggest that they may have been the key initial mechanisms which ensured the survival of puny *Homo sapiens* in a tough, hostile environment until our nervous system developed to the point where it could make a significant contribution (Bookchin, 1995a, pp.21-34).

Fortunately, long gone are the days when all caring happened through informal processes. Rightly, we have developed a vast array of formal structures and processes to help people - policies, laws, regulations, funding programs, services, resources, organisations, professions and the like. 'Rightly', because we are sufficiently civilised as a nation to want to try to ensure that all people get the help they need no matter who they are or where they live, and 'fortunately' because we are sufficiently wealthy to aim to achieve this goal.

At the conceptual level, interaction between formal and informal care is an example of *dialectically-related* frameworks (Bookchin, 1995b, pp.5-15). On the one hand, we can conceive of social care as being provided through formal societal structures, according to formalised laws and rules, by functionaries employed in relatively clearly-defined roles who are informed by sophisticated ideological, conceptual and theoretical frameworks, data sets and other information produced through systematic research. But we can also think of social care as an ongoing expression of interaction between people who are responding to each other subjectively, spontaneously and passionately as whole human beings on the basis of intuition, life experience and informal normative systems.

The point is that how we think about social care results partly from our recognition that these (and other) dialectically-related frameworks are relevant to what we are trying to do and from our efforts to relate them together. Nowhere is this more clearly evident than for the rural practitioner. The framework which was presented in Chapter 8 as community-oriented practice is derived partly from juxtaposing formal and informal care and analysing the interaction between them at a conceptual level. Community-oriented practice is not a well-ordered, nicely-integrated theory but a framework which is neither complete nor even internally consistent. To the extent that it reflects the reality of living and working in the same community for a particular practitioner, the framework helps to meaningfully pattern one's experiences and organise one's thoughts about what is going on and about what can be done. As such, it also helps guide one's action. Community-oriented practice is not fixed - it is a dynamic, evolving and inevitably incomplete product of interaction among dialectically-related systems of ideas.

We, in the formal sector, have come to view the universe of social care primarily though a formal lens. The increasingly opaque windows through which we peer are made of the same substance as the formal structures which envelop us. We have established an 'institution' of 'social welfare' and filled it with organisational structures and procedures, trained professionals, fragmented programs, elaborate equipment, sophisticated databases, learned writings, proficient reports, endless memoranda and so on. Without doubt these have made, and will continue to make, valuable contributions to human well-being. But in our thinking and, partly due to our thinking, in reality, the institution has become increasingly detached from the totality of human life, from spontaneous support processes, from community, and from other sectors involved in managing social and economic change. We have come to view social care more and more narrowly as a product of societal structures and let fade the idea that it is also an expression of human community. We have increasingly focused on only one 'side' of the dialectic - care which is provided through the *gesellschaftlich* interaction which so dominates (at least numerically) most Australians' experience of life. The other side - the *gemeinschaftlich* interaction which characterises our intimate social networks and, at least for some rural people, which forms the fabric of their community-embedded existence - has receded from view. For us, the dialectic has become lopsided.

Dialectic interaction involves practitioners, managers, planners, policy formulators, scholars and researchers wrestling with counterpoised systems of ideas in relation to their work. As they do so, they frequently generate new insights - new fusions of ideas which had at first appeared to be contradictory.

Of course, *dialectic interaction* at the conceptual level reflects and, in turn, is reflected in real world processes. Formal and informal caring structures and processes are *interrelated* in reality as well as dialectically related at a conceptual level. For example, people 'out there' are discussing what happens to them in the formal system - whether they should seek formal help, what 'the social worker' said, whether to notify 'the authorities' of suspected child abuse, whether to claim an income security provision and so on. Some people are actively stopping others from seeking protection, as in some domestic violence situations, and sometimes they are interfering with their receipt of income security entitlements. Similarly, the meeting of a community group with a funding official has more often than not been preceded by numerous informal discussions in pubs and private homes about community needs and about how to prepare the funding proposal.

To some degree, formal and informal care carry on more or less in isolation from each other. This is especially true of informal care. On her own initiative, Mrs Brown cooks meals for Mrs Jones because she is too ill to do so herself. Bill calls his mate in Cairns when he is depressed. Bob and Joan accommodate their daughter and her young children because she can't afford her own housing. At a community level, people get sufficiently irate about local social issues to form a committee or press for action from elected officials. They continue to get together to discuss, argue about, and perhaps take action against proposed new developments because of what they imagine will be the consequences for their social, emotional and material well-being. The formal network carries on in isolation from informal care less frequently, although income security payments provide one example.

Formal and informal structures and processes not only interrelate - we have also developed a *technology* for managing their interaction. For instance, in Chapter 7, I reviewed a number of mechanisms for linking informal and formal care. Similarly, Table 6.5 presented a number of social care development functions and tasks which involve linking participative horizontal interaction with vertical planning processes.

Dialectic interaction and *interrelatedness* also weave their way through the discussion of rural life in Chapters 3 and 8. With regard to dialectics, rural life has been conceptualised in terms of community *and* the existential individual, so much so that the very concept of 'community' was defined as an ever fluid product of interaction between the two. Other dualities have been identified at the level of the individual including, for example, individual distinctiveness *and* social belongingness, visibility *and* anonymity, freedom *and* constraint. Similarly, at the community level we find interaction between concepts of place *and* culture, *gemeinschaft and gesellschaft*, horizontal *and* vertical, normative constraint *and* support for self-expression.

Although it takes less intellectual effort and may be more fashionable to paint rural communities as constraining social places characterised by *gemeinschaft* interaction and horizontal ties, and governed by stark and strong social, political and normative structures, it is also wrong. They are geographic localities (by and large) where the many dialectic dramas of individual and community are played out. This is clearly so for the social care practitioner who stands at the intersection of horizontal *and* vertical ties, *gemeinschaftlich and gesellschaftlich* interaction, visibility *and* anonymity, belonging *and* distinctiveness, constraint *and* challenge, spontaneity *and* professionalism. The 'and' is emphasised because it is the key - rural communities are where dualities interact to create individual and social realities within a continually changing kaleidoscope of interactional shades.

The interrelatedness of rural living also comes through in Chapter 3. There are two levels: the individual and the collective. At the individual level, people interact with their respective 'worlds'. For each of us, this is a unique world which the individual continually creates as, indeed, it creates the individual. It was suggested that, for most of us, the four modes of world - self, social, natural and spiritual - come together to form a singularity where all rest on the same core set of 'lived' assumptions. One such assumption, that people do or should dominate their world, is common in dominant Western ideology. This translates in respective modes into self-control, vertical power structures, control over nature, and a hierarchical form of spirituality ruled at the top by an omniscient and omnipotent supreme being (Norgaard, 1994, pp.182-4). The same, of course, holds at the collective, or cultural, level of analysis.

In our thinking and in our practice, we who populate formal social care structures have done fairly well at addressing the interrelatedness of people with their social and 'self' worlds, although we have barely begun to fathom how what we do relates with their natural and spiritual worlds. In Australia, as elsewhere, this failure has been most apparent in our treatment of indigenous people. But the issue goes beyond indigenous concerns. As suggested in Chapter 3, we have also failed to respond adequately and appropriately to the severing of the relationships of many farmers with their land when they are forced to sell up. Theoretically, empirically and in our technology we urgently need to address these relationships.

Other interrelationships have surfaced at the collective, or community, level. These include, for instance, those amongst residents, between local organisations, and within local social support networks. We have also discussed the interrelatedness of place, culture and nature; of local social, political and power structures; and of political and media processes. And, in Chapter 2, we discussed interrelationships at the local level between the economy, patterns of land use, physical infrastructure and industry, as well as the interrelatedness of global, national, regional and local market forces.

The third key concept, *managed interaction,* takes us into the *technology* of social care. Figure 4.1 offered a broad framework for understanding social care based on notions of *dialectic interaction, interrelatedness* and *managed interaction.* This framework identified four social care arenas:

- direct practice;
- formal structures, models and strategies;
- social care development; and
- social policy.

Cutting across all arenas are a number of dialectics including horizontal *and* vertical ties, formal *and* informal care, *gemeinschaftlich and gesellschaftlich* interaction, and individual *and* community focus. Each of these translates into *dialectic interaction* between systems of ideas within each of the four arenas. The framework specifies, for instance, that the direct service practitioner is embedded in community *and* responsive to individual needs; that the community-based organisation is a product of community structures, processes and perspectives *and* of individual and family needs; and that the role of the social care developer incorporates both social planning *and* participative community development.

The *dialectic interaction* of other counterpoised frameworks informs the technological issues discussed in Chapters 5 to 8. Prominent among these is the conceptual tension between a rational, linear, systematic, data-driven, objective, technical view of social care and a spontaneous, messy, participative, intuitive, subjective and responsive approach. This is most apparent in relation to the counter-positioning of the neat, linear, tough-minded approach of social planning with the process-embedded participative artistry and messiness of community development described in Chapter 6. It is also implicit in how we view direct practice - as technical, scientific, objective professionalism counterpoised with spontaneous, intuitive, subjective human responsiveness.

The framework presented in Figure 4.1 goes beyond dialectics into interrelatedness. Part 2 illustrates the interrelatedness of:

- economic, infrastructure, industry, social care and land use planning at the local level; and
- central structures and processes, such as government funding bodies, with those at the periphery, such as local community-based organisations.

So far, we have discussed what 'is'. We can also envisage what 'can be' and identify strategies aimed at establishing and maintaining what we hope for according to our social justice aims. The latter is what I mean by *technology*. When we write about, research and discuss this technology we are dealing with *conceptualised technology*. *Applied technology* - putting the concepts into practice - will be discussed later.

Many of the recommendations made in Part 2 are ways of trying to manage conceptual dialectics and, because of this, they can appear to be contradictory. But dialectics is not the same as contradiction. For where frameworks are dialectically related there is the potential for some integration at a higher conceptual level. However, the idea of managing dialectics also implies that practitioners frequently have to live with frameworks (and realities) which simply don't quite fit together.

Some recommendations in Part 2 were produced by juxtaposing 'technological' and 'human' frameworks. For example, the community developer was advised to engage in rational, linear, data-based planning *and* facilitate the more complex process of community participation. Similarly, the *RAATSICC* program, described in Chapter 7, brought into the same administrative frame spontaneous interactional processes amongst indigenous women *and* some highly systematic and regulated formal program rules. In Chapter 8, practitioners were advised to participate in community life *and* maintain some boundaries between their personal and professional lives. The polarities involved in these examples are not contradictory. Each recommendation is an attempt to manage (not *control*) the interaction between dialectically-related, or counterpoised, frameworks.

The resulting conceptual tension translates into tension in the real world through the practitioner who experiences the process as an unharmonious and uncomfortable juggling act where apparent contradictions constantly surface to be 'resolved' to the extent that they can be. This is the lot of the practitioner who is trying to participate in the community and maintain some autonomy; of the community developer who tries to relate participative processes with systematic local area planning; and of the resource officer who sits in the wings while community leaders run their own workshop knowing that, at some point, what they produce may well be inconsistent with existing funding program rules. Again, it is the 'and' which is crucial - the 'and' which arises from dialectic interaction between frameworks which, at the same time, both reflect and are reflected in reality. The technology is not consistent because the real world isn't.

Much of the social care technology presented in this book is an attempt to manage the interrelatedness of structures and processes involved in social care. There are some exceptions. For example, developing income security programs so that they are more responsive to the circumstances of farmers and other self-employed rural people really only requires action by central organisations. Similarly, placing greater emphasis on *rural targeting* and *developmental* frameworks in Commonwealth and State policies can also be done within the formal sector alone. For the most part, however, our existing technology tries to manage interaction between various components of social care arrangements and their relationships with other structures and processes. These include interaction between:

- formal *and* informal caring;
- central *and* peripheral structures - especially central *and* local service provision organisations, and central funding bodies *and* community-based organisations;
- local social care organisations;
- vertical social care structures;
- local people *and* organisations involved in the various 'regional development' sectors;
- central *and* locally-based regional planning bodies; and
- rural practitioners *and* their communities.

Strategies designed to manage interaction between formal and informal sources of care include some of the service models presented in Chapter 7, such as linking people with their personal support networks, establishing geographically-extended, mutual aid groups, supporting key natural helpers, and resourcing spontaneous informal support through subsidies and access to technology. A number of other service models designed to manage interaction between central and peripheral organisations were also presented in Chapter 7. These included, for example, non-local specialist visiting services, such as child development experts, linking with local organisations, such as schools and hospitals.

The community services development model of the *Queensland Department of Families, Youth and Community Care* which was discussed in Chapter 7 comprises a number of strategies to manage the interaction of central funding bodies with locally-based organisations. And many of the coordinating and integrating strategies presented in Tables 7.2 and 7.3 involve partnerships between local organisations (e.g., case conferences and shared management committees) and between central organisations (such as lead agencies and clearing-houses).

Much has been written here about managing the interaction between the various sectors and organisations involved in regional change. These include, for example, joint involvement in local area planning and social impact assessment and establishing integrated regional development organisations.

Finally, many technologies were suggested in Chapter 8 to manage the interaction between practitioners and local community structures and processes. These include strategies for working with power structures and various joining techniques.

Thus far, I have only addressed *conceptual technology*. This is what we write about, discuss, teach, research and codify into various laws, regulations, guidelines and handbooks. What about *the doing*? And how does *the doing* - or the *applied technology* (putting the concepts into practice) - relate to what I have called *conceptual technology*? Here I draw on Hegel's (1969) dialectic of *the real, the actual* and *the potential*. *The real* encompasses 'what is' - including that which is *actual* (or actually going on at the time), and what is there *in potential* (or that which can become *actual*). For example, whilst a practitioner might be working cooperatively with a local chamber of commerce in its efforts to stimulate the local economy (*actuality*), the same practitioner also has the capacity to institute a number of social action conflict strategies (*potentialities*). These *potentialities* may or may not be *actualised*, but the failure to actualise them does not make them any the less *real*.

Now, in two senses *conceptual technology* is real *in potential*. First, we verbalise, teach, research and write about it, and some of it is codified into various laws, regulations, guidelines and handbooks. It only needs to be applied (or done) to become actual. Second, the various pieces of *conceptual technology* also contribute to the furnishings of a practitioner's mind. (In this context, practitioners comprise all those who practice formal social care - social planners, social policy formulators, community developers and managers as well as direct service practitioners.) Here they lie in waiting, so to speak, as potentialities. It is only when the practitioner does things, engages in concrete actions such as radical change strategies, joining with an elite power group or telling Mrs Jones about her neighbour's situation that they become actual.

The point of this brief philosophical interlude is that people - real human beings - are at the interface of *conceptual technology* and actual social care processes. If people don't actualise the technology it simply doesn't happen - regardless of the prescriptions of textbooks and handbooks. This is a far cry from the view that practitioners are mere knowledge applicators. They are much more than this. They are aware, thinking, feeling human beings who are continually influenced by a host of real world processes. It is people who, in the final analysis, choose to do or don't do various things - who do or don't act this way or that as they interact with a client, participate in a local area planning meeting, supervise staff or manage a service program.

At any given moment practitioners possess a large number of *conceptual technologies*. These come from a variety of places - their employing organisations, their professional associations, other professional reference groups, their own personal stories, the communities in which they live, literature they have read and education programs in which they have participated.

Education programs warrant further comment. Most professional social care training programs in Australia have four deficiencies in relation to rural social care. First, and most obviously, they are insufficiently rural. Their key concepts, frameworks and knowledge bases do not include those which have been prominent in this book. Nor are the perspectives, methods and approaches they teach. Concepts such as place, community, ecology and the interrelatedness of social care with other sectors are absent. So, too, is material concerning service designs, regional development, local area planning and managed interaction.

Second, courses and those who teach them are frequently too one-sided with respect to many of the dialectics which permeate this book. Too often, it seems, dialectic issues are polarised into 'this or that' ideology, theory, research design or practice approach, and one side or the other is promulgated. For instance, the relatively fixed, hierarchical social structures of many rural communities are frequently set in opposition to the ideology of equal rights which is implicit in the concept of social justice and students are exhorted to be on the 'side' of social justice. The problem is not that we shouldn't be committed to social justice. It is the polarisation of this against a stereotype of 'traditional' social values which is often unjustifiably attributed to rural community leaders. For instance, I once overheard an academic colleague remark to a group of social work students that "rural social work would be okay if it wasn't for the 'rednecks'". Because rural community leaders are thus set aside as the enemy, many practitioners find it difficult to work with them and the social work profession has, with only one or two notable exceptions (such as Martinez-Brawley, 1990b), failed to develop technologies to help them do so.

Third, social care education is insufficiently interrelational. We have failed, for instance, to prepare practitioners to participate in multi-sector planning and to relate central structures with peripheral processes. The pity is that social justice perspectives are not being assertively and authoritatively contributed to the planning processes which have such major impacts on the well-being of rural communities and the people who live in them.

Fourth, we educators have largely failed to realise that helping students to develop *technological potentialities* involves far more than simply telling them 'stuff'. Establishing a potentiality which, for the practitioner, is a powerful viable option which can compete on more or less equal terms with those derived from elsewhere - notably their employing organisations, their personal socialisation and some local power elites - involves a complex and gradual process of assimilation (Cheers, 1980). This failure to internalise viable technologies is particularly problematic for new rural practitioners who can find themselves in an organisational and professional void. On the one hand, they have not integrated relevant course material to the point where they can use it confidently and spontaneously in day-to-day practice situations. However, because they are far away from central management, they also lack the immediate, compelling presence of organisational imperatives.

Coevolution and Inter-sector Relatedness

Returning to the theme of *interrelatedness*, we lack frameworks which interrelate the various sectors of human society - social structure, political structure, economy, culture, ecology, ideology, spirituality, care and, as a facet of this, social care. We also need action strategies - *managed interaction technologies* - which derive from these frameworks. Bits of each have been presented throughout this book - some conceptual linkages have been identified and some concrete strategies presented. However, at this stage we seem to have more of the latter, which is understandable because applied issues are the most pressing. Still, without conceptual frameworks, our action will be patchy and somewhat 'hit or miss'.

Coevolutionary approaches, such as Norgaard's (1994), show some promise for conceptually organising inter-sector interrelatedness. In essence, Norgaard's formulations rest on two fundamental propositions. First, and most obviously, each sector interacts with the others. Culture interacts with the natural environment, and the local economy with political and social structures. Second, over time, each changes, or *evolves*, in interaction with the others. This is clearly so in the 'natural' world, or *first nature* (Bookchin, 1995a, pp.16-8) - hummingbirds have developed longer beaks as the flowers they feed on have become deeper. This idea can be extended to interaction between human beings (*second nature*) and the 'natural' environment - as, for example, when European methods of agriculture changed Australia's geography which, in turn, radically altered human settlement patterns on this continent.

The idea of *coevolution* can also be extended to the interrelatedness of facets of human society. As suggested in Chapter 1, our system of formal social care evolved to its present form - residual, reactive, formal, fragmented and highly structured - in interaction with the evolution of:

- economic patterns (capitalism);
- political structures (a federal system of government);
- an ideological system (Cartesian, incorporating individualism, isolationism and fragmentation);
- the natural environment (a largely arid continent with localised areas of high fertility);
- social structure (power differentials);
- culture (predominantly European derived); and
- spirituality (Judeo-Christianism, with its emphasis on hierarchy, domination and monotheism).

Some different kinds of coevolutionary interaction can be identified. Only six will be mentioned briefly here for illustrative purposes. They are organised according to three dimensions: *congruence-incongruence, complementarity-conflict*, and *continuity-discontinuity*.

Congruence occurs when various sectors have similar structures because they derive from a common ideology. For example, the individualism of capitalism is congruent with the primary focus of Australia's formal social care arrangements on individuals and nuclear families. *Incongruence*, on the other hand, occurs where sectors are structured differently because they operate according to different ideologies. For example, the participatory collectivism of community development can be difficult to integrate with the linear, data-based approach of regional planning.

Complementarity holds where sectors are different but mutually reinforcing. The hummingbird/flower is a good example from the natural world. Providing low-cost public housing for young people (social care) in an area experiencing large rent increases because of rapid growth in tourism (economy) provides an example from human society. Public housing fuels the economy because it forestalls potential resistance to economic development and because it helps keep young people in the region to serve as casual employment fodder for the tourist industry. In turn, economic growth creates the need for public housing and, where the local political structure is sympathetic, some funding for it. *Conflict*, on the other hand, occurs where sectors undermine each other. For instance, recent Australian history provides many instances where people who are focused on environmental concerns or social issues have actively conflicted with economic developers.

Continuity happens when all sectors continue in their established evolutionary directions. In contrast, *discontinuity* occurs where the established evolutionary direction of one or more sectors is broken, or severely disrupted either by the evolution of other directions or by an external force. Perhaps the transformation of social care in response to economic rationalism and industry restructuring in the 1980s is an example of the former. The intervention of an external force is vividly illustrated by the European invasion of the continent which radically disrupted the evolutionary directions of most facets of indigenous communities.

Because coevolutionary theory has been developed primarily in relation to *first nature* (the 'natural' world), rather than *second nature* (human beings), theorists usually advocate a focus on coevolution within local geographic areas. However, given their interconnectedness, a more useful *social coevolutionary* framework would encompass local, regional, State, national and global levels. Despite this, as the evolution of local area and regional planning in Australia demonstrates, there are many good reasons for suggesting that in this country *managed coevolution* should be regionally focused and regionally located.

Social Justice and the Ethicscape

In Chapter 1, the purpose of social care was defined in terms of human rights and the distribution of power and resources. Thus formulated, social justice stands as a worthy ideal but, in the final analysis, without any supporting argument as to why it is more worthy than others, such as a culturally integrated, or racially pure, society where some have more rights than others. Where does the ideal of social justice come from? Is it merely that socially-inclined people in Western middle classes think it is good? Or is it somehow implicit in human nature and human society?

Nor does our concept of social justice relate immediately to visions of purposes in other sectors. How does it fit, for instance, with notions of enhancing ecological diversity, or ecological, social, cultural and spiritual sustainability, or peace? If all sectors are coevolutionary then action in each will be more effective when it moves in similar rather than opposing directions. What we need is a broader vision for the planet and the human race from which purposes in all sectors can be derived. As Booth (1995, p.124) pointed out, it is imperative that we actively define the vision and take charge of what he called the 'ethicscape'.

> We invent our own meanings and so make our own nature. We are constrained by old stories and theories, but not determined by them. We can create new ones. .... Human 'nature' is there to be written, and rewritten, and reinventing our human future will be shaped by whether and how we reinterpret the past. And it is the future of the next few tumultuous generations that ... [we] ... must desperately worry about, because if it all goes wrong few will have the luxury of speculating about the eternal questions concerning philosophical foundations. (Booth, 1995, p.126)

We have to work out what kind of human society we want, how we want it to relate to the rest of the universe, and set to work at actualising our vision. If we leave this to chance, there may well be no human society at all and not much left of the planet.

One such vision is of a caring, peaceful human society which respects and cultivates ecological, cultural, social and spiritual diversity using all the ingenuity, technology, knowledge and capacity for rational thought at its disposal. But what makes this more worthy and achievable than other visions? There are two main supporting arguments. First, we have ample ecological, social and political evidence to suggest that if we don't actively move in this direction, the survival of the human race, the planet and its other inhabitants are at risk. Second, the various postmodernisms aside, the *potential* for this kind of society has been there (*real*) from the very beginnings of *first nature* (Bookchin, 1995a, pp.228-56, 1995b). The big picture of history suggests that this vision has been, and continues to be, slowly actualised, despite the many setbacks, side-tracks and cul-de-sacs, and the periodic actualisation of other just as real alternative potentialities such as we saw with Nazi Germany. The first major actualisation of this vision occurred with the evolution of *second nature* (human beings) through the development of our capacities for self/world-awareness, rational thought, creativity, artistic expression, ingenuity (creative complex problem solving), and caring about and for each other and for the rest of nature. With this came the ability to be responsible for human action, for its consequences and for coevolution itself. According to this argument, human society and, through this, *first nature* has, in the final analysis, slowly been actualising this vision.

But there is no guarantee that this potentiality, and not some other, will come to rule in the future. The responsibility for trying to ensure that it does falls to human beings because it is only we who can conceive of the responsibility in the first place and who have the capacity to intentionally do something with it. Regardless of whether one agrees with this particular vision, it provides one way to locate social justice within a broader ethicscape which incorporates the aspirations of related sectors.

Beyond Welfare

Australia provides a case study of the difficulties which traditional Western approaches to social care have had coping with the needs, contexts and disadvantages of rural people. The same story could be recounted for many other nations. When welfare practitioners, managers, planners and policy formulators moved seriously into rural Australia in the 1980s, they were at a loss to know how to deal with what was, to them, a new reality. They were 'bushed' because their conceptual and applied technologies were not as effective as they had been in urban areas.

Moving beyond Australia and rural contexts, Western welfare has not solved, or even significantly reduced, the major problems facing the human race. Hunger and starvation have continued to increase despite the fact that the world produces enough food for everyone. In 1994, the Save the Children Fund reported that 13,000 children were dying daily from diarrhoea, yet could be saved by a simple inexpensive daily sachet of salts and sugar. In 1993, Galtung (p.688) reported that 40,000 children were dying each day from preventable diseases and malnutrition. Poverty continues unabated and has increased over the last 30 years in most countries. Throughout the world, the distribution of wealth has become increasingly obscene. Unemployment has climbed to previously unacceptable levels in many developed countries - permanently, we are told, by political and economic power brokers. In one of the wealthiest countries in the world, one-third of Australia's youth are unemployed, mostly for the long term, and the life span of many indigenous people is 20 years less than the national average. Mental illness has increased this century in most Western countries as more and more people fail to find meaning in their lives and fall into the void of schizophrenia or the suicidal abyss of depression and despair.

Traditional Western social welfare has failed rural Australians because it is founded on wrong assumptions about human life, ignorant of what is known about rural living and isolated from related sectors. We have become confused about our purposes and how these relate to broader visions for the human race and the planet's other inhabitants. The philosophically ill-founded Cartesian view of the human being as a fragmented, objectified, commodified, disengaged and tragically lonely astronaut in a space capsule has not solved the problems of human living. Human life is subjective, more or less integrated, and embedded in physical, social, cultural and spiritual worlds. Ideologically, social care is concerned with developing and preserving equal human rights and changing the distribution of power and resources so that this is possible. As professionals, and as human beings, we have an obligation to contribute to the ongoing, deliberate construction of the human ethicscape.

Empirically, rural living is embedded in the sense, and reality, of local and geographically-extended communities. In rural areas, social care is entwined with other sectors, including market and political forces, the natural world, shared spirituality, health care and education. In their day-to-day practice, practitioners have to identify, understand and work with these realities, and for this they need useful frameworks and strategies. In Chapter 4, social care was located within the inter-sectoral framework of managed, sustainable regional change and, in the present chapter, social ecology and coevolutionary theories were identified as potentially useful conceptual tools to help us understand the interrelationships involved. Throughout this book, approaches to rural social care have been developed from such frameworks, more useful philosophical assumptions, clearer ideological commitments and more empirically-grounded knowledge of rural life.

Essentially, social care is an expression of human community. To limit the concept to resources provided through formal organisational structures is the wrong starting point. All social care practitioners - direct service workers, managers, social planners, community developers, policy formulators and researchers - focus on, and work through, interaction between people. Inevitably, they, too, are within the interaction, contributing to the expression of human caring. They are located where the various dialectics of human community are played out, marshalling the formal and informal resources which people need to handle their lives as best they can.

The practitioner stands where horizontal and vertical ties intersect, where individuals merge with their local and geographically extended communities, where individual responsibility and community commitment meet, where formal and informal care interact, and where social well-being interfaces with market forces, political processes, shared spirituality, physical well-being and education. The social care practitioner is the human being who, inevitably imperfectly, must navigate between the pristine tidiness of theoretical formulations and the messiness of real world demands within this sea of human interaction.

Bibliography

Aboriginal and Torres Strait Islander Commission (ATSIC) (1993), *Social Justice Issues for Aboriginal People in North Australia*, ATSIC, Darwin.
Alexander, I. (1994), 'DURD Revisited? Federal Policy Initiatives for Urban and Regional Planning 1991-94', *Urban Policy and Research 12(1)*, 6-26.
Alston, M. (ed.) (1991a), *Family Farming Australia and New Zealand*, Keypapers No.2, Centre for Rural Social Research, School of Humanities and Social Sciences, Charles Sturt University - Riverina, Wagga Wagga.
_____ (1991b), 'Women's Place in the Future of Agriculture', in M. Alston (ed.), *ibid.*, 97-104.
_____ (1992), 'Editorial: Rural Australia', *Australian Social Work 45(2)*, p.2.
_____ (1995), *Women on the Land: The Hidden Heart of Rural Australia*, UNSW Press, Sydney.
Anderson, J. (1997), *Media Release: Federal Government gives Farm Sector "AAA" Rating*, 14th September, Parliament House, Canberra.
Aoun, S., Underwood, R. and Rouse, I. (1994), 'A Pilot Study of Psycho-social Morbidity in Rural General Practice', in D. McSwan and M. McShane (eds.), *Issues Affecting Rural Communities*, Rural Education Research and Development Centre, James Cook University of North Queensland, Townsville, 110-6.
Arensburg, C.M. (1955), 'American Communities', *American Anthropologist 57*, 1143-62.
Arnstein, S. (1969), 'A Ladder of Citizen Participation', *Journal of the American Institute of Planners*, July, 216-24.
Australian Bureau of Agricultural and Resource Economics (ABARE) (1992), *Commodity Statistical Bulletin 1992*, ABARE, Canberra.
Australian Bureau of Statistics (ABS) (1990), *Index of Economic Resources*, ABS, Canberra.
_____ (1991a), *1991 Census of Population and Housing*, ABS, Canberra.
_____ (1991c), *CDATA with MapInfo*, ABS Cat.No. 2721.0-8, ABS, Canberra.
_____ (1994), *Socio-economic Index for Areas*, ABS, Canberra.
_____ (1997), *Australian Demographic Statistics, September Quarter*, ABS Cat.No. 3101.0, ABS, Canberra.
Australian Catholic Social Welfare Commission (ACSWC) (undated), *Evaluation of the Skills and Requirements of Rural Human Service Organisations*, ACSWC, Curtin.
Australian Council of Social Service (ACOSS) (1993a), 'An Overview of the Report on Local Government and Social Justice: Key Issues for Developing Local Government's Social Justice Role', in ACOSS, *Local Government and Social Justice, Final Report of the Project on Local Government in a Time of Regional Change*, ACOSS, Sydney, i-x.
_____ (1993b), *Local Government and Social Justice, Final Report of the Project on Local Government in a Time of Regional Change*, ACOSS, Railway Square, NSW.
_____ (1994), ACOSS Charities Inquiry Submission, *Impact*, June, p.1 and p.10.

Australian Farm Journal (1993), February.
Australian Government Commission of Inquiry into Poverty (1975), *Poverty in Australia, Volume 1 - First Main Report*, Australian Government Commission of Inquiry into Poverty, AGPS, Canberra.
Australian Science and Technology Council (1993), *Research and Technology in Tropical Australia, Draft Report*, AGPS, Canberra.
Ayres, J.S. and Potter, H.R. (1989), 'Attitudes toward Community Change: A Comparison between Rural Leaders and Residents', *Journal of the Community Development Society 20(1)*, 1-18.
Bailey (1978), *Consultative Arrangements and the Co-ordination of Social Policy Development*, Task Force on Co-ordination in Welfare and Health, AGPS, Canberra.
Bates, E. (1983), *Health Systems and Public Scrutiny - Australia, Britain and United States*, Croom Helm, London.
Bates, V.E., Clarke, F.W. and Bertsche, J.W. (1980), 'Developing Comprehensive Community Helping Systems in Boom Towns: The Potential of Informal Helping', in J. Davenport III and J.A. Davenport (eds.), *The Boom Town: Problems and Promises in the Energy Vortex*, University of Wyoming, Laramie.
Bell, C. and Newby, H. (1972), *Community Studies: An Introduction to the Sociology of the Local Community*, Praeger, New York.
Benedikston, K., Manning, S., Moran, W. and Anderson, G. (1990), *Participation of Ragian County Farm Households in the Labour Force*, Occasional Publication 27, Department of Geography, University of Auckland, Auckland.
Benzaken, D. (1995), 'Social Impact Assessment in Environmental Decision Making Processes', *Northern Radius 2(3)*, 9-13.
Blacksell, M., Clark, A., Economides, K. and Watkins, C. (1988), 'Legal Services in Rural Areas: Problems of Access and Local Need', *Progress in Human Geography 12(1)*, 47-65.
Blanchard, A. and Lin, M. (eds.) (1987), *Social Work in a Changing Society*, Proceedings, 20th National Conference of the Australian Association of Social Workers, AASW Ltd., Canberra.
Bone, R. et al. (1993), *The Needs of Young People in the Whitsunday Shire*, Welfare Research and Studies Centre, James Cook University of North Queensland, Townsville.
Bookchin, M. (1995a), *Re-enchanting Humanity: A Defense of the Human Spirit against Anti-humanism, Misanthropy, Mysticism and Primitivism*, Cassell, London.
_____ (1995b), *The Philosophy of Social Ecology: Essays on Dialectical Naturalism*, Second Edition, Blackrose Books, Montreal.
Booth, K. (1995), 'Human Wrongs and International Relations', *International Affairs 71(1)*, 103-26.
Braglio Luther, V. (1994), 'Clues to Community Survival: A Curriculum for Leadership Development', in D. McSwan and M. McShane (eds.), *op cit.*, 339-42.
Breed, C. (1987), 'Rural Aboriginal Women: What Do They Want and How Do They Want It', in P. Dunn (ed.), *Community Welfare Services: A Rural Focus*, Riverina and Murray Neighbourhood Centres Group, Wagga Wagga, 147-52.
Bryant, L. (1991), 'Farm Family Displacement', in M. Alston (ed.), *op cit.*, 81-96.
_____ (1992), 'Social Aspects of the Farm Financial Crisis', in G. Lawrence, F. Vanclay and B. Furze (eds.), *Agriculture, Environment and Society: Contemporary Issues for Australia*, Macmillan, South Melbourne, 157-72.

Buck, R. (1982), *Personal Communication to E.E. Martinez-Brawley.*
Burnley, I.H. (1981), 'Population Change and Social Inequalities in Sparsely Populated Regions in Australia', in R.E. Lonsdale and J.H. Holmes (eds.), *Settlement Systems in Sparsely Populated Regions: The United States and Australia*, Pergamon, New York, 105-24.
Bush, R. (1990), 'Rural Youth Suicide', *Rural Welfare Research Bulletin No.6*, 25-7.
Buxton, E.B. (1976), 'Delivering Social Services in Rural Areas', in L.H. Ginsberg (ed.), *Social Work in Rural Communities: A Book of Readings*, Council on Social Work Education, New York, 29-38.
Callaghan, B. (1993), 'Planning and Social Infrastructure Provision', Discussion Paper Number Two, in Australian Council of Social Service, *op cit.*, 75-109.
Camasso, M.J. and Moore, D.E. (1985), 'Rurality and the Residualist Social Welfare Response', *Rural Sociology 50*, 397-408.
Campbell, A., Converse, P.E., and Rodgers, W.L. (1976), *The Quality of American Life: Perceptions, Evaluations and Satisfactions*, Russell Sage Foundation, New York.
Campbell, H. and Phillips, E. (1993), 'The Uncoupling Thesis: A Critical Appraisal', *Regional Journal of Social Issues 27*, 47-9.
Carter, J. and Jones, T. (1989), *Social Geography*, Edward Arnold, London.
Cass, B. (1991), *The Housing Needs of Women and Children*, Discussion Paper, National Housing Strategy, AGPS, Canberra.
Castles, I. (1995), *Year Book Australia 1995*, ABS, Canberra.
Centacare Australia and Australian Catholic Social Welfare Commission (Centacare) (1993), *A New Approach to Welfare Services in Rural and Remote Areas of Australia*, Centacare Australia and ACSWC.
Cheers, B. (1980), 'Things and Theories', *Journal of Contemporary Social Work Education 3*, 99-107.
_____ (1985), 'Aspects of Interaction in Remote Communities', *Australian Social Work 38(3)*, 3-10.
_____ (1990a), 'Mr. Silly Feet', *Families in Society: The Journal of Contemporary Human Services 71*, 246-51.
_____ (1990b), 'Rural Disadvantage in Australia', *Australian Social Work 43(1)*, 5-13.
_____ (1991), 'Problems of Families in Remote Towns', *Australian Social Work 44(3)*, 37-41.
_____ (1992a), 'Rural Social Work and Social Welfare in the Australian Context', *Australian Social Work 45(2)*, 11-21.
_____ (1992b), *Social Support in Small Remote Towns in Far North and North-west Queensland, Australia: Implications for Human Services*, unpublished PhD thesis, James Cook University of North Queensland, Townsville.
_____ (1993a), 'Remote Region Social Developers', *Regional Journal of Social Issues 27*, 59-77.
_____ (1993b), 'Roads and People', *Rural Society 3(1)*, 12-5.
_____ (1995), *Integrating Social and Economic Development in Regional Australia*, Critical Social Justice Paper No.2, Centre for Social and Welfare Research, James Cook University of North Queensland, Townsville.
_____ (1996), *Global Change and Rural People*, Monograph Series No.2, Centre for Development Studies, Edith Cowan University, Perth.
_____ (1997), *Social Support in Remote Areas of Australia*, unpublished paper, School of Social Work and Social Policy, University of South Australia, Adelaide.

_____ and Harris, K. (1995), *We Can't Pass Go: Non-mainstream Education and Training for Young People in Townsville/Thuringowa*, Centre for Social and Welfare Research, James Cook University of North Queensland, Townsville.

Cheers, B. and Yip, K. (1994), *The Needs of Young People in the Hinchinbrook Shire*, Welfare Research and Studies Centre, James Cook University of North Queensland, Townsville.

Childs, A.W. and Melton, G.B. (eds.) (1983), *Rural Psychology*, Plenum Press, New York.

Christenson, J.A. (1984), '*Gemeinschaft* and *Gesellschaft*: Testing the Spatial and Communal Hypotheses', *Social Forces 63*, 160-8.

Cities Commission (1973), *A Recommended New Cities Programme for the Period 1973-1978*, Parliamentary Paper No.223, AGPS, Canberra.

Clark, D. (1994), 'Health and Welfare Needs of Remote Area Women', *Rural Society 4(3/4)*, 22-9.

Clark, J. (1995), 'The State, Popular Participation, and the Voluntary Sector', *World Development 23*, 593-601.

Coleman, M. (1987), *Providing Government Services: Opportunities and Constraints*, paper presented at the Rural Australia Symposium: The Future of Non-metropolitan Australia, Albury.

Collier, K. (1984), *Social Work with Rural Peoples: Theory and Practice*, New Star Books, Vancouver.

Collingridge, M. (1991), 'What is Wrong with Rural Social and Community Services?', *Rural Society 1(2)*, 2-6.

Commonwealth Department of Foreign Affairs and Trade (1993), *Composition of Trade: Australia, 1992*, AGPS, Canberra.

Commonwealth Department of Human Services and Health (1995), *Youth Suicide in Australia: A Background Monograph*, AGPS, Canberra.

Coombs, H.C. (1993), 'Black Society is not Mired in Failure: the Debate on Aboriginal Affairs', in H.C. Coombs, *Issues in Dispute: Aborigines Working for Autonomy*, NARU, Australian National University and *The Age* and *The Canberra Times*, Darwin, 12-6.

Cooper, S. (1992), *Farm Wars: The Battles Confronting Australian Farming*, Schwartz and Wilkinson, Melbourne.

Coorey, L. (1988), *Domestic Violence and the Police: Who is being Protected? A Rural Australian View*, University of Sydney Printing Service, University of Sydney, Sydney.

Cotterell, J.L. (1984), 'Social Networks of Mining Town Women', *Australian Journal of Social Issues 19*, 101-12.

Cottrell Jnr, L.S. (1983), 'The Competent Community', in R. Warren and L. Lyon (eds.), *New Perspectives on the American Community*, Dorsey Press, Homewood, Illinois, 401-12.

Courtenay, P.P. (1982), *Northern Australia: Patterns and Problems of Tropical Development in an Advanced Country*, Longman Cheshire, Melbourne.

Cox, D. and Veteri, D. (1992), *Developing Links with Rural Victoria: An Information and Discussion Paper*, Victorian Council of Social Service and Office of Rural Affairs, Melbourne.

Craig, R.A. and Killen, A.E. (1984), 'Farm Families: A Focus for Australian Rural Social Work?', *Australian Social Work 37(1)*, 19-26.

Cribb, J. (1994), 'Farewell to the Heartland', *The Australian Magazine February 12-13*, 10-6.
Crittenden, R. and Lea, D. (1989), 'Whose wants in 'Needs Based Planning'?, Some Examples of Unwritten Agendas from the Provincial Integrated Rural Development Programmes of Papua New Guinea', *Public Administration and Development 9*, 471-86.
Crofts, D. (1992), *Integrated Planning for Housing, Employment and Services - The Role of Local Government in Building Better Cities*, paper presented to the Sustainable Cities Conference, Canberra.
Cullen, T., Dunn, P. and Lawrence, G. (eds.) (1990), *Rural Health and Welfare in Australia*, Centre for Rural Social Research, Charles Sturt University, Wagga Wagga.
Curtis, A., Birckhead, J. and De Lacy, T. (1995), 'Community Participation in Landcare Policy in Australia: the Victorian Experience with Regional Landcare Plans', *Society and Natural Resources 8*, 415-30.
Dale, A. (undated), *Key Concepts in Local Area Planning*, Social Impact Assessment Unit, Department of Family Services and Aboriginal and Islander Affairs, Brisbane.
_____ (1994), 'Delivering Community Services in Rural Communities: Problems and Prospects', in D. McSwan and M. McShane (eds.), *op cit.*, 329-35.
_____ (1995), *Social Impact Assessment in Queensland: Why Practice Lags Behind Legislative Opportunity*, paper presented to the Queensland Environmental Law Association (QUELA), Port Douglas.
Department of Aboriginal Affairs (1986), *Aboriginal Statistics 1985*, AGPS, Canberra.
Department of Community Services (DCS) (1986), *Low Incomes and Social Issues in Rural and Provincial Australia*, DCS, Canberra.
Department of Families, Youth and Community Care (DFYCC) (1997), *RAATSICCP Calendar*, DFYCC, Brisbane.
Department of Family and Community Services (DFACS) (1993), *RAATSICCP Services Progress Summary 1993*, DFACS, Brisbane.
_____ (1994), *RAATSICCP Services Progress Summary 1994*, DFACS, Brisbane.
_____ (1995), *North Queensland Community Services Development Regional Profile*, DFACS, Brisbane.
Department of Health, Housing and Community Services (DHHCS) (1992), *Annual Report*, DHHCS, Canberra
Department of Housing and Regional Development (1994), *Business Investment and Regional Prosperity: the Challenge of Rejuvenation*, Department of Housing and Regional Development, Canberra.
Department of Immigration and Ethnic Affairs (1984), *Australia: Statement prepared for the International Conference on Population*, Mexico City, August, AGPS, Canberra.
Department of Primary Industries and Energy (1995), *The Rural Book*, AGPS, Canberra.
Department of Prime Minister and Cabinet (1992), *Housing and other Services in Rural and Remote Areas*, Report No.4, Social Justice Research Program into Locational Disadvantage, AGPS, Canberra.
_____ (1994), 'The Mabo Case and the Native Title Act', in I. Castles, *op cit.*, ABS, Canberra, 49-52.
Department of Social Security (1995), *Information Handbook: A Guide to Payments and Services*, DSS, Canberra.

DeSantis, M. et al. (1994), *Leadership and Regional Economic Development*, paper presented at the Annual Meeting of the North American Regional Science Meetings, Niagara Falls, Ontario.

Dickey, B. (1980), *No Charity There: A Short History of Social Welfare In Australia*, Nelson, Melbourne.

Dillman, D. and Tremblay Jr., K. (1977), 'Population Redistribution, Migration and Residential Preferences', *Annals of the American Academy of Political and Social Sciences 429*, 130-44.

Disney, J. (1992), *Regional Development and Australia's Future*, The Annual Earle Page Lecture, University of New England, Armidale.

Dixon, J. (1987), 'The Dilemma of Community Management', in P. Dunn (ed.), *op cit.*, 169-90.

Dodson, M. (1993), *Aboriginal and Torres Strait Islander Social Justice Commission First Report*, AGPS, Canberra.

Douglas, D. (1989), 'Community Economic Development in Rural Canada: A Critical Review', *Plan Canada 29(2)*, 28-46.

Dunn, P. (1982), *Personal Communication*.

_____ (ed.) (1987), *Community Welfare Services: A Rural Focus*, Riverina and Murray Neighbourhood Centres Group, Wagga Wagga.

_____ (1989), 'Rural Australia: Are You Standing in it? Putting some Definition into "Rural"', *Rural Welfare Research Bulletin No.2*, 12-3.

_____ (1990), 'Rural Older Persons: Some Issues and Implications', in T. Cullen, P. Dunn and G. Lawrence (eds.), *op cit.*, 111-31.

_____ and Williams, C. (1992), Human Services Delivery to the Elderly, *Rural Society 2(1)*, 10-2.

Dusevik, T. (1995), 'Outback blacks face 'Fourth World' lifespans', *The Weekend Australian June 24-25*, 7.

Eakins, S.K. and Kleven, S.L. (1988), 'Inter-church Ministries of Nebraska: The Farm Crisis Response Network', *Human Services in the Rural Environment 12*, 29-32.

Edgerton, J.W. (1983), 'Models of Service Delivery', in A.W. Childs and G.B. Melton (eds.), *op cit.*, Plenum Press, New York, 275-303.

Elderton, C. (1992), *A Discussion Paper on Coordination, Community Development Planning and Evaluation*, Northern Australia Development Unit, Darwin.

Epps, R. (1994), 'The Chemistry of Economic Development in Rural Australia: Proposed Methodologies', *The Australian Journal of Regional Studies No.8*, December, 12-29.

_____ and Sorensen, T. (1993), 'Introduction', in T. Sorensen and R. Epps (eds.), *Prospects and Policies for Rural Australia*, Addison Wesley Longman Australia, Melbourne, 1-6.

Ernst, J. (undated), *Community Development: Back to Basics*, Outer Urban Research and Policy Unit, Victoria University of Technology, Melbourne.

Etzioni, A. (1989), 'The "Me First" Model in the Social Sciences is too Narrow', Editorial, *The Chronicle of Higher Education, February 1*, A44.

Fagan, D., Kennedy, F. and Short, J. (1996), 'High Court's Decision Angers Farmers, Miners', *The Australian, Tuesday December 24*, 1.

Fattahipour, A. (1991), 'The Malays' Quest for a Muslim Identity', in S. Sewell and A. Kelly (eds.), *Social Problems in the Asia Pacific Region*, Booralong Publications, Brisbane, 188-208.

Fenby, B.L. (1980), 'Social Work in a Rural Setting', in H.W. Johnson (ed.), *Rural Human Services: A Book of Readings*, F.E. Peacock, Inc., Itasca, Illinois, 149-53.
Filson, G. and McCoy, M. (1993), 'Farmers' Quality of Life: Sorting Out the Differences by Class', *The Rural Sociologist 13(1)*, 15-37.
Fine, M. (1995), 'Community-Based Services and the Fragmentation of Provision', *Australian Journal of Social Issues 30*, 143-61.
Fischer, C. (1982), *To Dwell Among Friends: Personal Networks in Town and City*, The University of Chicago Press, Chicago.
Fitzwarryne, P. and Fitzwarryne, C. (1982), *Health Education Programmes in Rural Areas: Evaluation of a Demonstration Project*, Health Research Associates, Canberra.
Foley, P.W., Fyffe, R.G.B. and Grichting, W.L. (1986), *Sugar People take a Caning: A Report on the Impact of the Decline of the Sugar Industry on Families in the Mulgrave Shire, North Queensland*, Department of Behavioural Sciences, James Cook University of North Queensland, Townsville.
Frankenburg, R. (1966), *Communities in Britain, Social Life in Town and Country*, Penguin Books, Baltimore.
Freilich, M. (1963), 'Toward an Operational Definition of Community', *Rural Sociology 28*, 117-27.
Freudenberg, W.R. and Jones, R.E. (1991), 'Criminal Behaviour and Rapid Community Growth: Examining the Evidence', *Rural Sociology 56*, 619-45.
Froland, C., Pancoast, D.L., Chapman, N.J. and Kimboko, P.J. (1981), *Helping Networks and Human Services*, Sage, Beverly Hills.
Galtung, J. (1993), 'Peace', in J. Kreiger (ed.), *The Oxford Companion to the Politics of the World*, Oxford University Press, Oxford.
Ganguli, M., Gilby, J., Seaberg, E. and Belle, S. (1995), 'Depressive Symptoms and Associated Factors in a Rural Elderly Population - The Moveis Project', *American Journal of Geriatric Psychiatry 3*, 144-60.
Gilbert, N. and Specht, H. (1981a), 'Emergence of the Institution', in N. Gilbert and H. Specht (eds.), *The Emergence of Social Welfare and Social Work*, Second Edition, F.E. Peacock, Itasca, Illinois, 18-21.
_____ (eds.) (1981b), *The Emergence of Social Welfare and Social Work*, Second Edition, F.E. Peacock, Itasca, Illinois.
Ginsberg, L.H. (1977), 'Rural Social Work', in J.B. Turner et al. (eds.), *Encyclopedia of Social Work, 17th Issue, Vol.2*, NASW, Washington, D.C., 1229-34.
Gleed, S. (1996), *Symbiosis: A Study of Northern Territory Missions and Government, 1910-1940*, unpublished Master of Social Policy thesis, Department of Social Work and Community Welfare, James Cook University of North Queensland, Townsville.
Glover, J. and Woollacott, T. (1992), *A Social Health Atlas of Australia*, ABS, Canberra.
Goodfellow, M. (1983), 'Reasons for Use and Nonuse of Social Services Among the Rural Elderly', *Human Services in the Rural Environment 8(4)*, 10-6.
Gray, A. (1988), *Aboriginal Child Survival: An Analysis of Results from the 1986 Census of Population and Housing*, Occasional Paper, ABS, Canberra.
Gray, I. (1991), 'Family Farming and Ideology: Some Preliminary Explorations', in M. Alston (ed.), *op cit.*, 55-68.
Griffith, D.A. (1994), 'A Northern Territory Approach to Quantifying "Access Disadvantage" to Educational Services in Remote and Rural Australia', in D. McSwan and M. McShane (eds.), *op cit.*, 311-4.

Hadley, R. and Hatch, S. (1981), *Social Welfare and the Failure of the State*, Allen and Unwin, London.

Hadley, R. and McGrath, M. (1984), *When Social Services are Local; The Normanton Experience*, Allen and Unwin, London.

Harber, K. and Payton, G. (1978), *Heinemann Australian Dictionary*, Second Edition, Heinemann Educational Australia, Richmond.

Hardiman, M. and Midgley, J. (1982), *The Social Dimensions of Development*, Wiley, Chichester.

Harper, S. (1989), 'The British Rural Community: an Overview of Perspectives', *Journal of Rural Studies 5(2)*, 161-84.

Harris, K., Cheers, B. and Hatte, E. (1993), *South Townsville Inner City Village Project: Final Summary and Recommendations, South Townsville Inner City Village Project*, Welfare Research and Studies Centre, James Cook University of North Queensland, Townsville.

Hart, J. (1995), 'The Challenge of Remote Area Social Work: A Pacific Island Experience', *Australian Social Work 48(2)*, 39-45.

Hays, T. (1996), *Personal Communication*.

Hegel, G.W.F. (1969), *Hegel's Science of Logic*, translated by A.V. Miller, Allen and Unwin, London.

Henshall Hansen Associates (1988), *Small Towns Study in Victoria*, Department of Agriculture and Rural Affairs, Melbourne.

Heyman, S.R. (1983), 'Problems in Program Development and the Development of Alternatives', in A.W. Childs and G.B. Melton (eds.), *op cit.*, 233-73

Hil, R., Wilkinson, R. and McMahon, J. (1996), *The Employment Needs of People with Disability in the Whitsunday Shire*, CSAWR Research Report No. 4, Centre for Social and Welfare Research, James Cook University, Townsville.

Holmes, J.H. (1984), 'Australia: The Dilemma of Sparse Population and High Expectations', in G. Enyedi and R.E. Lonsdale (eds.), *Rural Public Services: International Comparisons*, Westview Press, Boulder, Colorado, 163-84.

_____ (1985), 'Policy Issues Concerning Rural Settlement in Australia's Pastoral Zone', *Australian Geographical Studies 23*, 3-27.

Hudson, P. (1989) *North Western Australian Coastal Aboriginal Settlements in 1989*, Northern Australia Research Unit (NARU), Australian National University, Darwin.

_____ (1991), 'Tourist Development and Community Attitudes in North Western Australia: Case Studies of Broome and Exmouth', in I. Moffatt and A. Webb (eds.), *North Australia Research: Some Past Themes and New Directions*, NARU, Darwin.

_____ (1992), 'Affirmative Action for Rural and Remote Northern Australia and its Implications for Housing', *Queensland Housing Conference Papers*, Queensland Shelter, Brisbane.

_____ and Jensen, P. (1991), *Remote Towns and Regions in Australia: An Overview and Some Observations*, Proceedings, Pacific Regional Science Conference, Cairns.

Humphrey, C.R. and Wilkinson, K.P. (1993), 'Growth Promotion Activities in Rural Areas: Do they make a Difference?', *Rural Sociology 58(2)*, 175-89.

Humphreys, J.S. (1985), 'A Political Economy Approach to the Allocation of Health Care Resources: The Case of Remote Areas of Queensland', *Australian Geographical Studies 23*, 121-8.

_____ (1993), 'Planning for Services in Rural Australia', *Regional Journal of Social Issues 27*, 10-9.

Hurley, F. (1994), 'Regional Development Policy in the Big Picture', *The Australian Journal of Regional Studies No.8*, December, 1-11.

IINA Torres Strait Islanders Corporation (IINA) (1996), *Proposed Plan of Action for the Prevention of Child Abuse and Neglect in Torres Strait Islander Communities*, IINA, Torres Strait Islands.

Industry Commission (1994a), *Charitable Organisations in Australia: An Inquiry into Community Social Welfare Organisations: Draft Report*, Industry Commission.

_____ (1994b), *Charitable Organisations in Australia: An Inquiry into Community Social Welfare Organisations - Overview: Draft Report*, Industry Commission.

_____ (1995), *Industry Commission Report into Charitable Organisations in Australia*, AGPS, Canberra.

Interorganizational Committee on Guidelines and Principles for Social Impact Assessment (1993), *Guidelines and Principles for Social Impact Assessment*.

Janovich, M. (1967), *The Community Press in an Urban Setting*, Phoenix Books, New York.

Jayasuriya, L. and Lee, M. (eds.) (1994), *Social Dimensions of Development*, Proceedings of the Inaugural Conference of the WA Inter-University Consortium for Development Studies, Paradigm Books, Bentley.

Jeffreys, H. and Munn, P. (1996), 'Tumby Bay - An Integrated Community Development Approach for Managing Change', *Rural Society 6(1)*, 3-13.

Jones, A. (1993), *The Evaluation of the Mackay Regional Council for Social Development Pilot Project July 1991-September 1992: Final Report*, Andrew Jones Pty Ltd., Brisbane.

Jones, G. (1980), 'Nature makes no Leaps', in R. Hadley and M. McGrath (eds.), *Going Local: Neighbourhood Services*, National Council of Voluntary Organization, Bedford Square Press, London.

Jose, N. (1985), 'Cultural Identity', in S. Graubard (ed.), *Australia: The Daedalus Symposium*, Angus and Robertson, Sydney.

Keating, P. (1994), *Working Nation: The White Paper on Employment and Growth*, AGPS, Canberra.

Keith, P.M. (1980), 'Demographic and Attitudinal Factors Associated with Perceptions of Social Work', *Sociology and Social Welfare 7*, 561-70.

Kelley, P. and Kelley, V. (1985), 'Supporting Natural Helpers: A Cross-Cultural Study', *Social Casework 66*, 358-67.

Kenny, S. (1994), *Developing Communities for the Future: Community Development in Australia*, Nelson, Melbourne.

Kivett, V.R. (1983), *Affinal and Consanguineal Kin as a Social Support for the Rural Elderly*, paper of the Journal Series of the North Carolina Agricultural Research Services, Raleigh, NC, 1983.

_____ (1985), 'Aging in Rural Society: Non-kin Community Relations and Participation', in R.T. Coward and G.R. Lee (eds.), *The Elderly in Rural Sociology*, Springer, New York, 79-104,

_____ (1988), 'Older Rural Fathers and Sons: Patterns of Association and Helping', *Family Relations 37*, 62-7.

Korte, C. (1980), 'Urban-Nonurban Differences in Social Behaviour and Social Psychological Models of Urban Impact', *Journal of Social Issues 36(3)*, 29-51.

_____ (1983), 'Help-Seeking in a City: Personal and Organizational Sources of Help', in A. Nadler, J.D. Fisher and B.M. De Paulo (eds.), *New Directions in Helping*,

Vol.3: *Applied Perspectives on Help-Seeking and -Receiving*, Academic Press, New York, 355-71.

Larson, D.K. (1989), 'Transitions of Poverty amidst Employment Growth: Two Nonmetro Case Studies', *Growth and Change 20*, 19-34.

Lawrence, G. (1987), *Capitalism and the Countryside: The Rural Crisis in Australia*, Pluto Press, Leichhardt, Sydney.

_____ and Hungerford, L. (1994), 'Rural Restructuring: Sociological Meaning, Social Impacts and Policy Implications', in D. McSwan and M. McShane (eds.), *op cit.*, 280-6.

Lawrence, G. and Share, P. (1993), 'Rural Australia: Current Problems and Policy Directions', *Regional Journal of Social Issues 27*, 3-9.

Lawrence, G. and Vanclay, F. (1992), 'Agricultural Production and Environmental Degradation in the Murray-Darling Basin', in G. Lawrence, F. Vanclay and B. Furze (eds.), *op cit.*, 33-59.

_____ and Furze, B. (eds.) (1992), *Agriculture, Environment and Society: Contemporary Issues for Australia*, Macmillan, South Melbourne

Lawrence, G. and Williams, C. (1990), 'The Dynamics of Decline: Implications for Social Welfare Delivery in Australia', in T. Cullen, P. Dunn and G. Lawrence (eds.), *op cit.*, 38-59.

Le Heron, R. (1991), 'Perspectives on Pluriactivity', in M. Alston (ed.), *op cit.*, 25-33.

_____, Roche, M. et al. (1991), 'Pluriactivity in New Zealand's Agro-commodity Chains', *Proceedings, Rural Economy NA and Society Section, Sociological Association of Aotearoa (NZ) Conference*, Agribusiness and Economics Research Unit, Lincoln University, Discussion Paper No.129, 41-55.

Lea, D. and Wolfe, J. (1993), *Community Development Planning and Aboriginal Community Control*, North Australia Research Unit Discussion Paper No.14, NARU, Darwin.

Lee, G.R. and Cassidy, M.L. (1981), 'Kinship Systems and Extended Family Ties', in R.T. Coward and W.M. Smith (eds.), *The Family in Rural Society*, Westview Press, Boulder, Colorado, 57-71.

_____ (1985), 'Family and Kin Relationships of the Rural Elderly', in R.R. Coward and G.R. Lee (eds.), *The Elderly in Rural Society*, Springer, New York, 151-69.

Lee, G.R. and Whitbeck, L.B. (1987), 'Residential Location and Social Relations among Older Persons', *Rural Sociology 52(1)*, 89-97.

Lewis, S. (1990), 'Rural Population and Workforce', in D.B. Williams (ed.), *Agriculture in the Australian Economy*, Third Edition, Sydney University Press, Sydney.

Lichter, D.T., Johnston, G. and McLaughlin, D.K. (1994), Changing Linkages between Work and Poverty in Rural America, *Rural Sociology 59*, 395-415.

Lichter, D.T. and McLaughlin, D.K. (1995), 'Changing Economic Opportunities, Family Structure and Poverty in Rural Areas', *Rural Sociology 60*, 688-706.

Lieber, M.D. (1990), 'Lamarckian Definitions of Identity on Kapingamarangi and Pohnpei', in J. Linnekin and L. Poyer (eds.), *Cultural Identity and Ethnicity in the Pacific*, University of Hawaii Press, Honolulu, 71-101.

Lifeline (1992), *A Response to the Drought: A Report of the Activities of Lifeline's Rural Support Unit*, Lifeline, Brisbane.

Lipsky, M. and Lounds, M. (1976), 'Citizen Participation and Health Care: Problems of Government Induced Participation', *Journal of Health Politics, Policy and Law 1(1)*.

Lockie, S. (1994), 'Farmers and the State: Local Knowledge and Self-help in Rural Environmental Management', *Regional Journal of Social Issues* 28, 24-36.

Loder, L.F. (1965), *Report of the Committee of Investigation into Transportation Costs in Northern Australia*, Mimeo, Canberra.

Lohse, H. (1992), 'Actual and Attempted Suicides in Broken Hill', *Youth Studies 11(1)*, 33-8.

Long, K. (1987), 'Clubs: Small Communities in the Big City', *The Atlanta Constitution November 20*, 38.

Long, N. (1977), *An Introduction to the Sociology of Rural Development*, Tavistock, London.

Lonne, R.E. (1990), 'Beginning Country Practice', *Australian Social Work 43(1)*, 31-9.

_____ (1996), *Personal Communication*.

Lonsdale, R.E. (1981), 'Drawing Conclusions from an Examination of Two Nations', in R.E. Lonsdale and J.H. Holmes (eds.), *op cit.*, New York, 377-86.

_____ and J.H. Holmes (eds.) (1981), *Settlement Systems in Sparsely Populated Regions: The United States and Australia*, Pergamon, New York.

Lorenz, F.O. et al. (1993), 'Economic Conditions, Spouse Support, and Psychological Distress of Rural Husbands and Wives', *Rural Sociology* 58, 247-68.

Luloff, A.E. (1990), 'Community and Social Change: How do Small Communities Act?', in A. Luloff and L. Swanson (eds.), *American Rural Communities*, Westview Press, Boulder, Colorado, 214-27.

_____ and Wilkinson, K.P. (1979), 'Participation in the National Flood Insurance Program: A Study of Community Activeness', *Rural Sociology* 44, 137-52.

Lundin, R. and Arger, G. (1994), 'Rural Isolation: Technologies for the Delivery of Education and Training', in D. McSwan and M. McShane (eds.), *op cit.*, 157-63.

MacPherson, S. (1982), *Social Policy in the Third World*, Allanhead, Osmun, New Jersey.

_____ (1994), 'Can we turn Social Science into Social Development Studies?', in L. Jayasuriya and M. Lee (eds.), *op cit.*, 185-203.

Madden, R. (1993), Discussion Paper Number One - Social Justice and Local Government - Identifying the Issues, in ACOSS, *op cit.*, 1-74.

Madden, R. (1994), *National Aboriginal and Torres Strait Islander Survey 1994 Detailed Findings*, ABS, Canberra.

Magill, R.W. and Clark, T.N. (1975), 'Community Power and Decision Making: Recent Research and its Policy Implications', *Social Service Review* 49, 33-45.

Manning, C. and Cheers, B. (1995), 'Child Abuse Notification in a Country Town', *Child Abuse and Neglect: The International Journal* 19, 387-97.

Marsden, D. and Oakley, P. (1982), 'Radical Community Development in the Third World', in G. Craig, N. Derricourt and M. Loney (eds.), *Community Work and the State*, Routledge and Kegan Paul, 153-63.

Martin, K.E. and Wilkinson, K.P. (1984), 'Local Participation in the Federal Grant System: Effects of Community Action', *Rural Sociology* 49, 374-88.

Martinez-Brawley, E.E. (undated), *Social Services in Spain: The Case of Rural Catalonia*, Department of Sociology, The Pennsylvania State University, University Park.

_____ (1980), 'Rural Social Work Tenets in the U.S. and Latin America', *Community Development Journal 15(3)*, 166-78.

_____ (1982), *Rural Social Work and Community Work in the U.S. and Britain*, Praeger, New York.

_____ (1986), 'Community-oriented Social Work in a Rural and Remote Hebridean Patch', *International Social Work 29*, 349-72.

_____ (1987), 'Rural Social Work', in *Encyclopedia of Social Work No.17*, National Association of Social Workers, Washington, D.C., 521-37.

_____ (1989), *Community Oriented Social Work: Some International Perspectives*, unpublished address, Rural Human Services Leadership Conference, Syracuse, New York.

_____ (1990a), *Have We Arrived? Rural Practice Tenets, Myths and Realities*, unpublished Keynote Address, National Rural Social Work Institute, Fredonia, New York.

_____ (1990b), *Perspectives on the Small Community: Humanistic Views for Practitioners*, NASW Press, Silver Spring, MD.

_____ and Blundall, J. (1989), 'Farm Families' Preferences toward the Personal Social Services', *Social Work 34*, 513-22.

_____ with Buck, R.C. (1990), 'Locality and Localism Reconsidered', in E.E. Martinez-Brawley, *Perspectives on the Small Community: Humanistic Views for Practitioners*, NASW Press, Silver Spring, MD, 81-104.

_____ and Delevan, S.M. (1991), *Considerations on Integrative Structures, Conditions and Alternative Models for County Human Services Delivery*, Pennsylvania Rural Counties Project, Department of Sociology, Social Work Program, The Pennsylvania State University, University Park, Pennsylvania.

Mathers, C. (1995), 'Mortality Patterns of Urban, Rural and Remote Populations in Northern Australia', *People and Place 3(2)*, 15-24.

May, R. (1958a), 'Contributions of Existential Psychotherapy', in R. May, E. Angel and H.F. Ellenberger (eds.), *Existence: A New Dimension in Psychiatry and Psychology*, Simon and Schuster, New York, 37-91.

_____ (1958b), 'The Origins and Significance of the Existential Movement in Psychology', in R. May, E. Angel and H.F. Ellenberger (eds.), *ibid.*, 3-36.

McCullough, B.J. (1995), 'The Relationship of Family Proximity and Social Support to the Mental Health of Older Rural Adults: The Appalachian Context', *Journal of Aging Studies 9*, 65-81.

McDonald, E. and Bullis, H. (1991), *Barriers to Effective Service Delivery in Rural and Remote Areas*, unpublished paper, Rural and Remote Areas Unit, Department of Health, Housing and Community Services, Darwin.

McGranahan, D.A. (1984), 'Local Growth and the Outside Contacts of Influentials: An Alternative Test of the 'Growth Machine' Hypothesis', *Rural Sociology 49*, 530-40.

McKenzie, B. (1987), 'Social Problems: The Government Response and its Consequences', in P. Dunn (ed.), *op cit.*, 68-90.

McLennan, W. (1995), *Australian Standard Geographical Classification (ASGC)*, Edition 2.5 (effective 1/7/95), Cat.No.12160, ABS, Canberra.

_____ (1996), *Year Book Australia*, ABS, Canberra.

_____ (1997), *Year Book Australia*, ABS, Canberra.

McSwan, D. and McShane, M. (eds.) (1994), *Issues Affecting Rural Communities*, Rural Education Research and Development Centre, James Cook University of North Queensland, Townsville.

Melton, G. B. (1983), 'Ruralness as a Psychological Construct', in A.W. Childs and G. B. Melton (eds.), *op cit.*, 1-13.

Menneghan, T.M. (1976), 'Clues to Community Power Structures', *Social Work 21*, 126-30.

Mercier, J.M., Paulson, L. and Morris, E.W. (1988), 'Rural and Urban Elderly: Differences in the Quality of the Parent-Child Relationship', *Family Relations 37*, 688-72.

Merton, R.D. (1957), *Social Theory and Social Structure*, Free Press, Glencoe, Illinois.

Midgley, J. (1981), *Professional Imperialism: Social Work in the Third World*, Heinemann, London.

_____ (1986a), 'Community Participation: History, Concepts and Controversies', in J. Midgley, A. et al., *Community Participation, Social Development and the State*, Methuen, London, 13-44.

_____ (1986b), 'Community Participation, the State and Social Policy', in J. Midgley et al., *ibid.*, 145-60.

_____ (1986c), 'Introduction: Social Development, the State and Participation', in J. Midgley et al., *ibid.*, 1-11.

_____ et al. (1986), *Community Participation, Social Development and the State*, Methuen, London.

Midgley, M. (1989), *Wisdom, Information and Wonder: What is Knowledge For?*, Routledge, London.

Miller, M.K. and Luloff, A.E. (1981), 'Who is Rural? A Typological Approach to the Examination of Rurality', *Rural Sociology 46(Winter)*, 608-25.

Minuchin, S. (1974), *Families and Family Therapy*, Tavistock, London.

Mollah, W.S. (1993), 'Towards Sustainable Agriculture: Environmental Contexts, Constraints and Scales as a Guide', in T. Sorensen and R. Epps (eds.), *op cit.*, 57-76.

Monk, J.J. (1980), 'Social Change through Education: Problems of Planning in Rural Australia', in W.P. Avery, R.E. Lonsdale and I. Volgyes (eds.), *Rural Change and Public Policy: Eastern Europe, Latin America and Australia*, Pergamon, New York, 129-55.

Moran, P. and O'Connor, K. (1981), 'Change in the Location of Primary Schools in the Wimmera, Victoria, 1947-1976', in R.E. Lonsdale and J.H. Holmes (eds.), *op cit.*, 262-75.

Morganthauw, T. et al. (1981), 'America's Small Town Boom', *Newsweek, July 6*, 26-37.

Morton Consulting Services Pty. Ltd. (1990), *Rationalisation: Rural Local Government and Human Services*, The Local Government Association of Queensland (Inc.), Brisbane.

Mues, C., Roper, H. and Ockerby, J. (1994), *Survey of Landcare and Land Management Practices 1992-93*, Research Report 94.6, ABARE, Canberra.

Munn, P. (1993), 'Locally Based Resource Funding: the AAP Revisited', *Rural Society 3(3)*, 14-5.

Musgrave, W.F. (1987), 'Economic, Demographic and Other Influences', in *Rural Australia Symposium 1987*, TRDC Paper No.151, TRDC, Armidale.

Mushi, S.S. (1981), 'Community Development in Tanzania', in R. Dore and Z. Mars (eds.), *Community Development*, Croom Helm, London, 139-244.

Nachtigal, P.M. (1994), 'Rural Schools, Rural Communities: An Alternative View of the Future', in D. McSwan and M. McShane (eds.), *op cit.*, 145-50.

National Board of Employment, Education and Training (1991), *Toward a National Education and Training Strategy for Rural Australians*, AGPS, Canberra.

National Housing Strategy (1992), *Background Paper No.12*, AGPS, Canberra.
Nichol, B. (1990), 'What is Rural? - The Debate Continues. "Rural" and "Remote", and the Question of Definition', *Rural Welfare Research Bulletin No.4*, 4-5.
Norgaard, R.B. (1994), *Development Betrayed. The End of Progress and a Coevolutionary Revisioning of the Future*, Routledge, London.
Northern Territory Department of Lands and Housing (1993), *Rental Values in the Northern Territory*, Northern Territory Department of Lands and Housing, Darwin.
Nyerere, J.K. (1968), *Freedom and Socialism*, Dar es Salaam, Oxford University Press, Dar es Salaam.
O'Brien, D.J. and Hassinger, E.W. (1992), 'Community Attachment among Leaders in Five Rural Communities', *Rural Sociology 57*, 521-34.
O'Brien, D.J., et al. (1991), 'The Social Networks of Leaders in More and Less Viable Rural Communities', *Rural Sociology 56*, 699-716.
Ockwell, A. (1990), 'The Economic Structure of Australian Agriculture', in D.B. Williams (ed.), *Agriculture in the Australian Economy*, 3rd Edition, Sydney University Press in association with Oxford University Press, South Melbourne, 27-49.
Office of Northern Development, Commonwealth Department of Housing and Regional Development (1994), *Towards the Development of a North Australia Social Justice Strategy: Final Report*, OND, Darwin.
Office of Rural Affairs (1991), *Study of Government Service Delivery to Rural Communities*, Ministry of Ethnic, Municipal and Community Affairs, Victorian State Government, Melbourne.
Office of Rural Communities (1994), *Queensland Rural Services Directory*, ORC, Brisbane.
Osgood, M.H. (1977), 'Rural and Urban Attitudes toward Welfare', *Social Work 22*, 41-7.
O'Toole, K. (1993), 'Replacing Rurality with Human Services in Victorian Local Government', *Rural Society 3(3)*, 8-13.
Parkum, K. (1983), 'Joiners and Doers: A Study of Why People Volunteer for and Actively Participate in Community Health Planning', *Pennsylvania Sociological Society*, Pennsylvania.
Patterson, S.L. et al. (1988), 'Effectiveness of Rural Natural Helpers', *Social Casework 69*, 272-9.
Pearson, R.R. (1985), *A Short History of a Small Place*, Ballantine Books, New York.
Platt, E. and Brentnall, B. (1985), *Results of a Questionnaire sent to Nurses Working in Areas where there is no Resident Doctor*, unpublished paper presented at the Third National Conference of the Remote Area Nurses Association, Townsville.
Poole, D.L. and Daley, J.M. (1985), 'Problems of Innovation in Rural Social Services', *Social Work 30*, 338-44.
Powell, R.A. (1987), 'Rural Employment', in *Rural Australia Symposium 1987*, TRDC Paper No.151, The Regional Development Centre, Armidale.
Powers, R.C. (1967a), 'Power Actors and Social Change, Part 1', *Journal of Cooperative Extension 5*, 153-63.
_____ (1967b), 'Power Actors and Social Change, Part 2', *Journal of Cooperative Extension 5*, 238-73.
Puckett, T.C. and Frederico, M. (1992), 'Examining Rural Welfare Practice: Differences and Similarities between Rural and Urban Settings', *Australian Social Work 45(2)*, 3-10

Putman, R.D. (1993), 'The Prosperous Community', *The American Prospect, Spring*, 36-42.
Queensland Community Services and Health Industries Training Council Inc. (1996), *Real Skills for Real Workplaces. 1996 Industry Training Plan For The Community Services and Health Industries*, Queensland Community Services Health Industries Training Council Inc., Brisbane.
Queensland Office, ABS (1985), *Queensland Yearbook*, ABS, Brisbane.
Quixley, S. (1993), 'Responding to Young People's Needs', *Impact 24(4)*, 18-20.
Radford, A.J. (1981), 'Community Action: A Rural Survey and Its Outcome', in A. Howe (ed.), *Towards an Older Australia*, University of Queensland, St. Lucia.
Rank, M.R. and Hirschl, T.A. (1988), 'A Rural-Urban Comparison of Welfare Exits: The Importance of Population Density', *Rural Sociology 53*, 190-206.
Raper, M. (ed.) (1994), *The Independent Social Security Handbook: A Practical Guide for Advisers*, Second Edition, Pluto Press Australia, Leichhardt.
Reese, M. and Malamud, P. (1981), 'Our Town in 1981', *Newsweek, July 6*, p.28.
Reid, M. and Solomon, S. (1992), *Improving Australia's Rural Health and Aged Care Services*, National Health Strategy Background Paper No.11, AGPS, Canberra.
Reynolds, M. (undated), *Local Government - The Challenge of Devolution*, unpublished paper, Department of Behavioural Sciences, James Cook University of North Queensland, Townsville.
Riches, G. (1993), *Commitment to Welfare in the New Reality*, Critical Social Justice Paper No.1, Welfare Research and Studies Centre, James Cook University of North Queensland, Townsville.
Rivera, F.G. and Erlich, J.L. (1981), 'Neo-Gemeinschaft Minority Communities: Implications for Community Organization in the United States', *Community Development Journal 3*, 189-200.
Roberts, B. and Thorsheim, H. (1982), 'The Approach of Social Ecology: A Partnership of Support and Empowerment', *Journal of Primary Prevention 3*, 140-3.
Rodgers, W. (1979), *Residential Satisfaction in Relationship to Size of Place*, Institute for Social Research, Ann Arbor, Michigan.
Rolley, F. and Humphreys, J.S. (1993), 'Rural Welfare - The Human Face of Australia's Countryside', in T. Sorensen and R. Epps (eds.), *op cit.*, 241-57.
Romans, S.E. et al. (1992), 'Social Networks and Psychiatric Morbidity in New Zealand Women', *Australian and New Zealand Journal of Psychiatry 26*, 485-92.
Rumley, D. (1983), 'Ideology, Regional Policy and Applied Geography: The Case of the Kimberley', Western Australia, *Australian Journal of Social Issues 1*, 233-44.
Rural and Remote Areas Unit, Department of Health, Housing and Community Services (1991), *Innovative Service Models in Rural and Remote Areas*, unpublished paper, DHHCS, Darwin.
Rural Industries Research and Development Corporation (RIRDC) (1992), *Addressing the Issues of Rural Towns: R&D Opportunities Available for RIRDC to Fund*, RIRDC, Canberra
Sacco, M. (1994), 'Skills and Requirements of Rural Human Service Organisations', in D. McSwan and M. McShane (eds.), *op cit.*, 99-103.
Sackville, R. (1973), 'Social Welfare in Australia: The Constitutional Framework', *Federal Law Review* 5, 248-64.
Salt, B. (1992), *Population Movements in Non-metropolitan Australia*, Coopers and Lybrand Consultants, Melbourne.
Samyia, L. (1987), 'Rural Women's Access to Services', in P.Dunn (ed.), *op cit.*, 115-46.

Saunders, P., Newby, H. and Bell, C. (1978), 'Rural Community and Rural Community Power', in H. Newby (ed.), *International Perspectives in Rural Sociology*, Wiley, Chichester.

Save the Children Fund (1994), *Saving Lives with Salt and Sugar*, Observer, March.

Saw, C. (1994), 'Replacing Rurality with Human Services', *Rural Society 4(3/4)*, 37-8.

Schindeler, E. (1993), *Working for Social Justice in Rural and Remote Queensland*, OND, Darwin.

Schmalenbach, H. (1961), 'The Sociological Category of Communion', in T. Parsons et al. (eds.), *Theories of Society: Foundations of Modern Sociological Theory*, The Free Press of Glencoe, New York.

Scott, J.P. and Roberto, K.A. (1985), 'Use of Informal and Formal Support Networks by Rural Elderly Poor', *The Gerontologist 25*, 624-30.

_____ (1987), 'Informal Supports of Older Adults: A Rural-Urban Comparison', *Family Relations: Journal of Applied Family and Child Studies 36*, 444-9.

Sharp, D. and Inwald, S. (1986), *Community Development and Community Management*, unpublished paper, Sydney.

Sher, J. and Sher, K.R. (1994), 'Beyond the Conventional Wisdom: Rural Development as if Australia's Rural People Really Mattered', in D. McSwan and M. McShane (eds.), *op cit.*, 9-32.

Smailes, P.J. (1995), 'The Enigma of Social Sustainability in Rural Australia', *Australian Geographer 26(2)*, 140-50.

Smallwood, G. (1994), 'Issues Affecting Rural Communities from an Indigenous Perspective', in D. McSwan and M. McShane (eds.), *op cit.*, 305-7.

Smith, B. (1987), 'Developing Appropriate Strategies in the Bush', in A. Blanchard and M. Lin (eds.), *op cit.*, 242-60.

_____ (1989), *Welfare Service Delivery: Options for Remote Areas*, NADU Occasional Paper No.2, Northern Australia Development Unit, Darwin.

_____ (1993), 'Regionalisation,: Resuscitating or Restricting the Country?', *Rural Society 3(2)*, 12-3.

Smith, G. and Smith, W. (1987), 'Mobile Counselling', in A. Blanchard and M. Lin (eds.), *op cit.*, 106-10.

Smith, N. (1984), *Uneven Development: Nature, Capital and the Production of Space*, Basil Blackwell, Oxford.

Sorensen, T. (1993a), 'Approaches to Policy', in T. Sorensen and R. Epps (eds.), *op cit.*, 274-89.

_____ (1993b), 'The Future of the Country Town: Strategies for Local Economic Development', in T. Sorensen and R.Epps (eds.), *ibid.*, 201-40.

_____ (1994), 'Working Nation: A New Approach to Regional Development?', *The Australian Journal of Regional Studies No.8*, December, 39-48.

_____ and Epps, R. (eds.) (1993), *Prospects and Policies for Rural Australia*, Longman Cheshire, Melbourne.

_____ (1994), *Leadership and Local Development: Dimensions of Leadership in Four Central Queensland Towns*, paper presented to the Institute of Australian Geographers Conference, Townsville.

South Australia Health Commission (1988), *A Social Health Strategy for South Australia*, South Australian Health Commission, Adelaide.

Stayner, R. and Reeve, I. (1990), *'Uncoupling': Relationships between Agriculture and the Local Economies of Rural Areas in NSW*, TRDC, Armidale.

Sturmey, R. and Edwards, H. (1991), *The Survival Skills Training Package. Community Services and Health Workforce in Rural and Remote Areas: Needs and Recommendations Study*, University of New England, Armidale.

Sundet, P.A. and Mermelstein, J. (1987), 'Why aren't Farmers Banging Down Agency Doors?', *Public Welfare, Summer*, 15-9.

Symons, G. (1992), *Future Directions and Policy Issues for the Northern Territory*, Department of Health and Community Services, Darwin.

Takaya, Y. (1995), 'The Starting Point of International Cooperation', *Technology and Development 8*, 5-9.

Taskforce on Regional Development (1993), *Developing Australia: A Regional Perspective, Volume 1*, AGPS, Canberra.

Taylor, J. (1987), *Access to Women's Services in Rural Areas*, paper presented at the 20th National Conference of the Australian Association of Social Workers, AASW, Perth.

Taylor, J. and Roach, L. (1994), *The Relative Economic Status of Indigenous People in New South Wales, 1986-91*, Discussion Paper No.55/1994, Centre for Aboriginal Economic Policy Research, Australian National University, Canberra.

Taylor, R.J., Chatters, L.M. and Mays, V.M. (1988), 'Parents, Children, Siblings, In-laws, and Non-kin as Sources of Emergency Assistance to Black Americans', *Family Relations 37*, 298-304.

The Advertiser (1997), 'Attitudes of MPs 'are in the 19th century'', *The Advertiser, Friday, May 9*,13.

Thomas, D. (1971), *Collected Poems 1934-1952*, J.M. Dent and Sons Ltd., London.

Tomlinson, D.D. and Tannock, P.D. (1982), *Review of the Assistance for Isolated Children's Scheme*, Commonwealth Department of Education, Canberra.

Tonnies, F. (1955), *Community and Society*, Harper and Row, New York.

Torzillo, P.J. et al. (1995), 'Invasive Pneumococcal Disease in Central Australia', *The Medical Journal of Australia 167*, 20 February, 182-6.

Trattner, W.I. (1981), 'The Background', in N. Gilbert and H. Specht (eds.), *op cit.*, 22-31.

United Nations (UN) (1975), *Popular Participation in Decision Making for Development*, UN, New York.

_____ (1981), *Popular Participation as a Strategy for Promoting Community Level Action and National Development*, UN, New York.

Urey, J.R. and Henggeler, S.W. (1983), 'Interaction in Rural Families', in A.W. Childs and G.B. Melton (eds.), *op cit.*, 33-44.

Vidich, A.J. and Bensman, J. (1960), *Small Town in Mass Society*, Anchor Books, Garden City, New York.

Wade-Marshall, D. (1982), 'And Deborah Will Talk to the Women', in P. Loveday (ed.), *Service Delivery to Remote Communities*, NARU, Darwin, 69-77.

Walker, A. (1983), *In Search of our Mothers' Gardens*, Harcourt Brace Jovanovich, San Diego.

Walmsley, D.J. (1980), *Social Justice and Australian Federalism: An Inquiry into Territorial Justice and Life Chances in Australia*, Department of Geography, University of New England, Armidale.

_____ and Sorensen, A.D. (1993), *Contemporary Australia: Explorations in Economy, Society and Geography*, Second Edition, Longman Cheshire, Melbourne.

Walsh, P. (1993), *Community Participation in Planning: A Human Services Perspective*, Queensland Council of Social Service Inc., Brisbane.

Warnock, G. (1967), *Contemporary Moral Philosophy*, Macmillan, London.
Warren, R.L. (1963), *The Community in America*, First Edition, Rand McNally, Chicago.
Watson, C. (1992), 'An Ecologically Unsustainable Agriculture', in G. Lawrence, F. Vanclay and B. Furze (eds.), *op cit.*, 19-32.
Wellman, B. (1979), 'The Community Question: The Intimate Networks of East Yorkers', *American Journal of Sociology 84*, 1201-31.
Whittington, B. (1985), 'The Challenge of Family Work in a Rural Community', *The Social Worker/Le Travailleur Social 53*, 104-7.
Wild, R.A. (1974), *Bradstow: A Study of Status, Class and Power in a Small Australian Town*, Allen and Unwin, London.
_____ (1983), 'Communication, Power and the Country Press', *Regional Journal of Social Issues 12*, 1-7.
Wilkinson, K.P. (1989), 'Community Development and Industrial Policy', *Research in Rural Sociology and Development 4*, 241-54.
_____ (1991), *The Community in Rural America*, Greenwood, New York.
Williams, C.J. and McHugh, J. (1993), 'Growing Old in Rural North Queensland', *Rural Society 3(2)*, 2-6.
Williams, C.J. and McMahon, A. (1995), *The Human Service Needs of Older People in the Whitsunday/Airlie Beach Area, North Queensland*, Department of Social Work and Community Welfare and Centre for Social and Welfare Research, James Cook University of North Queensland, Townsville.
Willits, F.K., Bealer, R.C. and Crider, D.M. (1982), 'Persistence of Rural/Urban Difference', in D.A. Dillman and D.J. Hobbs (eds.), *Rural Society in the U.S.: Issues for the 1980s*, Westview Press, Boulder, Colorado.
Wilson, R. (1995), 'Families Hold Key to Teen Self-esteem', *Week-end Australian June 24-25*, p.7.
Wong, L. (1990), 'Reassessing Rural Health Policy', *Health Issues 24*, September, 31-4.
Yap, K.S. (1990), 'Community Participation in Low-income Housing Projects: Problems and Prospects', *Community Development Journal 25(1)*, 56-67.
York, R., Denton, R. and Moran, J. (1989), 'Rural and Urban Social Work Practice: Is There a Difference?', *Social Casework 70*, 201-9.
Zapf, M.K. (1993), 'Remote Practice and Culture Shock: Social Workers Moving to Isolated Northern Regions', *Social Work 38*, 694-704.

Index

008 numbers 178, 199

Aboriginal and Torres Strait Islander Commission (ATSIC) 55
Aborigines 37-8
    disadvantage 38-43
access to services 171-4
accountability
    critique of current methods 190-1
    economic rationalism 6
    horizontal accountability 190
    improving 191
    vertical accountability 190-1
actual, the 265-7
adjustment to rural practice
    phases 249
    strategies 249-50, 252
advocacy 126, 128, 154, 185
Agriculture - Advancing Australia policy 114-5
animateur 234-5
anonymity in rural practice 245-6
applied technology 265
Australia
    economy 27-9
    geography 23
    government 23-4
    politics 23-4
    population 24-6
    settlement patterns 24-7
availability of services 170-1

boundaries
    administrative 207
    geographic 207
    inter-professional 229
    national grid 207
    practitioner-client roles 229-30
boundary issues 229-30
brokerage 194, 196
care 17

central point services 193-200
centralisation
    Australian welfare 5-9, 53, 57, 264
    services 175-6
centre, the 181-2
centre-periphery relationships 182-5, 264
child abuse 149, 173
circuit services 197, 200
coevolution
    dimensions 268-70
    human responsibility 270-1
    meaning 268
co-location 196, 198
combined services funding 198
commencement of rural practice 247-52
commodification 62
communication technology 50-1, 85-6
community
    cohesion 68
    commitment 67-8
    communication technology 50-1
    community entitivity 67-8
    conflict 85
    defining 67-8, 73
    dialectic interaction 260-1
    gemeinschaft interaction 71-3
    gesellschaft interaction 71-3
    horizontal ties 73-5
    identification 67
    indigenous communities 55-6
    interrelatedness 260-2
    investment 67-8
    ownership 10, 150
    participation 10, 147-53
    social development 18, 102
    solidarity 76
    vertical ties 75
community assessment 250-1
community-based organisations
    issues 185-8

management 185-8
  recommendations 187-8
  staffing 185
community development
  approaches 143-5
  definition 142
  need for in rural Australia 58
  processes 143-5
  values 142
community energising 234
community focus
  services 180-1
  social policy 100
community gate-keepers 77-8
community leadership
  'cosmopolitan' leaders 146
  horizontal and vertical ties 146
  issues 146-7
  'local' leaders 146
community-oriented practice
  boundary issues 229-30
  community energising 234
  confidentiality 230-3
  conscientisation 234
  defined 221-3
  generalism 223-5
  joining 240-3
  localism 225-8
  model 221
  mutuality 222
  politicisation 234
  power structures 235-40
  practitioner rewards 244-5
  prevention 223
  proactivity 222
  stress 245-9
community participation
  community identification 149
  community ownership 149
  consultation 148
  definition 147
  delegated power 147-8
  horizontal ties 151
  importance in rural areas 148-50
  informing 148
  ladder of participation 147-8
  negotiation 148
  partnership 148
  state responses 151-2

  vertical ties 151-2
community services development 55-6, 183-5
community services planning 137-8
computer technology 199
conceptual technology 263
confidentiality 230-3
conflict in rural communities 84-5
conscientisation 234
Consultative Rural Finance Forum 114
coordination
  horizontal 208-11
  services 10, 207-14
  vertical 208-10, 212-4
cosmopolitans
  leaders 80-2
  working with 237-8
Country Women's Association 236
craft social service paradigm 180
created relationships 204
Cross Program Funding Initiative 189
culture shock in rural practice 248-9

development as a social policy framework 95
dialectic interaction 257-61
dialectically-related frameworks 257-61
Disaster Relief Payments 115
disorientation period 249
Drought Relief Payment 114

economic development
  definition 103
  social care development 100-2
economic rationalism 6, 47
economic reductionism 94
education, professional 10-1, 175-6, 266-7
electronic media 199-200
elite power structures 239-40
embedded relationships 197, 204-6
Emergency Relief Funds 115
entitivity 67-8
Exceptional Circumstances Relief Payment 114

factionalism 85
Family Payments 114

Farm Business Improvement Program 114
Farm Family Restart Scheme 113-5
Farm Household Support Scheme 111-5
Farm Management Deposit Scheme 114, 116
first nature 268-70
focus of services 180-1
fragmentation
   human living 62
   services 180
   social welfare 7-9
funding
   cross-program 188-90
   formulae 188-90
   models 188-90
   pooled funding 189

gemeinschaft interaction
   definition 71-2
   rural social care 96-7, 259
generalism
   community-oriented practice 223-5
   stress 246-7
generic services 194, 196
gesellschaft interaction
   defining 71-3
   rural social care 96-7, 259
globalisation
   Australian economy 45-9
   economic market 45-9
   rural Australia 45-9
   social welfare 15
gossip 77-8
grief and loss phase of adjustment 249
Griffith Service Access Frame 14

honeymoon phase of adjustment 249
horizontal ties
   accountability 190
   community 73-5
   community leadership 146
   community participation 151
   definition 73-4
   rural social care 97-100
   service coordination 209-11
   service integration 209-11
   social care development 153-4

   social care practice 74-5, 97-100
   social development 97-100
housing issues
   Aborigines 119-23
   access 119-23
   affordability 119-23
   appropriateness 123-5
   availability 119-23
   caravan parks 126-7
   entrapment 119
   information 125
   location 122
   principles 127-9
   quality 123
   representation 126
   Torres Strait Islanders 119-23
human rights 16-7, 270

ideology, definition 89
income security
   critique 116-7
   policy directions 117-8
   programs 109-16
indigenisation 225-6
indigenous Australians
   capitalism 38
   change 54-6
   coevolution 269
   culture 38
   disadvantage 7, 38-43
   European invasion 38, 54-5
   land rights 43-5, 55
   population 37-8
   social welfare 54-5, 59
influence 80-3
informal care 201-6
   formal care 203-6, 258-61
   linking strategies 203-6
information
   hubs 77
   needs of organisations 178-9
   needs of rural people 176-8
   provision strategies 177-80
innovation 224
in-reach services 196-7, 198-200
integrated service approaches 195-6
integration of services 206-15
   horizontal 208, 210-11
   vertical 208, 212-4

inter-professional boundaries 229
interrelatedness 257-63
isolation, definition 13

Job Search Allowance 112
joining 240-3

key helpers 197, 204-5

ladder of community participation 147
Landcare Program 138
leadership in rural communities 146-7
local area planning
    community services 137-8
    corporate plan 136
    definition 136
    environmental planning 138
    housing 128
    industry development 138
    infrastructure planning 139
    land use planning 139
    planning schemes 136
    regional planning 137
    strategic planning 136
local influentials 81, 237-8
localism
    centre-periphery 181-5
    coevolution 269
    community-oriented practice 221-3
    housing 127-8
    localism-centralism debate 181-5
    services 181-5
    social care 57
locality-based community, definition 67-8

Mabo, Eddie 43
mainstreaming 94-5
managed coevolution 270
managed interaction 257, 262
    formal and informal care 260
    technologies 262
managed, sustainable regional change
    definition 106
    framework 107
    presentation 103-7
market processes
    change 45-9
    rural impacts 45-9

media
    community power structures 87-9
    roles 87-9
    social debate 87-8
migration, urban to rural 122
models of service delivery
    classification 196-7
    presentation and analysis 193-206
multiple practitioner roles 245-6
multi-purpose service models 194-200
mutual aid networks 197, 204

Native Title Act 43-5
Natural Disaster Relief Scheme 115-6
natural helping
    access to services 172
    key helpers 197, 204-5
    linking services 10, 15, 203-6
    natural social networks 66
    natural support networks 66
    rural compared with urban 201-2
    rural people 201-6
natural world
    estrangement from 62-3
    social welfare 9, 54
network care 200-6
Newstart Allowance 111
non-government organisations 152-3
    advocacy 154-5,
    social care development 154-5, 158

one-stop shops 179, 195
ongoing service models 194-8
out-reach service models 193-8

Parenting Allowance 114
participation 147-53
    housing 128
Partner Allowance 114
periphery, the 181-2
pluralist power structures 239-40
pluriactivity
    meaning 49
    social policy responses 59
political economy arguments 36-7
politicisation 234
potential, the
    meaning 265
    human society 271

power 80-3
power actors 80-2, 235
power structures
  definition 82
  social change 82-3
  typology 82-3
  working with 235-40
practice, rural social care 219-53
practice wisdom 222
professionalisation
  services 175-6
  welfare 9, 15
programatic approaches 206-7
program-based services 98
provision-based services 9
public housing 93, 119,125, 269

rationalisation of services 6
reactive residualism 95
real, the 265
regional councils for social
  development 214-5
regional development 103
regional planning 137
regional social development
  commission 215
regional social plans 214-5
regionally-based services
  coordination 206-15
  integration 206-15
  relevance 174-6
relevance of services
  increasing 176
  issues 174-6
Remote Area Aboriginal and Torres
  Strait Islander Child Care Program
  184-5
Remote Area Allowance 115
Remote Area Rebates 115
Remote Areas Children's Funding
  Package 189
remoteness
  defining 13-4
  implications 85-6
  servicing 26
rental housing programs 121-2
reorganisation and adjustment 249
residential care 124
responsiveness 94, 145, 263

Restart Re-establishment Grant 113,
  115
role-related key helpers 197, 204-5
Royal Flying Doctor Service 195
Rural Adjustment Scheme 111-2
Rural Agents program 179, 189
rural Australia
  diversity 27, 152, 175
  economy 27-9
  education 32-3, 58
  essential services 33
  global market 45-9
  health 31-2, 58-9
  housing 30-1
  income levels 30
  living costs 30
  population 24-7
  population shifts 48, 51-2
  poverty 30
  settlements, classification of 28
  social problems 33
  unemployment 31
  welfare failure 53-4
  work 49-50
  workforce 27-9
rural communities
  conformity 77-9
  constancy 77
  culture 69-71
  deviancy 78
  distinctiveness, sense of 75
  economic base 69
  gemeinschaft and *gesellschaft*
  interaction 71-3
  horizontal and vertical ties 73-5
  identity, sense of 75
  liberation 79-80
  material form 69-71
  nature 69-71
  normative expectations 77-8
  politics 84
  significance, sense of 76
  social provisions 75-80
  solidarity 76-7
  visibility 76
  'we-ness' 76-7
Rural Communities Program 114
rural, defining 11-2
rural disadvantage

analysis 29-37
explanations 35-7
services 170-1
rural targeting 95
rural-urban continuum 12-3
rural youth access centres 198

satellite service models 193-5, 196
second nature 268-9, 271
service hubs 196-8
service technology 257
social care
   arenas 262
   definition 17
   dialectic interaction 262-3
   expression of community 15, 96-7, 258
   function of government 96-7,
   gemeinschaft interaction 259
   gesellschaft interaction 259
   horizontal ties 97-100
   ideology 61-6
   indigenous people 59
   meaning 258-9
   responsibility of community 66
   social development 18
   technology 263-4
social care development
   constraints 153-7
   defining 131, 153
   description 153-8
   economic development, and 100-2
   functions and tasks 158-9, 161-8
   government, role of 154
   horizontal ties 153-4
   non-government organisations 154-5
   participation 147-53
   technology 262
   vertical ties 153-4
social care practice
   rural compared with urban 219-21
   rural practice 219-53
social care wisdom 176, 222
social citizenship 15-6
social development
   community cohesion 102
   conceptual limitations 18
   economic development 57, 262-3

horizontal ties 99
social care 18
vertical ties 99
social ecology 273
social impact assessment 139-42
social justice
   definition 15-7
   visions of human society 270-1
social networks 66, 86-7
social planning 56-7, 131-42
   definition 131-2
   frameworks 132-3
   information required 134-5
social policy frameworks 93-5
social welfare
   conceptual problems 14-5
   failure in rural Australia 53-4
sociological imagination 247
Special Benefit 115
special purpose accommodation 123-5
specialisation of services 175
specialised service models 194-5, 196-7
spiritual world 9, 54, 61, 65
staffing
   issues 11, 191-3
stigmatisation, impacts on service access 172
support networks
   linking services 9, 15, 53, 195-7, 201-6
   rural people 86-7
supports of practitioners 252
sustainability 103-4
sustainable, integrated regional development
   conceptual limitations 103-5
   defining 103-5

technology of social care 263-7
terra nullius, doctrine of 38, 43
threshold arguments 35-6
Torres Strait Islanders 37-43
   disadvantage 38-43
transportation 85

unintegrated services 195-6
urbanisation
   Australia 24-6

Australian welfare 3-11
urbo-centricity
　services 174-6
　social policy framework, as a 93-4

vertical coordination of services 208-9, 212-4
vertical segregation of services 175
vertical ties 73-5
　community leadership 146-7
　community participation 151-3
　coordination of services 208-9, 212-4
　defining 73-5
　integration of services 210-9
　rural communities 73-5
　rural social care 97-9
　social care development 153-4
　social care practice 73-5, 97-100
　social development 97-100
　vertical accountability 190-1
video conferencing 199-200

visiting practitioners 243-4
visiting services, models of 193-6
volunteers 197, 204

Western ideology
　assumptions 14-5, 61-6
　critique 61-6
　indigenous people 7, 65-6
　social welfare 4-5, 8, 61-6
Wik
　Judgement 44-5
withdrawal and depression phase 249
women's shelters 124
world
　concept 63-6
　interrelatedness 261

youth, rural
　housing issues 120-4
　service access 172
　social planning 132-3
　suicide 31, 94, 144, 199